CHURCH, CHANGE
AND REVOLUTION

PUBLICATIONS OF
THE SIR THOMAS BROWNE INSTITUTE
LEIDEN

(WERKGROEP ENGELS-NEDERLANDSE BETREKKINGEN)

NEW SERIES, No. 12

PUBLISHED FOR THE SIR THOMAS BROWNE INSTITUTE

E.J. BRILL/LEIDEN UNIVERSITY PRESS
LEIDEN 1991

CHURCH, CHANGE AND REVOLUTION

TRANSACTIONS OF THE FOURTH ANGLO-DUTCH CHURCH HISTORY COLLOQUIUM (EXETER, 30 AUGUST-3 SEPTEMBER, 1988)

EDITED BY

J. VAN DEN BERG AND P. G. HOFTIJZER

E.J. BRILL

LEIDEN · NEW YORK · KØBENHAVN · KÖLN

1991

This paper in this book meets the guidelines for permanence and durability of the Committee on Production Guidelines for Book Longevity of the Council on Library Resources.

Library of Congress Cataloging-in-Publication Data

Church, change, and revolution: transactions of the fourth Anglo-
   Dutch church history colloquium, Exeter, 30 August-3 September 1988
   / edited by J. van den Berg and P. G. Hoftijzer.
        p.   cm.—(Publications of the Sir Thomas Browne Institute;
   new ser., no. 12)
      Organized by the British Sub-Commission of the Commission
   internationale d'histoire ecclésiastique comparée and held at the
   University of Exeter.
      Includes index.
      ISBN 90-04-09350-8
      1. Revolutions—Religious aspects—Christianity—History of
   doctrines—Congresses. 2. Church history—Congresses. 3. England—
   Church history—Modern period, 1485- —Congresses. 4. Netherlands—
   Church history—Congresses. I. Berg, Johannes van den, 1922- .
   II. Hoftijzer, P. G. (Paul Gerardus) III. Commission internationale
   d'histoire ecclésiastique comparée. British Sub-Commission.
   IV. Series.
   BT738.3.C58   1991
   270—dc20   90-24670
                                                        CIP

ISSN   0920-5551
ISBN   90 04 09350 8

PRINTED IN THE NETHERLANDS

CONTENTS

vi

ACKNOWLEDGEMENTS

We wish to thank all those who have made possible the publication of this volume of essays: the Stichting Dr Hendrik Muller's Vaderlandsch Fonds, the Ir S.E.D. Enschedé Stichting, and a third sponsoring organisation, which prefers to remain unknown. Furthermore we thank Professor J.K. Cameron (St. Andrews), chairman of the British Sub-Commission of the Commission Internationale d'Histoire Ecclésiastique Comparée for the assistance he gave during the preparation of this volume and for his willingness to write the 'Introduction'.

J. van den Berg
P.G. Hoftijzer

LIST OF CONTRIBUTORS

J. van den Berg, Emeritus Professor of Church History, Leiden University.

J.A. Bots, Professor in the History of Ideas, University of Nijmegen.

F.G.M. Broeyer, Lecturer in Church History, University of Utrecht.

James K. Cameron, Emeritus Professor of Ecclesiastical History, University of St. Andrews.

Jane E.A. Dawson, Lecturer in Modern History, University of St. Andrews.

I.M. Green, Lecturer in Modern History, the Queen's University, Belfast.

P.G. Hoftijzer, Lecturer at the Sir Thomas Browne Institute, University of Leiden.

A. Jelsma, Professor of Church History, Theological University of the Reformed Churches, Kampen.

F.R.J. Knetsch, Emeritus Professor of Church History, University of Groningen.

M.E.H.N. Mout, Professor of History, Leiden University.

Andrew Pettegree, Lecturer in Modern History, University of St. Andrews.

P. Raedts, Lecturer in Church History, Catholic Theological University, Utrecht.

Johanna Roelevink, Institute of Netherlands History, The Hague.

Michael J. Wilks, Professor of History at Birkbeck College, University of London.

INTRODUCTION

In 1988 it was fitting that the fourth Anglo-Dutch Ecclesiastical History symposium, organised by the British Sub-Commission of the Commission Internationale d'Histoire Ecclésiastique Comparée (CIHEC) and held appropriately at the University of Exeter, should have as its central theme the Church and Revolution. In the course of its almost two thousand years' history the Church has been no stranger to reformation, political change and revolution. Set in the world it could not but be affected by the world nor could it itself, given its nature, fail to exert a variety of influences on social and political as well as on ecclesiastical events. By all of the great revolutions in the Western world its life has been profoundly affected and the course of its history directed. While the Church had itself brought to bear on every period of profound change its own distinctive and often determinative contribution. Aspects of these twin features blend together the essays that make up this record of academic co-operation.

The theme of the symposium is admirably set by Professor Michael Wilks in his wide ranging opening lecture 'Rebellion and Revolution: A Lockeian Theme and Pre-Reformation England'. In the only strictly medieval contribution to the symposium Dr. P. Raedts discusses the place of apocalypticism in the First Crusade; apocalyptic expectations usually played an important part in times of change and revolution, as later contributions also will show. For his contribution to the symposium Professor A. Jelsma compares in a delightful article the ways in which the main Protestant Books of Martyrs treat the role of women and puts forward some interesting explanations.

Dr. M.E.H.N. Mout examines the development of armed resistance in the Revolt of the Netherlands and argues that it arose out of pragmatism rather than from a conscious development of resistance theories. Also that in its origins it in some particulars pre-dates and is independent of the works of Scottish Calvinists and French monarchomachs. In the matter of resistance the Dutch Calvinists were opposed by some of their fellow Dutch exiles in London. The development of a resistance theory on the basis of Scripture by John Knox's one time colleague, Christopher Goodman, is the subject of Dr. Jane Dawson's original and closely argued article while Dr. Andrew Pettegree examines in detail the varieties of involvement of the Calvinist exiled Churches in the Reformation in the Netherlands *Wonderjaar*, 1566, and their role in forming the climate of opinion within the Dutch evangelical movement.

Dr. I.M. Green in his essay '"England's Wars of Religion"? Religious Conflict and the English Civil Wars' discusses the relationship between the Church and revolution in England and draws attention to the variety of ways in which today's historians are debating the events. Was there in fact a 'Puritan Revolution'? What part politically was played by theological ideas? How politically substantial or important were the differences in the opinions held? Should the English Civil War not, as John Morrill suggests, be regarded as 'the last of the Wars of Religion' rather than as 'the first of the European revolutions'? The discussion centres on, but by no means is confined to, England. The force of religious issues such as Arminianism and Millenarianism, Laudianism and Congregationalism, some of which are raised in other essays are all evaluated in this analytical study.

Appropriately several papers are concerned with various aspects of the 'Glorious Revolution'. Professor Hans Bots examines the relations between William III and his fellow Calvinists in the Low Countries and presents what he regards as 'tentative findings'. Stress is placed upon the Stadholder-King's 'zeal for toleration' which can also be paralleled in his relations whith his fellow Calvinists in Scotland. The connections between the political events in Britain and the contemporary and strongly anti-Catholic apocalypticism set out in Professor J. van den Berg's article brings to light an important but insufficiently explored feature of contemporary religion. He draws out, for example, the connections between the thought of Drue Cressener and the Huguenot theologian Pierre Jurieu whose defence of the Glorious Revolution and the Dutch part in it are among the subjects dealt with by Professor F.R.J. Knetsch in his essay. Jurieu was indeed one among many who made significant use of what we might now not unfairly describe as the popular pamphlet in order to defend, in opposition to Pierre Bayle and for the benefit of his persecuted French co-religionists, the English Revolution. An advocate of toleration and irenicism his literary and theological activities deserve to be much better known.

In Anglo-Dutch relations, particularly in the spheres of education and religion, it would be difficult to exaggerate the role of the printing press and the book trade. In his article, necessarily restricted to the period of the Glorious Revolution, Dr. P.G. Hoftijzer sheds new light on this absorbing subject. After 1688 the Dutch booksellers increased their already strong hold on the English market particularly in the sale of theological and related works, which however, was by no means a one way traffic. The remaining two articles are more restricted in scope in

CAMERON — INTRODUCTION   3

that they primarily centre on Utrecht. Dr. F.G.M. Broeyer examines
William III's relations with the Church in Utrecht after the French occupation of 1672-73 and Dr. Johanna Roelevink discusses the roles of
two Utrecht professors in the Dutch Patriot Revolt at the end of the
eighteenth century.

The members of the British Commission, on whom the responsibility
for arranging the symposium fell, are deeply grateful to their Dutch colleagues for their active participation, proving once again not only that
the world of scholarship transcends national boundaries, but also that
the study of history and especially of church history cannot but be enriched by international co-operation.

To the authors and editors sincere thanks is expressed and to the Sir
Thomas Browne Institute for undertaking the responsibility of publication.

St. Andrews   James K. Cameron.
1989

REBELLION AND REVOLUTION:
A LOCKEIAN THEME AND PRE-REFORMATION ENGLAND

Michael Wilks

Whilst the rest of Europe prepared to commemorate the bicentenary of the French Revolution, perfidious Albion sought to upstage the event by celebrating the tercentenary of the English Revolution of 1688-89 (having been too preoccupied to bother very much about the true English Revolution of the 1640s). 'But when', queried Eric Hobsbawm recently, 'did a reputable English historian last refer to the so-called "Glorious Revolution" of 1688?'[1] To him the term revolution cannot be applied to a single political event, but should only be used of a total social change. In accepted modern terminology to have a revolution means to create a new state, or at least a new constitution and a new sovereignty, to produce that *novus ordo saeculorum* proclaimed by the American colonists when they successfully achieved what is now regarded as the first of the modern revolutions.[2] Yet even the quickest glance along the bookshelves of recent publications on the seventeenth century not only demonstrates a general acceptance of Christopher Hill's description of it as a 'century of revolution', but also adds 'and rebellion' as if the use of both terms will ensure that one of them is right.[3] Indeed, a cynic might say that there is no essential difference between them, since a revolution is merely a rebellion which succeeds, and a rebellion is a revolution which fails (and could cite John Locke in support[4]). But most people today would probably agree that a rebellion is simply a protest against the operation of a political system without wishing to change that system itself, whilst the requirement of a revolution is that it demands a new system altogether. A more sophisticated analysis would suggest that there should be a threefold division between a *revolt*, which is objecting to an administrative system but is not seeking the removal of the head, just as the English Peasants' Revolt of 1381 claimed that it was a rising on behalf of Richard II against the unjust operation of the manorial system; a *rebellion*, in which the aim is the replacement of the head—but the operative word is replacement: another king is brought in (as in 1689), and the monarchy remains; and a *revolution* like the French and Russian Revolutions, in which the monarchy itself was to be abandoned. As the Duke of Liancourt said to Louis XVI in 1789, 'This is not a revolt, sire, this is a revolution': and events showed that it meant both the removal of the head of State (and the head of the head) and the creation of a new State itself. But in seventeenth-century England the Civil War produced what was meant to be a new State, the Commonwealth, and was condemned afterwards as a 'Great Rebellion', whereas the reassertion of Parliamentary control and a change of rulers in 1689 (with little of the popular upsurge now deemed to be necessary) was a 'Glorious Revolution'.

It is sometimes said that during the sixteenth century there was only one successful political revolution; the revolt of the Netherlands against Spain, the abdication of Philip II in 1581, and the creation of the Dutch Republic. It was a revolution which took everybody by surprise, even the Dutch themselves, and it left them gravely embarrassed at the thought that they might have done something improper. They therefore did their best to maintain that it never happened. They refused to acknowledge that they had created a new State. They insisted that they were simply continuing the old State under its traditional guardians, the provincial estates, although as Professor Kossmann has pointed out,[5] they had in fact created a federal republic which it was impossible to classify in terms of existing political theory. The sixteenth century made no real provision for new forms of government, let alone new forms of State, and the essentially conservative Dutch had no intention of making a contribution of that sort. The real literature of revolt at this period was a product of the French religious wars, where ironically it made little difference in the long run to the onward march of the monarchy towards absolutism. Let me hasten to add, in deference to our conference chairman, that I have not forgotten John Knox and Mary, Queen of Scots (who indeed could forget them?), but I shall try to suggest in this paper that the overturning of that monstrous regiment of female rule might be better seen in the context of the long series of English revolts which took place between 1300 and 1500, and which were used by numerous writers in seventeenth-century England as historical justification for the right of a people to depose its king. Of these the most influential was undoubtedly John Locke.

Although Locke published his *Two Treatises of Government* in 1689 on his return to London after five years of exile in the Netherlands, and the stated purpose of the work was 'to establish the Throne of our Great *Restorer*, Our present King William, to make good his Title in the Consent of the People',[6] Peter Laslett has shown conclusively that the justification of popular revolution in the *Second Treatise* had been initially drafted some ten or more years earlier (even before the attack on Filmer and the Divine Right of Kings in the *First Treatise*), and must therefore be seen

in relation to his efforts between 1679 and 1682 to assist his patron, the
Earl of Shaftesbury, to persuade the childless Charles II to exclude his
staunchly Roman Catholic brother, James, Duke of York, from the succession to the English throne.[7] Locke's theory of revolution must accordingly be assessed against the background of the politics leading to the
Exclusion Crisis in the first instance, and beyond that the aftermath of
the Civil War, rather than the deposition of James II. It was the revolution of the 1640s which shaped his thinking. Although his family were
Somerset landed gentry, his father had been a Parliamentary captain;
as a schoolboy aged sixteen Locke himself had been within earshot of
the execution of Charles I; and his first published work was an ode in
praise of Oliver Cromwell for his victory over the Dutch in 1653. Like
Shaftesbury, he hurriedly accommodated himself to the restoration of
the Stuarts. But in 1660 he was heavily influenced by Hobbes, and took
the view that it did not really matter very much whether 'the magistrate's crown drops down on his head immediately from heaven or is
placed there by the hands of his subjects.'[8] Even this nod in favour of
Divine Right had largely vanished twenty years later when in the *Second
Treatise* he made the existence of the monarchy a matter for Parliamentary preference rather than the will of God.

Given the uncertainties of his earlier views, it is perhaps curious that
Locke should be so adamant that his theory of justifiable resistance was
a long-standing and traditional part of the English constitution. But the
basis of his constitutional theory was old enough: a Roman and
medieval, Ciceronian and Gelasian, distinction between legislative authority and executive power. According to Locke this division was essential in a civil society, a true state—which he termed a 'constituted commonwealth', a state with a proper, popularly approved constitution.[9] At
once he got himself into the position of appearing to say that there was
no state in France, because this distinction did not exist in the government of Louis XIV.[10] What he meant of course was not that there was
no civil government in France, but that there was no government as he
had defined it. Under the terms of his own definition there needed to be
two separate bodies, one to make the laws and one to administer them,
in English terms a Parliament and a royal administration. Naturally,
nothing is ever simple in England: and here 'the executive is vested in a
single person who also has a share in the legislative'.[11] In other words
the king is also one of the estates, a part of Parliament—'the king in
Parliament'—so that no law can be made without his consent. It was
easier, Locke found, when dealing with England, to lapse into medieval
terminology, which was itself proof that one was dealing with an ancient
constitution. The social contract, which had taken men out of the state

of nature by an agreement amongst the members, had created a mystical body known as a commonwealth or Leviathan, a being with a will of its own which always operated for the public good.[12] This mysterious entity, the 'State' in our language, now has a double representation: it is made actual in practice by Parliament when it is sitting and by the king alone when it is not.[13] The first act of society, he writes, is the fundamental one of establishing a legislative, and it is in the legislative that the members of a commonwealth are made one and combined together into a coherent living body.[14] But when the king alone is acting, he becomes the 'image, phantom or representative person of the commonwealth', acting by the will of society declared in its laws, and therefore has no power or will but that of the law.[15] Otherwise he becomes a mere private person with no power, since no one is obliged to obey a private will. It is almost a paraphrase of John of Salisbury, combined with the enhanced role of Parliament as the *communitas regni* which it had acquired by the fourteenth century.[16]

Locke appears then, in these passages, to be doing little more than describe the operation of the English constitution as he saw it in his own time. Parliament, as the legislative body which has little other capacity beyond that of making law, does not need to be in existence all the time, and it would not be convenient for it to be in permanent session; whereas the function of the crown as executive is to handle all the day to day business of government, to convoke and dissolve the legislative at appropriate times, and to activate emergency powers, the powers of prerogative, to provide for the public good in such cases where unforeseen circumstances make it unsafe to apply existing fixed laws, i.e. the power to act illegally in an emergency.[17] It all seems so commonplace and so boring that the reader is mentally jolted to find that Locke now moved on to the question of what should be done if either legislative or executive exceeds its powers and there is conflict between Parliament and king, with the attendant problem of who is to judge between them. The answer, says Locke in a famous phrase, must be to appeal to heaven, for there is no judge on earth superior to them (again very medieval language).[18] The people at large have no power under the positive human law of the constitution to deal with either a delinquent king or a tyrannical Parliament: but 'by a law antecedent and paramount to all positive laws of men', by divine and natural law,[19] the people may resort to force, putting themselves into that state of war which alone can determine matters which have no judge on earth. It is up to each individual to decide when this state of war exists.[20] God and nature, he declares, will never allow a man so to abandon himself that he neglects his own preservation.[21]

Locke is as much concerned here to explain and justify the Civil War, although that in itself might be taken as a barely veiled threat to the government of Charles II. But talking about a divine-natural right of the great majority of the population to go to war faced Locke with the awful problem that he seemed to be advocating a return to the state of nature and, worst of all, that the state of nature was one of war—which could only demonstrate that Hobbes was right after all.[22] It was something which could not possibly be allowed: and Locke hastily took refuge in two very important distinctions (following the old principle of the medieval canonists, when in doubt, draw distinctions). In the first place, he said, 'he that will speak with any clearness' (a sure sign that he was about to say something confusing) 'about the dissolution of government, ought first to distinguish between the dissolution of society and the dissolution of government'. The downfall of the government does not entail the demise of the State as a political society.[23] Men in the state of nature formed themselves into a political society by an act of association: the individuals turned themselves into a corporate body, the mystical entity of Leviathan, by a social contract amongst themselves, that which 'makes the community and brings men out of the loose state of nature into one politic society'.[24] But they did this without thereby creating a government as such. That required a further agreement—a political as opposed to a social contract—in other words a trust.[25] But until that was established, society—the State—existed so to speak by itself. It was something which could not be destroyed, unless it was obliterated by a foreign power's conquest, which would wipe out the existing state; or the individual removed himself to a new state of nature somewhere else, for example by emigrating to America.[26] As regards internal politics, however, all that had to be considered was the dissolution of the government, when either the legislative or the executive broke faith with society, betrayed the State, and put an end to the trust that the people had placed in them. Theirs was, as he put it in another famous phrase, a fiduciary power only.[27] They held their power in trust for the good management and administration of the realm: and if they failed in their duties they could be dismissed like the stewards of any estates. It was the language of estate management,[28] and illustrates the way in which Locke saw the kingdom as a piece of property, a landed inheritance which should be cultivated and improved during their lifetimes by the landed proprietors—what the Middle Ages would have called the 'natural men' of the kingdom, the landed aristocracy and gentry.

It is not my purpose here to get involved in Locke's theory of property rights as an essential part of his idea of the state of nature. But it is perhaps relevant to mention the way in which Locke constructed his state of nature so that it reflected the world of the seventeenth-century gentleman and merchant. Claiming that what he said was justified by both divine and natural law, Locke depicted a thoroughly unequal, quasi-feudal society of landowners and labourers, regulated by men who had become wealthy by the enclosure of comman land;[29] who had numerous servants and workers (including slaves[30]); who had a duty of care[31] towards their families, to whom they were obliged to pass on their estates by inheritance,[32] and towards their other dependents under the obligations of charitable acts (like the Poor Laws); and who had a natural right to act as justices against those who would disturb the peace and infringe the rights of others to life, liberty and the enjoyment of their property.[33] In other words society already existed by divine-natural right long before it became necessary to enforce natural law on a national scale by bringing in government, a system of law, judgement and armed enforcement, which could also regulate the supply of land as the population expanded and the amount of available land contracted. Government, politics, matters determined by human law, were things simply added on, additional,[34] to a naturally organised society. Government was an inherently temporary arrangement placed on top of a natural society, ancient, fundamentally stable and of long standing. Once more Locke was not being particularly original: the notion of political institutions added on to nature, and so subject to natural law, had been well developed by Thomas Aquinas and has its roots in Cicero. But it meant for Locke that the men of the land, the landlords of the realm, began with an enormous advantage over those non-natural, artificial elements, Parliament and king. Since Parliament was largely composed of landed gentry, merchants and lawyers and aristocracy, it was really the monarchy which incurred and bore the brunt of this theory of government as a very limited additional feature of society.

This relationship is reflected in Locke's discussion of what to do if either the legislative or the executive broke its trust and thereby terminated the political contract.[35] If the members of Parliament sought to become arbitrary and dispose of the lives, liberties and fortunes of their subjects, illegally invading their rights or property,

> the Community perpetually retains a Supream Power of saving themselves from the attempts and designs of any Body, even of their Legislators, whenever they shall be so foolish, or so wicked, as to lay and carry on designs against the Liberties and Properties of the Subject.[36]
>
> In these and the like Cases, when the Government is dissolved, the People are at liberty to provide for themselves, by erecting a new Legislative, differing from the other, by the change of Persons, or Form, or both as they shall find it most for their safety and good. For the Society can never, by the fault of another, lose the Native and Original Right it has to preserve itself ....[37]

At one point Locke tries to argue that Parliamentary denial of property rights would be tantamount to an invasion, so that the social contract itself might be dissolved, bringing death to the commonwealth and a return to the state of nature. But his whole treatment of the subject is vague, and to my mind inconsistent.[38] The replacement of a king acting arbitrarily against the common good is on the other hand treated with enthusiasm and at length, and is really a much more interesting blend of precedent and ingenuity.

The traditional medieval answer to the problem of a king acting arbitrarily against the well-being of the subjects whom he had sworn to protect was to pretend that he did not exist—in the hackneyed phrase 'rex non recte regendo, non est rex sed tyrannus'.[39] The tyrant was not, by definition, a king: there was therefore no problem involved in acting against him. His tyranny had created a presumptive vacancy, and there literally was no one for his subjects to obey. The feudal right of *diffidatio* or 'legalised rebellion', perhaps best articulated by the thirteenth-century *Song of Lewes*, relied heavily on the equation of king with *iustitia*, so that (to quote Bracton) 'non enim est rex ubi dominatur voluntas et non ea'.[40] On the contrary, said John of Salisbury in the preceding century, the tyrant by his tyranny has committed treason against the State, the *res publica*, and therefore the people have a legal obligation to embody the law in themselves, to take up arms and, if necessary to kill, the tyrant: it would be an act of treason in itself not to rise against him. A century later Thomas Aquinas made the same point when he described the tyrant as guilty of sedition against society, who put himself into the same category as the usurper, one who had no right to be there—and therefore in a rightful sense literally was not there. The people, said Thomas, can rebel against him and will not themselves be committing a seditious act.[41] This, basically, is Locke's own position,

> What then, Can there no Case happen wherein the People may of right, and by their own Authority help themselves, take Arms, and set upon their King, imperiously domineering over them? None at all, whilst he remains a King. 'Honour the King' (I *Pet.*, ii.17), and 'he that resists the Power, resists the Ordinance of God' (*Rom.*, xiii.2), are Divine Oracles that will never permit it. The People therefore can never come by a Power over him, unless he does something that makes him cease to be a King. For then he divests himself of his Crown and Dignity, and returns to the state of a private Man, and the People become free and superior; the Power which they had in the Interregnum, before they Crown'd him King, devolving to them again. But there are few miscarriages which bring the matter to this state. After considering it well on all sides, I can find but two. Two Cases there are, I say, whereby a King, *ipso facto*, becomes no King, and loses all Power and Regal Authority over his People ...[42]

although he takes it a stage further. If, he maintains, the executive re-
sorts to government by will, that is, his own arbitrary will, and either
refuses to call or hinders the calling of Parliament, and governs by sheer
military force;[43] or if he ignores the safety of the realm by delivering his
country into the clutches of a foreign power[44] (by which he appears to
mean France or Spain, Catholic powers, whereas Protestant powers like
the Dutch, and later no doubt the Hanoverians, would come into the
very different category of friends whom the English would encourage to
be at home here); or if—following Hobbes—the executive is merely
negligent,[45] then the tyrant has deposed himself and the people may take
up arms against him. 'When a King has Dethron'd himself', Locke declares, 'and put himself in a state of War with his People, what shall hinder them from prosecuting him who is no King.'[46] This, moreover,
would not be a rebellion, but a revolution. On the contrary it would be
the king who was the rebel, who was committing rebellion by trying to
overturn the constitution: whilst it would be the people who would need
to have a revolution in order to turn the government of the kingdom
back to what it had been before the tyrant destroyed it. A rebellion, he
urged, is not against a person but an act contrary to authority founded
in the constitution. Accordingly anybody, Parliament or king alone, who
acts unconstitutionally 'are properly, and with the greatest aggravation,
Rebellantes, Rebels'.[47] So that if you are faced by a prolonged rebellion
by the government, the only thing the community can effectively do is
to have a revolution against that rebellion:[48] and a revolution means
precisely what it says, a revolving, a turning round and back again, a
cyclical action, which restores the constitution to what it had been before the government subverted it. Even if the replacement government
assumed a new form or composition, this was not to be regarded as a
new constitution, but essentially just a return. The English, Locke argued, are essentially conservative, and their desire is to preserve old
forms:

> This slowness and aversion in the People to quit their old Constitutions,
> has, in the many Revolutions which have been seen in this Kingdom ...
> still brought us back again to our old Legislative of King, Lords and Com-
> mons.[49]

Indeed the main feature of a revolution was its absence of novelty: it was
the most conservative thing there could be, and the best prevention
against arbitrary government, 'the best fence against Rebellion, and the
probablest means to hinder it'.[50]

To justify this Locke offered his readers a vision of the history of England as a constant series of happy returns to 'the old constitution'. There
had been many revolutions 'in this and former Ages ... And whatever

provocations have made the Crown be taken from some of our Princes Heads, they never carried the People so far, as to place it in another Line'.[51] Individual kings were removed from their thrones, but the hereditary kingship, the royal line of descent, survived. He was reminding his audience that despite the rigours of Tudor rule, in the course of the two centuries between 1300 and 1500 no less than five English kings had been deposed and killed with Parliamentary approval. Whilst it would be tedious to make a solemn investigation of each of these medieval 'revolutions' in turn, it is nevertheless worth making the point that these English depositions seemed, certainly with hindsight, to have followed a standard pattern (largely modelled on the removal of Edward II in 1327) and could therefore be represented as established constitutional practice. Then this in turn could be used to lend support to the myth that a recognized system of sovereignty shared between monarchy and Parliament had always existed.

Like all classical dramas, medieval depositions in England could be divided into three acts. The first was to recognise that the king ruled by divine right, that is to say, by virtue of hereditary descent. He was the direct choice of God, for only God can create an heir.[52] This served to get round the awkward point that the king in question had been accepted as a true, divinely approved ruler up to that point. But it also meant that it had then to be shown that the king in question was suddenly not a king and that a vacancy had occurred. In 1327 there had been some doubt about how to achieve this. The first attempt was to declare the throne vacant on the grounds that Edward II had gone to Wales and had thus deserted the realm of England. A baronial assembly at Bristol in October therefore declared a regency under his son, Edward III,[53] who then summoned a Parliament, which would declare Edward II deposed for absenteeism. Quite apart from the curiously circular logic involved here, and the positively ludicrous implications of making a visit to Wales grounds for deposition and the apparent insistence that no medieval king should leave his kingdom, the opposition then vitiated its own case by capturing the king and bringing him back to England (to Kenilworth in November). This had the advantage that the Parliament could now be re-summoned as if the king had done it. But it left Edward's royal authority unimpaired, and 'Touch not the Lord's Anointed' was still the basic difficulty to be overcome. This eventually had to be dealt with by forcing Edward to abdicate. Under a mixture of threats and persuasion he resigned the crown to his son: but he did so as an act of royal will,[54] and technically the royal supremacy remained inviolate.

Richard II in 1399 was both more difficult and less of a problem:

more difficult in that no king was more aware of his inviolability and immunity as vicar of God;[55] less of a problem in that there was now a precedent. Richard too was induced to make a voluntary act of renunciation and abdicate, although he took good care to resign his crown to God and not to the assembly of the estates of the realm which was summoned to be told of this.[56] Parliament however took the view that this royal determination to act by will (of which the abdication itself was the latest example) proved Richard's character as a tyrant,[57] and where there was a tyrant there was no king—so again there was a vacancy. In short, king and Parliament agreed to differ on the cause, but accepted the same result that the throne had been vacated. From then on this aspect became more perfunctory. In 1461 the vacancy was obtained by declaring that Henry VI was a usurper and had therefore never been king at all.[58] As this meant that England had not had a king for 62 years (and Henry V's conquest of France was a nonsense), the matter was not elaborated: and the victorious Edward IV preferred to require his Parliament to accept that Henry had simply been a tyrant and had automatically ceased to be a king.[59] It was not difficult to depict the feeble-minded Henry as incompetent, and so false to his coronation oath to give the kingdom good government. Similarly in 1483 the question of hereditary right and divine election was avoided altogether by declaring Edward V to be illegitimate, on the grounds that his mother's marriage to Edward IV was invalid.

Throughout, then, a spurious thread of constitutional propriety had been maintained: nothing had been done except by royal will or by the fiction that there was no king to will anything. But in each case this position was promptly negatived and repudiated by a second act of allowing Parliament a capacity to depose the king on the basis of popular right and to have him executed. In 1327 the January Parliament declared that Edward II was deposed by the agreement of lords, clergy and people because he was incompetent, had broken his coronation oath, refused to accept the advice of his feudal magnates, was an oppressor, and had created an emergency endangering the safety of the realm.[60] There was constant stress upon the theme of *vox populi, vox Dei*, and that it was the voice of the people that gave the laws their force.[61] Much the same shopping list of notorious crimes and tyrannical acts was alleged for the Parliamentary deposition of Richard II in 1399, and the popular right to rule a king invoked.[62] Both Edward II and Richard II were of course killed in prison within a few months. Henry VI on the other hand refused to be caught and was not executed until ten years later, following his deposition by Parliament in November 1461. That Parliament was in any case more concerned to pass enough enactments to allow Edward IV to succeed him. Whilst in 1483, before it was deemed permissible for Richard III to be crowned, Richard had himself elected by the three estates of the realm meeting in Parliament, Parliament being specifically defined as possessing the *auctoritas regni*.[63] Richard III's title was upheld as being in accordance with divine law, natural law and ancient custom, that is to say, by hereditary right, by popular/Parliamentary election, and by consecration and coronation. This third act, coronation, was dependent on papal approval. But on no occasion does there appear to have been papal opposition to this series of depositions. To the best of my knowledge nobody has ever made a detailed study of the papal reaction to these events, and one tends to get the impression that the curia merely trailed along in the wake of events and acquiesced in a series of *faits accomplis*. But the papacy always had its own reasons for disliking theocratic kings who claimed the right to act independently by the will of God, and there was a long tradition of papal support for archbishops of Canterbury as the leaders of aristocratic opposition to the crown. Reynolds in 1327 and Arundel in 1399 both fitted easily into this tradition. During the fifteenth century there was steady papal support for the Yorkist cause,[64] until 1485, when the legate's advice caused Rome to change sides, recognise Henry Tudor's title, and excommunicate anyone who rebelled against him.[65]

Of greater significance is the clash of constitutional principles evinced by the process followed in each of these depositions. The divine right of the king to remove himself was counterbalanced by the right of the people acting in accordance with natural law through their representatives to remove him. This belt and braces procedure was adopted less as a compromise than as an agreement to disagree. Yet it was fundamentally contradictory, and indicated that there was evident confusion in England about how the kingdom was supposed to be governed. Royal opposition to Parliamentary sovereignty was manifest in the way each new claimant tried to avoid any suggestion that he owed his throne to anybody but God. Edward III insisted that he ruled by virtue of his father's will that his son should succeed him.[66] Henry IV produced a whole battery of such arguments: there was not only Richard III's wish that his cousin should take the throne, but there was also his own right of descent from Henry III, and there was the *iudicium Dei*, God's arbitration, displayed by Henry's successful conquest of England.[67] Rather astonishingly, Parliament accepted the whole package of royalist claims, no doubt contenting itself with the thought that the reality was otherwise. In 1461 Edward IV, on the basis of hereditary right,[68] took the sceptre, had himself acclaimed, enthroned, and then crowned—before he called a Parliament to approve what he had done—and Henry VII simply reversed the entire process. To begin with, he killed the king first instead of waiting like Edward III, Henry IV, Edward IV and perhaps Richard III until the constitutional process was completed. He then claimed the throne entirely by divine right, partly on the grounds of inheritance (and he appears to have used the royal title before Bosworth Field), partly because his victory at Bosworth was a direct judgment by God in his favour, and he thanked God (a very papal phrase this) for committing the kingdom to his care.[69] Subsequent Parliamentary action was a mere declaratory assent, an acquiescence in God's will, not a consent which implied any Parliamentary right to refuse him. Henry Tudor became the first English king since the Norman Conquest to rule by inherited right and right of conquest alone.

Such constitutional contradictions were not of course peculiar to England. By the fourteenth century every possible theory of power from above and power from below existed in European thought, and older theories of divine sovereignty now existed alongside a wide variety of aristocratic and more broadly based conceptions of government derived from feudal law, Roman law and Aristotle, to which were added conciliar theories of several kinds.[70] In Italy both despotic and communal governments stood side by side, and were often interchangeable; and within all kingdoms there was to be found a mass of corporate bodies of every kind operating with principles of popular decision-making and elective headship.[71] To point to these mutual antagonisms was, however, of no help to Locke, who was insistent that true civil government was based on contract and consent.[72] Although he was aware that historically absolute monarchy was likely to have been the more normal form of government, and that in a great many states this originated from conquest,[73] he was forced to argue that there must have been a social contract, an act of political consent, subsequent to the event to legitimise that government.[74] Indeed, he declared that the first act of true statehood was the creation of the legislative, in this context the calling of the first Parliament.[75] Understandably he was a little vague about when all this had actually happened in England. He seems to have accepted that the Norman Conquest established at least a partial despotism by its subjugation of British and Saxons, but that the incorporation into one body, the capacity of the whole kingdom to act as a *populus*, came later.[76] He probably regarded Magna Carta and the de Montfort Parliament as important stages in legitimising the Conquest, since he was careful to cite two of the thirteenth-century sources much beloved by exponents of the fashionable idea of an 'ancient constitution' against the Stuart monarchy, Bracton[77] and the *Mirror of Justices*.[78] If Aquinas had been the sort of author he could have admitted to using, he could have found with him the principle that an absolute government can be validated by a later act of consent.[79] But in England his 'old original constitution'[80] appears to have been a much more recent development than the expression suggests. In the infancy of government, he tells us with a nod to Bodin, when the commonwealth was like a family, government was all prerogative[81] in the hands of a God-like person[82] — Filmer was right to that extent. But since society is a community of rational creatures, the people were increasingly able to advance their power for the common good, especially to deal with bad kings.[83] There was, however, no inherent conflict in this, he argued, because all things done rightly were done for the same purpose: *salus populi suprema lex*.[84] This had made it possible for a system of dual authority to have evolved in England by the later medieval period, a double majesty of royal prerogative and king in Parliament: power from above and power from below had come together in harmony. There was, to use medieval terminology, neither a regal monarchy by divine right nor a politic kingship limited by the natural rights of the people, but a blend of each. Locke, who was usually fairly unforthcoming about his sources, acknowledged that much of this came from Sir John Fortescue, the mid-fifteenth-century lawyer and royal adviser who sought to popularise the notion of a 'Lancastrian Constitution' (which he traced back to King Brutus and the men of Troy).[85] But Fortescue himself derived his terminology from Tholemy of Lucca, and the whole notion of a mixed constitution really came from Aquinas, who had claimed both natural and divine law justification for it, natural in that it was in agreement with the teaching of Aristotle, divine in that it was the system devised by Moses to govern the Israelites.[86]

But if this meant that Aquinas and other later medieval political writers were familiar with the principle of rebellion,[87] and could on occasion allow that rebellion might be justifiable, it is difficult to credit them with a theory of revolution. They could talk as both Aquinas and — to take just one example — Wyclif did of a non-seditious popular disturbance. The word used was *turbatio*, which carried with it the undertones of a disorderly crowd: Wyclif applied it to the Peasants' Revolt of 1381, for which he had some sympathy.[88] But the most that could be said was that this notion of *dis*order implicitly suggested an order to be returned to. Medieval sources were not going to supply Locke with a clear distinction between impermissible rebellion and acceptable revolution however much they could supply most of the rest of his constitutional theory. So where did Locke get his distinction from? The simple answer might seem to be Jean Bodin, who had not only distinguished between society and government (following Aristotle, he had argued that the form of government, the way the government was exercised, might be very diffe-

rent to the form of the State, the formal constitution of a political society[89]), but had also made a clear division between rebellions and revolutions. A rebellion in his view differed from a revolution in two ways: it
was a human arrangement, so that men could determine for themselves
whether they recognised a right to rebel. For instance a feudal constitution might very well include a written-in right of resistance, the right to
withdraw fidelity from an unworthy feudal superior who failed to provide justice and protection. But it sought to do no more than replace one
superior by a better one, a bad king by a good king. It did not seek to
do away with kings as such—and Bodin himself, who was after all writing a defence of sovereign majestey, was not prepared to countenance
such a right in a true state. Rebellion was by definition wrong, and so
could be no right in law. There was no political right of rebellion, no
humanly-determined constitutional means of overthrowing the
sovereign. Therefore, he argued, if resistance was unavoidable, the only
recourse was to go outside the constitution altogether and resort to a
non-political or pre-political right, a natural right, whose use would destroy the whole system and necessitate starting again. Nothing could
alter a people's natural right to have a revolution as a last resort. But it
would then be logically obligatory to change to a different kind of constitution. It would not make sense to destroy an absolute sovereign
monarchy and then create another, when the revolution itself would
have demonstrated that there really was popular supremacy.[90]

Although Bodin was clearly defining a right of revolution in a sense
which we can use today, he was still not using the term itself. In Book
IV he discussed the downfall, ruin or collapse of commonwealths (which
might happen because of sedition or general decay or simply because
they became top-heavy and fell over). But he talked about them under-
going a change or conversion (*conversio*) to a different type of rule.
Changes, 'conversiones rerumpublicarum seu imperiorum', took place
when the wheel of fortune turned.[91] This illustrates a further point about
the word 'revolution' itself. Its use in 1600 did not normally extend to
the political overturning of an established government. As a term it had
a perfectly respectable ancestry in later Latin, Old French and Middle
English: but it simply meant a circular motion, a revolving, a turning
round and back again. This did not debar it from having a political application in either classical or medieval usage,[92] but the word was usually applied to something like time, the annual turning or returning of
the seasons of the year, or the circular motion of the heavenly bodies.
Copernicus, Galileo and Newton duly used it of the turning of the earth
itself. Its political use, however, was slow to develop, particularly in

England, and when it did so it had two forms which tended, confusingly, to mean the opposite of each other.[93]

a) It could mean a violent event which produced a change in the situation, something akin to modern usage.[94] For example, Montaigne's *Essays* of 1595 applied it to the more shattering events of the French religious wars; the Neapolitan rebellion of 1647 against Spanish rule was described as a *rivolationi*; and in England it was used of the execution of Charles I. Harrington employed it in a way which Bodin might have accepted: 'political or social change could come from natural revolution within the State or by violent revolution like conquest from without.'

b) On the other hand a good deal of English seventeenth-century usage continued to use the term in the opposite sense of return to a former or lost condition. Both Shakespeare and Milton applied it to man's lost status which he might (or might not) regain. Again there were ample Italian precedents for this usage,[95] but the key English figures seem to have been Clarendon and Sir William Temple, who respectively described the return of the Stuarts under Charles II in 1660, and of the house of Orange to the United Provinces in 1672, as revolutions, a revival of 'ancient and lawful government'.

How far Locke was familiar with any of these usages, it is difficult to say, and it may not matter. Because in the *Second Treatise* he speaks unexpectedly warmly of King James I[96] and one may surmise that he would have come across the word 'revolution' when it was first used in the King James Bible, the Authorised Version, as a variant reading for three passages in the Old Testament (*Exod.*, xxxiv.22; I *Sam.*, i.20; II *Chron.*, xxiv.23), in each case for the completion of a cycle. Perhaps one of the most significant contributions to Locke scholarship in recent years has been John Dunn's study of the underlying religious character of Locke's thought[97] (despite Locke's insistence that he was only dealing here with *civil* government). Locke's description of the state of nature owed much to the Puritan work ethic, itself an appropriation of medieval, especially Cistercian theology, and the idea of man as the product of divine 'workmanship'.[98] His theory of a double contract may have been derived from the French Protestant tract *Vindiciae contra tyrannos*, very popular in seventeenth-century England; but the *Vindiciae* itself acknowledged that this was an elaboration of an Old Testament passage on the proper form of kingship for Israel as a *populus Dei*.[99] One should also bear in mind that there was a long tradition in England, going back at least to the fourteenth century, which saw England as the new Israel, and therefore adopted the Old Testament as the essential guide to the divinely approved polity[100]—a theme endlessly stressed by Puritan theology. One of the most striking features of Locke's *Treatises* is the extent to which Locke used quotation after quotation from the Old Testament to support what he was saying. He could hardly have avoided this in the *First Treatise*, which was mainly a refutation of Filmer and required a close study of *Genesis*. But Locke clearly regarded the Old Testament as something which would provide the model for his theory of government and revolution, for the right of everyman to appeal to heaven and go to war against a rebellious government. He repeatedly claimed the authority of *Judges* xi-xii, in which Jephtha ruled Israel as the ninth judge,[101] coming in from outside (from the land of Tob) to rescue Israel from its enemies by force of arms under a contract made with God. But the actual distinction between rebellion and revolution in the Old Testament as translated in English Bibles, especially the Authorised Version, and not to be found in these terms in the Vulgate, occurs in the first chapter of *Isaiah*. This is the great lament of the prophet about the way in which the people of Israel had become corrupt under the rule of the kings of Judah and had rejected God as their lord. They have become, we are told, an alienated and sinful nation,[102] their cities like Sodom and Gomorrah in which the pursuit of wealth by the rich has led to the oppression of the poor,[103] and their religious ceremonies, however elaborate, bring no pleasure to God and are rejected by him.[104] From top to bottom, from the soles of the feet to the head, there is no soundness in the kingdom.[105] In terms which call to mind John of Salisbury, it is declared that corruption begins at the top: both head and heart are faint and sickly, and when princes rebel against God, their people will soon revolt too.[106] Rebellion, we notice, is the act of a prince in the first instance.

But the second purpose of the *Isaiah* chapter is to prophesy that the true Israel remains with a small number. It endures with a saving remnant: a city of true faith and righteousness which, although now besieged by the ungodly 'like a lodge in a wilderness of cucumbers', will nevertheless be the means of purging and destroying the enemies of the Lord. They will redeem Israel, once again restoring the rule of true judges and wise counsellors.[107] Here I think we can begin to see the essential ingredient of what Locke thought a revolution should be a return to: a return to the paths of righteousness and the ways of the Lord, and the redemption of a corrupted Israel, or one about to be corrupted by its prince. The true aim of the revolution should be to restore the Reformation Settlement as set out by Hooker.[108] It is a truism that the Reformation was a revolution which removed the pope as head of the English church and replaced him with a king. In fact the term *reformatio* had been used in that sense ever since Barbarossa in the twelfth century demanded a 'reformatio Urbis et orbis' for that purpose in the Universal

Church. Demands for a *reformatio status Ecclesiae*, and return to goodness, had become commonplace during the later Middle Ages.[109] For example, when Adolf of Nassau was deposed by his princes in 1298 because he was negligent and useless, this was said to have been done *pro reformatione pacis*, for a return to safety and the harmony of the realm. Similarly within a decade the Austrian abbot Engelbert of Admont demanded another emperor to correct the excesses of the princes and to re-form the wholeness of a dissolute *status*, a goodness that had been dissolved. In all these cases there was the basic Augustinian assumption that a *de-formatio* had occurred, and this deformation accordingly required a Reformation, a re-forming or return to what was right.[110] It was a thesis elaborated at great length by John Wyclif in his demands for a reformation in the 1370s and 1380s: a 'restitutio Ecclesiae ad statum quem Christus docuit', and he harped upon the necessity for return.[111] · What England needed was a second Norman Conquest, he proclaimed, which would again put back all church lands into the hands of the king.[112] And once the Reformation had taken place in England, a host of writers from Tyndale to Hooker emphasised that nothing unusual or extraordinary had taken place: the new royal headship was nothing more than a return to what should have been, and indeed once was.

A rejection of papal supremacy and of Roman Catholicism generally was a major feature of the call for a return to the ancient constitution. As Christopher St. German had said the Reformation reasserted the old constitution *because* it was a rejection of the pope's usurpation of the rights of the English Parliament.[113] When the English Parliament followed precedents and deposed James II in 1688-89 the grounds stated for this was that he had been tyrannical, and so had deposed himself— witness his absence from the realm. Technically he should have been replaced by his heir, since James III already existed. But quite apart from the question of the suitability of a child to govern, bedpan or no bedpan, the real problem was that he too would be a Roman Catholic. What proved to be the last straw with James II was his deliberate intention, in the second Declaration of Indulgence, to create true toleration which would benefit Catholics above all. Yet even before he began work on the *Second Treatise*, Locke had defined toleration in a civil State to be something which had to be appropriate to a Godly society, so that not only was there to be no toleration for atheists, but equally there was to be none for those who recognised papal supremacy and were *ipso facto* potential traitors to Israel simply because they were Catholics. When he came to write the *Second Treatise* he could hardly condemn James, Duke of York, for tyranny since James was still several years away from being a king. But Marsilius of Padua had described heresy as rebellion, rebellion against the cross of Christ; and after him Wyclif had defined heresy as the worst kind of tyranny. So a Catholic James already fell into the category of a rebellious prince, whose future succession would necessitate a popular revolution back to the headship of the *ecclesia anglicana* by a true Reformed ruler who would conserve the principles of the Reformation. When in 1858 the American author William Henry Seward exclaimed 'all the world knows that revolutions now go backwards', the shade of Locke must have smiled ironically at this statement of the obvious.

[1] E.J. Hobsbawn, 'Revolution', *Revolution in History*, R. Porter and M. Teich (eds.), Cambridge, 1986, pp. 5-46, at p. 35.
[2] D. Close and C. Bridge (eds.), *Revolution. A History of the Idea*, Totowa (N.J.), 1985, pp. 1-3, criticising P. Calvert, *Revolution*, London, 1970 and *A Study of Revolution*, London, 1970, for applying the term to any violent change of government. See in general J. Dunn, *Modern Revolution*, 2nd ed. Cambridge, 1989.
[3] C. Hill, *The Century of Revolution, 1603-1714*, 2nd ed. London, 1980. For some recent examples of double usage: G.E. Aylmer, *Rebellion or Revolution? England 1640-1660*, Oxford, 1986; J.C.D. Clark, *Revolution and Rebellion. State and Society in England in the Seventeenth and Eighteenth Centuries*, Cambridge, 1986; Y.-M. Bercé, *Revolt and Revolution in Early Modern Europe* (translated from the French), Manchester, 1987. For continued use of the traditional terminology, see, e.g., H. and B. van der Zee, *1688. Revolution in the Family*, Harmondsworth/New York, 1988; W.A. Speck, *Reluctant Revolutionaries. England and the Revolution of 1688*, Oxford, 1988.
[4] John Locke, *Two Treatises of Government* [*TTG*], ed. P. Laslett, Cambridge, 1988 (Cambridge Texts in the History of Political Thought), ii.230: 'Nor let any one say, that mischief can arise from hence, as often as it shall please a busie head, or turbulent spirit, to desire the alteration of the Government. 'Tis true, such Men may stir, whenever they please, but it will be only to their own just ruine and perdition. For till the mischief be grown general, and the ill designs of the Rulers become visible, or their attempts sensible to the greater part, the People, who are more disposed to suffer, than right themselves by Resistance, are not apt to stir.' In 1691 Locke argued that the 'sluggish mass' would be slow to rise because most of the people were poor due to idleness and incapacity for thought and action: see E.J. Hundert, 'The Making of *Homo Faber*. John Locke between Ideology and History', *Journal of the History of Ideas*, 33 (1972), pp. 3-22 at p. 6.
[5] E.H. Kossmann and A.F. Mellink (eds.), *Text Concerning the Revolt of the Netherlands*, Cambridge, 1974.
[6] *TTG*, Preface.
[7] P. Laslett, 'The English Revolution and Locke's *Two Treatises of Government*', *Cambridge Historical Journal*, 12 (1956), pp. 40-55; and the Introduction to his editions of the texts (Cambridge, 1960, 1967, 1988). This much seems to be generally accepted, and the question now is how much earlier was the *Second Treatise* to the *First Treatise* of c. 1680. For attempts to push the date back to c. 1673, see R.W.K. Hinton, 'A Note on the Dating of Locke's *Second Treatise*', *Political Studies*, 22 (1974), pp. 471-78; K. Olivecrona, 'A Note on Locke and Filmer', *Locke Newsletter*, 7 (1976), pp. 83-93; M.P. Thompson, 'On Dating Chapter XVI of the *Second Treatise of Government*', *Ibid.*, pp. 95-100. Recent attempts to portray Locke as a radical populist—notably by Richard Ashcraft, *Revolutionary Politics and Locke's Two Treatises of Government*, Princeton, 1987, and *Locke's Two Treatises of Government*, London, 1987—are criticised by D. McNally, 'Locke, Levellers and Liberty: Property and Democracy in the Thought of the First Whigs', *History of Political Thought*, 10 (1989), pp. 17-40.

[8] P. Abram, *John Locke: Two Tracts on Government*, Cambridge, 1967, pp. 174-75.

[9] *TTG*, ii.149-59, also 143. The Roman distinction between *auctoritas* and *potestas* is illustrated by Cicero, *De re publica*, II.xxxii-xxxiii.56-57; *Jude*, 25; Gelasius, *Epistolae*, xii.2; although some later medieval writers also cited Aristotle, *Ethics*, vi.8, 1141b; *Politics*, iv.14, 1297b-98a.

[10] *TTG*, ii.174: 'and that Absolute Dominion, however placed, is so far from being one kind of Civil Society, that it is as inconsistent with it ....' See further T. Redpath, 'John Locke and the Rhetoric of the *Second Treatise*', in H. Sykes and G. Watson (eds.), *The English Mind. Studies Presented to Basil Willey*, Cambridge, 1964, pp. 55-78.

[11] *TTG*, ii.151.

[12] *TTG*, ii.98. For his insistence that all forms of political organisation and power can exist only for the common good, see ii.131, 'the power of the Society, or Legislative constituted by them, can never be suppos'd to extend farther than the common good'; also ii.3, 135, 159-68.

[13] *TTG*, ii.153.

[14] *TTG*, ii.212, continuing, 'This is the Soul that gives Form, Life, and Unity to the Commonwealth: From hence the several Members have their mutual Influence, Sympathy, and Connexion'; cf. ii.211, 'That which makes the Community, and brings Men out of the loose State of Nature, into one Politick Society, is the Agreement which every one has with the rest to incorporate, and act as one Body, and so be one distinct Commonwealth'; also ii.96-97.

[15] *TTG*, ii.151: 'But when he quits this Representation, this publick Will, and acts by his own private Will, he degrades himself, and is but a single private Person without Power, and without Will, that has any Right to Obedience; the Members owing no Obedience but to the publick Will of Society.'

[16] A.P. Monahan, *Consent, Coercion and Limit: The Medieval Origin of Parliamentary Democracy*, Leiden, 1987, pp. 118-20. In general see further E.H. Kantorowicz, *The King's Two Bodies: A Study in Medieval Political Theology*, Princeton, 1957; and for John of Salisbury in particular my 'John of Salisbury and the Tyranny of Nonsense', *Studies in Church History*, *Subsidia*, 3 (1984), pp. 263-86 at pp. 279f.; and p. 263 for the influence of the *Policraticus* in later medieval England.

[17] *TTG*, ii.135, 142, 145-67.

[18] *TTG*, ii.241-42: 'But farther, this Question, (Who shall be Judge?) cannot mean, that there is no Judge at all. For where there is no Judicature on Earth, to decide Controversies amongst Men, God in Heaven is Judge: He alone, 'tis true, is Judge of the Right ... But if the Prince, or whoever they be in the Administration, decline that way of Determination, the Appeal then lies no where but to Heaven.' Cf. *Policraticus*, viii.20; Aquinas, *De regimine principum*, i.6: 'Quod si omnino contra tyrannum auxilium humanum haberi non potest, recurrendum est ad regem omnium Deum, qui est adiutor in opportunitatibus in tribulatione.'

[19] *TTG*, ii.168; also ii.135: 'Thus the Law of Nature stands as an Eternal Rule to all Men, Legislators as well as others. The Rules that they make for other Mens Actions, must, as well as their own and other Mens Actions, be conformable to the Law of Nature, i.e. to the Will of God, of which that is a Declaration, and the fundamental Law of Nature being the preservation of Mankind, no Humane Sanction can be good, or valid against it.'

[20] *TTG*, ii.21: 'Where there is no Judge on Earth, the Appeal lies to God in Heaven. That Question then cannot mean, who shall judge? whether another hath put himself in a State of War with me, and whether I may ... appeal to Heaven in it? Of that I my self can only be Judge in my own Conscience, as I will answer it at the great Day, to the Supream Judge of all Men'; ii.241-42: 'But every Man is Judge for himself, as in all other Cases, so in this, whether another hath put himself into a State of War with him, and whether he should appeal to the Supreme Judge ... wherein the Appeal lies only to Heaven, and in that State the injured Party must judge for himself, when he will think fit to make use of that Appeal, and put himself upon it.'

[21] *TTG*, ii.168; also ii.172, although, as Locke points out here, this does not prevent

loss of life or liberty by action of the adversary in war. Cf. ii.233: 'Self-defence is a part of the Law of Nature; nor can it be denied the Community, even against the King himself.'

²² As indicated by R.H. Cox, *Locke on War and Peace*, London, 1960.

²³ *TTG*, ii.211; cf. ii.149: 'And thus the Community may be said in this respect to be always the Supream Power, but not as considered under any Form of Government, because this Power of the People can never take place till the Government be dissolved.' The capacity of political society generally, expressing itself through Parliament, to act independently after the demise of lawful royal power had been argued by George Lawson's *Politica* of c. 1660, which Locke read in 1679. See J.H. Franklin, *John Locke and the Theory of Sovereignty*, Cambridge, 1978, pp. 53f., and now C. Condren, *George Lawson's Politica and the English Revolution*, Cambridge, 1989.

²⁴ *TTG*, ii.97: 'And thus every Man, by consenting with others to make one Body Politick under one Government, puts himself under an Obligation to every one of that Society, ... or else this original Compact, whereby he with others incorporates into one Society, would signifie nothing, and be no Compact, if he be left free, and under no other ties, than he was before in the State of Nature'; also ii.211 (above, n. 14). For the contract as an act of incorporation see also ii.15, 89, 99, 106, 120, 121, 178. Without it 'the People become a confused Multitude, without Order or Connexion'; ii.219.

²⁵ *TTG*, ii.136, 221-22, 242

²⁶ *TTG*, ii.211: 'The usual, and almost only way whereby this Union is dissolved, is the Inroad of Foreign Force making a Conquest upon them. For in that Case, (not being able to maintain and support themselves, as one intire and independent Body) the Union belonging to that Body which consisted therein, must necessarily cease, and so every one return to the state he was in before, with a liberty to shift for himself, and provide for his own Safety as he thinks fit in some other Society.' Cf. ii.121: 'he is at liberty to go and incorporate himself into any other Commonwealth, or to agree with others to begin a new one, *in vacuis locis*, in any part of the World, they can find free and unpossessed.'

²⁷ *TTG*, ii.149, 156.

²⁸ Cf. Hundert, 'The Making of *Homo Faber*', p. 6.

²⁹ *TTG*, ii.32, 35; cf. 26, 48; and note his description of representatives elected by the people 'as the Fence to their Properties'; ii.222. For Locke's view of natural man as an acquisitive proprietor see C.B. Macpherson, *The Political Theory of Possessive Individualism*, Oxford, 1962.

³⁰ *TTG*, ii.28-29, 85-86. Despite his numerous condemnations of slavery in *TTG* as a concomitant of absolute government—e.g. i.1: 'Slavery is so vile and miserable an Estate of Man, and so directly opposite to the generous Temper and Courage of our Nation; that 'tis hardly to be conceived that an Englishman, much less a Gentleman, should plead for't'; also ii.22-24—his position is the quasi-Aristotelian one that Englishmen never should be slaves, whereas negroes, being barbarians, can be hunted as spoils of war and enslaved. See Laslett's editorial note, pp. 284-85; also M. Seliger, *The Liberal Politics of John Locke*, London, 1968, pp. 118f., and in J.W. Yolton, *John Locke: Problems and Perspectives*, Cambridge, 1969, pp. 27-29; McNally, 'Locke, Levellers, and Liberty', p. 22.

³¹ *TTG*, ii.5-6.

³² *TTG*, ii.182; and note 114-19 for Locke's claim that coming into an inheritance is an act of consent; also i.101-02.

³³ *TTG*, ii.7-8, 11-12, 18-19.

³⁴ Just as a man's labour 'added something to them more than Nature', ii.28, and so created private property.

³⁵ *TTG*, ii.222: 'Whensoever therefore the Legislative shall transgress this fundamental Rule of Society; and either by Ambition, Fear, Folly or Corruption, endeavour to grasp themselves, or put into the hands of any other an Absolute Power over the Lives, Liberties and Estates of the People; By this breach of Trust they forfeit the Power, the People had put into their hands, for quite contrary ends, and it devolves to the People,

who have a Right to resume their original Liberty, and, by the Establishment of a new Legislative (such as they shall think fit) provide for their own Safety and Security, which is the end for which they are in Society. What I have said here, concerning the Legislative, in general, holds true also concerning the supreame Executor, who having a double trust put in him, both to have a part in the Legislative, and the supreme Execution of the Law, Acts against both, when he goes about to set up his own Arbitrary Will, as the Law of the Society.' Similarly ii.212.

[36] *TTG*, ii.149.

[37] *TTG*, ii.220; cf. 227, and 243: 'So also when Society hath placed the Legislative in any Assembly of Men, to continue in them and their Successours, with Direction and Authority for providing such Successours, the Legislative can never revert to the People whilst that Government lasts: ... But ... when by the Miscarriages of those in Authority, it is forfeited; upon the Forfeiture of their Rulers, or at the Determination of the Time set, it reverts to the Society, and the People have a right to act as Supreme, and continue the Legislative in themselves, or erect a new Form, or under the old form place it in new hands, as they think good.'

[38] *TTG*, ii.222: 'whenever the Legislators endeavour to take away, and destroy the Property of the People, or to reduce them to Slavery under Arbitrary Power, they put themselves into a state of War with the People, who are therefore absolved from any farther Obedience, and are left to the common Refuge, which God hath provided for all Men, against Force and Violence'; cf. 212: 'And therefore when the Legislative is broken, or dissolved, Dissolution and Death follows,' because 'it is in their Legislative that the Members of a Commonwealth are united, and combined together into one coherent living Body. This is the Soul that gives Form, Life, and Unity to the Commonwealth.' Similarly in 211 we are told that 'Whenever the Society is dissolved, 'tis certain the Government of that Society cannot remain. Thus Conquerours Swords often cut up Governments by the Roots, and mangle Societies to pieces'. But this lies oddly with the right of the corporate People acting as 'the Society' in nn. 35-37 above to manage without a legislative or to establish a different one.

[39] J. Balogh, 'Rex a recte regendo', *Speculum*, 3 (1928), pp. 580-82.

[40] The best general summaries of feudal political thought remain A.J. and R.W. Carlyle, *History of Political Theory in the West*, 6 vols., Edinburgh/London, 1936, III, pp. 19-86, and W. Ullmann, *Principles of Government and Politics in the Middle Ages*, 3rd ed. London/New York, 1974, pp. 150-92. The only edition and translation of the *Song of Lewes* is by C.L. Kingsford (Oxford, 1890); for Bracton see below note 77.

[41] John of Salisbury, *Policraticus*, iii.15; Aquinas, *Summa theologiae*, II.II.xl.2 ad 3 and civ.6 ad 3; *Comm. in Sent.*, II.xliv.2.2: as a usurper, the tyrant may be killed—even if an oath of perpetual loyalty has been taken to him: 'Nec putanda est talis multitudo infideliter agere tyrannum destituens, etiam si eidem in perpetuo se ante subiecerat; quia hoc ipse meruit, in multitudinis regimine se non fideliter gerens *ut exigit regis officium*, quod ei pactum a subditis non reservetur'; *De regimine principum*, i.6.

[42] *TTG*, ii.237: as Locke says, he is quoting here William Barclay, *De regno et regali potestati adversus Monarchomachos*, iii.16, of which he bought another copy for the Earl of Shaftesbury in 1681; see Laslett, p. 419. Also ii.239: 'In whatsoever he has no Authority, there he is no King, and may be resisted.'

[43] *TTG*, ii.214-18; cf. ii.155: 'In all States and Conditions the true remedy of Force without Authority, is to oppose Force to it. The use of force without Authority, always puts him that uses it into a state of War, as the Aggressor, and renders him liable to be treated accordingly.' Similarly ii.232.

[44] *TTG*, ii.238.

[45] *TTG*, ii.219.

[46] *TTG*, ii. 239.

[47] *TTG*, ii.227, and 230, 237 for the definition of rebellion as 'overturning the constitution'.

[48] *TTG*, ii.225: 'Secondly, I Answer, such Revolutions happen not upon every little mismanagement in publick affairs ... But if a long train of Abuses, Prevarications, and

Artifices, all tending the same way, make the design visible to the People, and they cannot but feel, what they lie under, and see, whither they are going; 'tis not to be wonder'd, that they should then rouze themselves, and endeavour to put the rule into such hands, which may secure to them the ends for which Government was at first erected.'

49 *TTG*, ii.223.

50 *TTG*, ii, 226.

51 *TTG*, ii.223.

52 For a recent survey of the succession question see A.L. Brown, *The Governance of Late Medieval England, 1272-1461*, London, 1989, pp. 7-11.

53 T. Rymer, *Foedera*, Record Commission, London, 1816-19, II, p. 646. The *Modus tenendi Parliamentum*, 13, probably written originally in the 1320s, said that the absence of a king without good reason 'dampnosa et periculosa est toti communitati Parliamenti et regni'; N. Pronay and J. Taylor (eds.), *Parliamentary Texts of the Later Middle Ages*, Oxford, 1980, p. 72.

54 *Foedera*, London, 1704-35, IV, p. 243: 'Pur ceo que Sire Edward, n'adgairs Roi d'Engleterre, de sa bone volunte, et de commun conseil et assent des Prelatz, Countes et Barons, et autres Nobles, et tote la Communalte du Roialme, s'en est ouste del Governement du Roialme deveigne a Sire Edward, son Fiutz eyne, et Heir, et q'il governe Regne, et soit Roi Corone.'

55 See H.G. Wright, 'The Protestation of Richard II in the Tower in September, 1399', *Bulletin of the John Rylands Library*, 23 (1939), pp. 151-65. For Shakespeare's version (which was banned during the 1680s) see Kantorowicz, *King's Two Bodies*, pp.24-41, and here further literature. Also R.H. Jones, *The Royal Policy of Richard II. Absolutism in the Later Middle Ages*, Oxford, 1968.

56 *Rotuli Parliamentorum*, London, 1767, III, pp. 416-17; cf. M.V. Clarke and V.H. Galbraith, 'The Deposition of Richard II', *Bulletin of the John Rylands Library*, 14 (1930), pp. 125-55 at pp. 133, 146; according to the Dieulacres Chronicle 'Deo ius suum resignavit'. For discussion of the status of the assembly see the works cited by A. Tuck, *Richard II and the English Nobility*, London, 1973, pp. 220f.

57 *Rotuli Parliamentorum*, III, pp. 418-20; it was said that 'idem Rex nolens iustas Leges et Consuetudines Regni sui servare seu protegere, set secundum sue arbitrium Voluntatis facere quicquid desideriis eius occurrerit, quandoque et frequentius quando sibi expositi et declarati fuerant Leges Regni sui per Iusticiarios et alios de Consilio suo, et secundum Leges illas petentibus iustitiam exhiberet; Dixit expresse, vultu austero et protervo, quod Leges sue erant in ore suo, et aliquotiens in pectore suo: Et quod ipse solus posset mutare et condere Leges Regni sui'. This rule by will was declared to be 'in derogationem Status Parliamenti, et in magnum incomodum totius Regni, et perniciosum exemplum'. There was a further accusation that Richard intended to abolish Parliament altogether.

58 *Rotuli Parliamentorum*, V, p. 465; also John Benet's *Chronicle*, G.L. and M.A. Harriss (eds.), Camden Miscellany XXIV, *Camden Society*, 4th Series, 9 (1972), pp. 151-252 at p. 230. See further R.A. Griffiths, *The Reign of King Henry the Sixth: The Exercise of Royal Authority, 1422-1461*, London, 1981, who accepts that Henry was personally active in government until c. 1453.

59 For what follows see R.L. Storey, *The End of the House of Lancaster*, 2nd ed. Gloucester, 1986; J.R. Lander, *Conflict and Compromise in Fifteenth-Century England*, London, 1969. The bastardy proceedings against the children of Edward IV are discussed by C. Given-Wilson and A. Curteis, *The Royal Bastards of Medieval England*, London, 1986.

60 *Foedera*, II, p. 650. The articles of deposition which are recorded in Adam Orleton's *Apology* of 1334 may have been produced for propaganda purposes rather than official acts.

61 R.M. Haines, *Archbishop John Stratford: Political Revolutionary and Champion of the Liberties of the English Church, c. 1275/80-1348*, Toronto, 1986, p. 183, who indicates the concerted attack through their sermons by Orleton, Stratford and Reynolds; also *The Church and Politics in Fourteenth-Century England: The Career of Adam Orleton, c. 1275-1345*, Cambridge, 1978, esp. pp. 167-77.

[62] *Rotuli Parliamentorum*, III, p. 422; Richard was declared 'fuisse et esse inutilem, inhabilem, insufficientem penitus, et indignum; ac propter praemissa, et eorum praetextu, ab omni dignitate et honore regiis ... merito deponendum' by a Parliamentary tribunal 'per Pares et Proceres Regni Anglie Spirituales et Temporales, et eiusdem Regni Communitates omnes Status eiusdem Regni representantes'. When querying the authority of Henry IV's first Parliament of October 1399, Archbishop Arundel covered himself both ways: 'a cause de l'acceptation de la Renunciation fait par le dit Roy Richard, et de la Deposition de mesme le Roy Richard'; III, p. 415.

[63] Richard's first real Parliament of January 1484 received a declaration by him that 'the courte of parliament is of suche authorite, and the people of this land of suche nature and disposicion, as experience teacheth, that manifestacion and declaracion of any trueth or right made by the thre estates of this reame assembled in parliament, and by auctorite of the same, maketh, before all other thynges, moost feith and certaynte, and, quietyng mens myndes, removeth the occasion of all doubtes and sedicious langage. Therfore, at the request and by assent of the thre estates of this reame, that is to say, the lordes spirituelx and temporelx, and commens of this lande assembled in this present parliament by auctorite of the same, bee it pronounced, decreed and declared that oure said soveraigne lorde the kyng was and is veray and undoubted kyng of this reame of England'; *Rotuli Parliamentorum*, VI, pp. 241-42. The expression 'by authority of Parliament' is first recorded in 1433, and in 1453 Parliament declared that 'this high court of Parliament ... is so high and mighty in its nature, that it may make law, and that which is law it may make no law'. See further *The English Parliament in the Middle Ages*, eds. R.G. Davies and J.H. Denton, Manchester, 1981, esp. pp. 149f.

[64] For the papal legate's support for the Yorkists in 1460-61 see E.F. Jacob, *The Fifteenth Century*, Oxford, 1961, pp. 518-20.

[65] A.F. Pollard, *The Reign of Henry VII from Contemporary Sources*, Rpt. New York, 1967, I, p. 35; cf. S.B. Chrimes, *Henry VII*, London, 1972, p. 177.

[66] *Foedera*, II, p. 683.

[67] '... et eorum occasione Regnum Anglie cum pertinentiis suis vacare, prefatus Henricus Dux Lancastrie de loco suo surgens, ... dictum Regnum Anglie, sic ut premittitur vacans, una cum Corona ac omnibus membris et pertinentiis suis, vendicavit in lingua materna, sub hac forma verborum:

> In the name of Fadir, Son, and Holy Gost, I Henry of Lancastre chalenge yis Rewme of Yngland and the Corone with all ye membres and ye appurtenances, als I yt am disendit be right lyne of the Blode comyng fro the gude lorde Kyng Henry therde, and thorghe yat ryght yat God of his grace hath sent me, with helpe of my Kyn and of my Frendes to recover it: the whiche Rewme was in poynt to be undone for defaut of Governance and undoyng of the gode Lawes.

Postquam quidem vendicationem et clameum, tam Domini Spirituales quam Temporales, et omnes Status ibidem presentes ... absque quacumque difficultate vel mora ut Dux prefatus super eos regnaret unanimiter consenserunt'; *Rotuli Parliamentorum*, III, pp. 422-23. See further G.T. Lapsley, 'The Parliamentary Title of Henry IV', *English Historical Review*, 49 (1934), pp. 423-49, 577-606; reprinted in *Crown, Community and Parliament*, eds. H.M. Cam and G. Barraclough, Oxford, 1951, pp. 273-340.

[68] *Rotuli Parliamentorum*, V, p. 465. The claim was dependent on recognition of his father's claim—that the 'Coroune, Roial Estate, Dignitee and Lordship ... of right apperteynd to the seid noble Prynce Richard, Duc of York ... verry true and rightful heir to the throne'—which had been acknowledged by the lords in the previous year (1460) on the basis of his descent from Edward III, but was to remain in abeyance until the death of the illegal king Henry VI; *ibid.*, V, pp. 375-79. On this see now P.A. Johnson, *Duke Richard of York, 1411-1460*, Oxford, 1988.

[69] Edward Hall, *Chronicle*, ed. H. Ellis, London, 1809, p. 420.

[70] The importance of medieval political thought for the development of seventeenth-century constitutional theory has long been recognised, notably by the late C.H. McIlwain, *Constitutionalism, Ancient and Modern*, 2nd ed. Ithaca, 1958, and more recently D.W. Hanson, *From Kingdom to Commonwealth: The Development of Civic Consciousness in English*

Political Thought, Cambridge (Mass.), 1970. For the relationship between conciliar theory and the growth of the idea of popular sovereignty see F. Oakley, 'On the Road from Constance to 1688: The Political Thought of John Major and George Buchanan', *Journal of British Studies*, 1 (1962), pp. 1-31, and 'Figgis, Constance and the Divines of Paris', *American Historical Review*, 75 (1969), pp. 368-86, both reprinted in *Natural Law, Conciliarism and Consent in the Late Middle Ages*, London, 1984; B. Tierney, 'Medieval Canon Law and Western Constitutionalism', *Catholic Historical Review*, 52 (1966), pp. 1-17, and 'Divided Sovereignty at Constance: A Problem of Medieval and Early Modern Political Theory', *Annuarium Historiae Conciliorum*, 7 (1975), pp. 238-56, both reprinted in *Church Law and Constitutional Thought in the Middle Ages*, London, 1979; also *Religion, Law and the Growth of Constitutional Thought, 1150-1650*, Cambridge, 1982.

⁷¹ Ullmann, *Principles*, pp. 215-305; Q. Skinner, *The Foundations of Modern Political Thought*, Cambridge, 1978, vol. I; S. Reynolds, *Kingdoms and Communities in Western Europe, 900-1300*, Oxford, 1984; A. Black, *Guilds and Civil Society in European Political Thought from the Twelfth Century to the Present*, London, 1984.

⁷² E.g. *TTG*, ii.15: 'But I moreover affirm, That all Men are naturally in that State, and remain so, till by their own Consents they make themselves Members of some Politick Society; And I doubt not in the Sequel of this Discourse, to make it very clear; ii.99: 'And thus that, which begins and actually constitutes any Political Society, is nothing but the consent of any number of Freemen capable of a majority to unite and incorporate into such a Society. And this is that, and that only, which did, or could give beginning to any lawful Government in the World'; cf. ii.89, 95-99.

⁷³ See the discussion beginning *TTG*, ii.105: 'I will not deny, that if we look back as far as History will direct us, towards the Original of Common-wealths, we shall generally find them under the Government and Administration of one Man'; ii.175: 'Though Governments can originally have no other Rise than that before mentioned, nor Polities be founded on anything but the Consent of the People; yet such has been the Disorders Ambition has fill'd the World with, that in the noise of War, which makes so great a part of the History of Mankind, this Consent is little taken notice of: And therefore many have mistaken the force of Arms, for the Consent of the People; and reckon Conquest as one of the Originals of Government. But Conquest is as far from setting up any Government, as demolishing an House is from building a new one in the place. Indeed it often makes way for a new Frame of a Common-wealth, by destroying the former; but, without the Consent of the People, can never erect a new one.' See also ii.106.

⁷⁴ *TTG*, ii.106: 'Thus, though looking back as far as Records give us any account of Peopling the World, and the History of Nations, we commonly find the Government to be in one hand, yet it destroys not that, which I affirm, (viz.) That the beginning of Politick Society depends upon the consent of the Individuals, to joyn into and make one Society; who, when they are thus incorporated, might set up what form of Government they thought fit.'

⁷⁵ *TTG*, ii.134: 'the first and fundamental positive law of all Common-wealths, is the establishing of the Legislative Power ... This Legislative is not only the supream power of the Common-wealth, but sacred and unalterable in the hands where the Community have once placed it; nor can any Edict of any Body else, in what Form soever conceived, or by what Power soever backed, have the force and obligation of a law, which has not its Sanction from that Legislative, which the public has chosen and appointed.' The reform of Parliamentary representation is therefore frustrated and 'thought incapable of a remedy' because the constitution of the legislative is 'the original and supream act of the Society, antecedent to all positive Laws in it'; ii.157.

⁷⁶ *TTG*, ii.177-78: 'We are told by some, that the English Monarchy is founded in the Norman Conquest, and that our Princes have thereby a Title to absolute Dominion: Which if it were true, (as by the History it appears otherwise) ... But supposing, which seldom happens, that the Conquerors and Conquered never incorporate into one People, under the same Laws and Freedom.' As so often happens with Locke, the crucial issue is discussed in terms of its reverse. This section is allegedly about a lawful conquest (which he denies to William I) and the rights of the Norman invaders and their descen-

dants (whereas the real question is the rights of William's new subjects), and the whole matter is then blurred by pointing out that French and English were subsequently assimilated together into one people.

[77] *TTG*, ii.239: 'and if there needed authority in a Case where Reason is so plain, I could send my Reader to Bracton, Fortescue, and the Author of the Mirrour, and others; Writers, who cannot be suspected to be ignorant of our Government, or Enemies to it. But I thought Hooker alone might be enough ...'; cf. Laslett, pp. 77, 426. It has been suggested that the *De legibus et consuetudinibus Angliae* (ed. G.E. Woodbine, New Haven, 1915-42; trans. and rev. by S.E. Thorne, Cambridge [Mass.], 1968-77) may not be by Henry de Bracton, but by William de Ralegh or Martin Pateshul: the matter remains unresolved. For Bracton's theory see W. Fesefeldt, *Englische Staatstheorie des 13. Jahrhunderts. Henry de Bracton und sein Werk*, Göttingen, 1962; and extensive bibliography in C.J. Nederman, 'Bracton on Kingship Revisited', *History of Political Thought*, 5 (1984), pp. 61-77.

[78] This is presumably the *Mirror of Justice* (ed. W.J. Whittaker, Selden Society, London, 1895), apparently written in French in the thirteenth century by Andrew Horne, which was popularised by Coke and printed and translated in the 1640s, rather than the *Mirror for Magistrates* assembled by William Baldwin in the 1550s. It was also used in favour of William III by writers like Sir William Temple and John Toland. Like the *Modus tenendi Parliamentum* (ed. Pronay and Taylor, pp. 67, 80), it claimed the support of an Anglo-Saxon origin; see H.A. MacDougal, *Racial Myth in English History. Trojans, Teutons and Anglo-Saxons*, Montreal/Hanover/London, 1982, pp. 57-58, 73-77.

[79] *Comm. in Sent.*, II.xliv.2.2: 'qui enim per violentiam dominium surripit non efficitur vere praelatus vel dominus; et ideo cum facultas adest, potest aliquis tale dominium repellere: nisi forte postmodum dominus verus effectus sit vel per consensum subditorum vel per auctoritatem superioris.'

[80] *TTG*, ii.153-54, 223. There was considerable contemporary pride in England's unique retention of its 'original' constitution; see D.H. Pennington, 'A Seventeenth-Century Perspective', *The English Parliament*, eds. Davies and Denton, pp. 186-87. See further J.G.A. Pocock, *The Ancient Constitution and the Feudal Law. A Study of English Historical Thought in the Seventeenth Century*, Cambridge, 1957; also A. Pallister, *Magna Carta. The Heritage of Liberty*, London, 1971.

[81] *TTG*, ii.162.

[82] *TTG*, ii.166.

[83] *TTG*, ii.163.

[84] *TTG*, ii.158.

[85] *De laudibus legum Angliae*, XIII, ed. S.B. Chrimes, Cambridge, 1949, p. 32; *The Governance of England*, II, ed. C. Plummer, Oxford, 1885, p. 112; cf. Chrimes, *English Constitutional Ideas in the Fifteenth Century*, Cambridge, 1936, who maintains (p. 324) that Fortescue was merely stating a situation in which theory and practice co-incided. For discussion of Fortescue's borrowing from Aquinas and Tholemy see now N. Rubinstein, 'The History of the Word *Politicus* in Early Modern Europe', *The Language of Political Theory in Early Modern Europe*, ed. A. Pagden, Cambridge, 1987, pp. 41-56 at pp. 42-45 and 49-52.

[86] *Summa theologiae*, III.I.cv.1; also II.I.xcv.4. See further my *Problem of Sovereignty in the Later Middle Ages*, Cambridge, 1963, pp. 200-04; and for a direct relationship between Locke and Aquinas' pupil, John of Paris, see J. Coleman, '*Dominium* in Thirteenth- and Fourteenth-Century Political Thought and its Seventeenth-Century Heirs: John of Paris and Locke', *Political Studies*, 33 (1985), pp. 73-100.

[87] Even Marsilius of Padua, despite his insistence on the right of a community to correct and depose its *pars principans*, had a highly developed sense of the iniquity of rebellion against a good prince and condemned those who fell into the traditional category of *rebelles imperii*; *Defensor pacis*, II.xxvi.13-14. Similarly heretics were rebels against Christ: 'velut haereticos et crucis Christi rebelles'; II.xxvi.16.

[88] Aquinas, *Summa theologiae*, II.II.xlii.2 ad 3: 'regimen tyrannicum non est iustum; quia non ordinatur ad bonum commune, sed ad bonum privatum regentis: ut patet per Philos. in iii *Polit.* et in viii *Ethic.* Et ideo perturbatio huius regiminis non habet rationem

seditionis; nisi forte quando sic inordinate perturbatur tyranni regimen quod multitudo subiecta maius detrimentum patitur ex perturbatione consequenti quam ex tyranni regimine.' This follows Ciceronian usage of *perturbatio* for popular unrest. For Wyclif's attitude towards the Peasants Revolt see Wilks, *'Reformatio regni'*, *Studies in Church History*, 9 (1972), pp. 109-30 at pp. 125-27.

[89] *Six livres de la République*, ii.2 and 7, iv.7, vi.6. The English translation of 1606 is edited by K.D. McRae, New York, 1962. Cf. Aristotle, *Politics*, v.1, 1301b.

[90] *République*, i.8-10, iii.4, iv.7, v.1.

[91] *République*, iv.1-3; also his *Methodus*, 6, 'conversiones rerum publicarum' and 'conversiones imperio rerum'.

[92] Although Plato and Aristotle could talk of a change of constitutions by one *turning* into another one, it was Polybius' cyclical notion of constitutional change as something comparable to the slow turning of a wheel (*Histories*, VI.ix.10) which popularised the idea of political change as a revolving in Roman thought, e.g. Cicero, *De re publica*, I.xxix.45: 'quasi circumitus in rebus publicis commutationum'; II.xxv.45: 'Hic ille iam vertetur orbis, cuius naturalem motum atque circuitum a primo discite adgnoscere. Id enim est caput civilis prudentiae, in qua omnis haec nostra versatur oratio, videre itinera flexusque rerum publicarum, ...'

[93] For what follows see V.F. Snow, 'The Concept of Revolution in Seventeenth-Century England', *Historical Journal*, 5 (1962), pp. 167-74; and for earlier usage A. Hatto, '"Revolution". An Enquiry into the Usefulness of an Historical Term', *Mind*, 58 (1949), pp. 495-517. Hatto comments (p. 505) on the slow development of English and northern European usage.

[94] Thus the earliest known medieval example to date is Matteo Villani's *Cronica*, which not only employed *revoluzione* to refer to general political unrest (v.19, ix.34), but also used it for the removal of an oligarchic regime in Siena in 1355 and its replacement by a more popular one: 'la subita revoluzione fatta per gli cittadini di Siena' (iv.90).

[95] Most of the Italian examples of the fifteenth and sixteenth centuries cited by Hatto (pp. 502-04)—notably Guicciardini, but not Machiavelli—related to pro- or anti-Medici changes of government, and so had the implication of return or restoration built into them. Cf. F. Gilbert, *Machiavelli and Guicciardini. Politics and History in Sixteenth-Century Florence*, Princeton, 1964.

[96] See *TTG*, ii.200, where James is praised for distinguishing between a king and a tyrant, the king making 'a double Oath to the observation of the Fundamental Laws of the Kingdom' by means of a 'paction' comparable to that made by God to Noah after the Flood. For James (as he says here) this was of course essentially an act of self-limitation in the coronation oath. Also ii.133.

[97] J. Dunn, *The Political Thought of John Locke*, Cambridge, 1969. Hobbes' portrayal of the State in terms of Biblical exegesis is familiar; see now D. Johnston, *The Rhetoric of Leviathan*, Princeton, 1986.

[98] *TTG*, ii.6 and 56; also i.53-54 and 86.

[99] Stephanus Junius Brutus, *Vindiciae contra tyrannos*, translated into English in 1689 as *A Defence of Liberty against Tyrants*, ed. H.J. Laski, London, 1924 (Rpt. New York, 1972), p. 87; and p. 71 for the requirement of a double covenant in accordance with IV *Kings*, xi.17. The *Vindiciae* was publicly burnt at Oxford in 1683 as 'a damnable book destructive of the sacred person of a prince'.

[100] Wilks, 'Royal Patronage and Anti-Papalism from Ockham to Wyclif', *Studies in Church History, Subsidia*, 5 (1987), pp. 135-63 at pp. 148-53, and here further references. This seems to have developed in England as an adaptation of French theory.

[101] *TTG*, i.163, refers to 'the story of Jephtha, where he Articled *with* the People, and they made him Judge over them'; similarly ii.109. One may contrast the contract with the people here and James I's 'paction *to* the people' above note 96. The Jephtha story is then used by Locke to justify the popular 'appeal to heaven': 'Then they may appeal, as Jephtha did, to Heaven, and repeat their Appeal, till they have *recovered* the native Right of their Ancestors, which was to have such a Legislative over them, as the Majority should approve, and freely acquiesce in'; ii.176. Also ii.20 and 241.

30   WILKS — REBELLION AND REVOLUTION: A LOCKEIAN THEME

Isaiah, i.4. the Vulgate *abalienati* becomes 'they have gone away backward' in the Authorised Version, which compares with the Wyclif Bible's 'thei ben aliened awei bacward'. One is reminded of Marx's condemnation of the alienated capitalist as reactionary for trying 'to roll back the wheel of history'.

i.23 (princes): only the Geneva Bible had 'thy princes are rebellious', whereas Coverdale had made them traitors, and the Vulgate and Wyclif versions had merely talked of infidel princes; i.2, 5, 20 (people): both Coverdale and Geneva have 'rebellious' for the people in i.20, whilst the Vulgate reads 'Israel autem me non cognovit, et populus meus non intellexit ... addentes praevaricationem ... Quod si nolueritis et me ad iracundiam provocaveritis' for the relevant phrases in i.3, 5 and 20 respectively. Cf. the AV people with a revolting and rebellious heart for 'cor incredulum et exasperans' in the Vulgate version of *Jeremiah*, v.23.

i.8-9, 24-31. The actual term 'revolution' appears in the AV marginal notes to *Exodus*, xxxiv.22, I *Samuel*, i.20, II *Chronicles*, xxiv.23, although only in the traditional sense of the cycle of the year or the completion of a period of pregnancy, 'post circulum dierum' etc.

Locke's debt to Hooker is well known and freely admitted by him: *TTG*, ii.5, 15, 60-61, 90-91, 94, 111, 134, 239.

See my *Problem of Sovereignty*, pp. 47-48, 199.

Problem of Sovereignty, p. 237 for this and other examples.

De civili dominio, ed. J. Loserth, Wyclif Society, 1900f., ii.13, p. 153; also for example ii.14, pp. 179 and 182; ii.16, p. 232.

De civili dominio, ii.6, pp. 47-51.

J.W. Allen, *History of Political Thought in the Sixteenth Century*, London, 1928, pp. 165-68. For the importance of St. German's view of Parliament as the seat of royal power over both spiritual and temporal matters see now J. Guy, *Reassessing the Henrician Age. Humanism, Politics and Reform, 1500-1550*, Oxford, 1986.

JERUSALEM: PURPOSE OF HISTORY OR
GATEWAY TO HEAVEN?
APOCALYPTICISM IN THE FIRST CRUSADE

P. Raedts

Few names in the history of the Church can have stirred so many hearts and have given hope to so many people as has the name Jerusalem: vision of peace, dream of heaven, symbol of a new and better future here on earth. And never did expectations rise higher than in the days of the First Crusade, when hundreds of thousands left home and family to take the road to Jerusalem. They did so answering the call of Pope Urban II (1088-1099) who, at the Council of Clermont (1095), had summoned all Christian knights to liberate Jerusalem and the Holy Places from the hands of the Infidel.[1] The question that has been exercising the minds of many for a long time now is, why the Pope's call met with such an overwhelming and unexpectedly enthusiastic response.

A very popular theory runs as follows: a distinction should be made between two kinds of crusade, the knights' and the people's crusade. The knights took arms to defend the rights of the Church in Muslim territory and to recover the Holy Places. The people, who at that time suffered from the consequences of a series of famines, understood the Pope's call as the first of the trumpets signalling the end of history, when their sufferings would come to an end and legend would come to life, when the face of the earth was to be changed utterly. The liberation of Jerusalem would herald the beginning of the thousand-year realm under the reign of the Last Emperor, a time of happiness and plenty for all, only to be ended with the coming of Antichrist. So anxious were the poor for this to happen that it was they who rescued the crusade of the knights when it got bogged down by quarrels between the princes after the siege of Antioch in 1098. And it was they who got the army moving again end kept it on the road to Jerusalem. This interpretation was first forwarded by Alphandéry[2], and acquired its popularity in the English-speaking world through N. Cohn's *Pursuit of the Millennium*. In Cohn's book the People's Crusade became the first of a long series of similar movements which, surfacing in times of social and political crisis, became quite a regular feature of European history up to the days of Marxism and National Socialism.[3]

This interpretation of the First Crusade as a fundamentally apocalyptic movement, at least on the part of the people, has come in for quite some criticism, yet all major crusade historians pay tribute to it and admit that apocalyptic feeling played at least some part in rousing the people. More substantial objections were formulated by R. Lerner and B. McGinn. Lerner maintains that the expectation of an imminent end was not just an occasional feeling among the uprooted classes, but a chronological constant, affecting everyone all the time, part of the mental make-up of medieval man.[4] Although this may well be true for the later Middle Ages, the period to which Lerner refers in particular, it is doubtful whether the same can be said for the period before 1200. Even when writers of that earlier period speculated about the events at the end of history, it was not so much, because they thought that the end was near, but because they wished to stress the fact that in the present struggle, as e.g. the Investiture Contest, which gave rise to several apocalyptic prophecies, last values were at stake.[5]

From a different angle B. McGinn criticizes Cohn for not noticing that many apocalyptic texts were not violent or revolutionary at all but were, in fact, written to uphold the established social order, as was the case with many prophecies about the Last Emperor.[6] Although this point is quite important for the assessment of apocalyptic texts, it does not impinge upon Cohn's theory very much, because he is talking about apocalyptic movements not about texts, in other words about the ideology recipients, not the producers.[7] The question remains whether the First Crusade was an apocalyptic mass movement.

Before proceeding with the assessment of the evidence and a further look at the underlying theories I first want to draw attention to the fundamental distinction between apocalypticism and eschatology. Eschatological beliefs were common to all Christians insofar as everyone at the time not only believed that history would once come to an end but also, far more important, that each man would come to his own end long before. Worries about one's fate in the hereafter was a common feature of Christian piety, it caused a lot of anxiety and drove many people on the way to Jerusalem. The apocalyptic belief that the end of the whole world was at hand now was a different matter altogether and, I think, much rarer. The point must be stressed, because quite often scholars seem to confuse the two by taking all references in the sources to the Heavenly Jerusalem or to paradise for expectations of the end of history,[8] whereas it is quite clear that most contemporary authors say nothing more than that a visit to or the conquest of the earthly Jerusalem could bring people nearer to heaven.[9]

If we take this distinction into account, the evidence for apocalyptic tendencies becomes slender, to say the least. Ekkehard of Aura mentions, in passing, that during that heady summer of 1096 the rumour went round that Charlemagne had come to life again to lead the army on to Jerusalem.[10] And Guibert of Nogent suggests that the liberation of Jerusalem had set the stage for the coming of Antichrist.[11] But this is so clearly an effort to fit the amazing events of those years into a theological pattern that it can be dismissed as evidence for the mood of the people. Alphandéry relies for his argument almost completely on Raymond of Aguilers, chaplain to Raymond of St. Gilles and eyewitness to the whole event.[12] His chronicle of the crusade is, no doubt, filled with dreams, visions and other miracles and thus does impart the impression that the crusaders were in a constant mood of exaltation and in very close touch with the supernatural during their long and exhausting march. Yet it is not quite the same as living in the expectation that the end is near, for which I can find no clear indications.

There is a far more pressing reason, however, to query the apocalyptic character of the First Crusade. Apocalyptic movements are usually characterized by their extreme dualism. All of history is separated into the life and death struggle between good and evil, between the present age and the age to come. The participants consider themselves to be God's chosen ones, the soldiers of light, fighting the forces of darkness.[13] Within the group a collective sense of exhilaration prevails, individual feelings seem no longer important, it is the group that has been chosen to herald the future, not each separate individual.[14] The forces of darkness are usually identified with established institutions of the present, such as the Church or the state. The consequence is that in these groups ordinary rules of law and order usually cease to be binding, because they are being considered as the chains of slavery to be shaken off now that the time of freedom has come for God's Elect.[15] A most interesting example of this kind of disregard of the law is the movement around the seventeenth-century Jewish Messiah, the Sabbatai Zvi. All reports about him agree that, contrary to all of Jewish tradition, he pronounced the ineffable Name and applied it to himself, ate the fat of forbidden animals and did other things against the Lord and his Law, pressing his followers to do likewise.[16]

The unbridled enthusiasm, the sense of collective election, the disengagement from the ordinary, all these characteristic features of chiliastic movements are absent from the First Crusade. It may seem surprising to say so, as all sources speak about God's armies fighting the enemy of Christ.[17] Even the language of the Turks is described as devilish, in battle they howl and shout like demons.[18] The crusaders are seen as martyrs in a just and godly cause.[19] The crusade itself is described as a second Pentecost, it was a venture in which 'people from many nations and many tongues flocked together and were united like brothers under the love of God'.[20] Yet it seems the language of hindsight, of the time when it had become clear that a new page had been written in the book of the history of salvation, i.e. after the deliverance of Jerusalem.[21] The authors of the eyewitness accounts cannot conceal, even when bathing in the glow of victory, that during the march to Jerusalem the army was beset by doubts about the whole enterprise. During the Turkish siege of Antioch the gates had to be locked and guarded from the inside, or very few would have remained. But even so many priests and laymen fled the city.[22] All authors are convinced that the army was victorious not because of its valour or merits, but because of God's infinite mercy.[23] They seem sometimes rather surprised that despite their many failings things went right after all, which is a far cry from the atmosphere of self-glorification which is so characteristic of apocalyptic movements.

Moreover these fears persisted right up to the end. The crusaders felt in constant need of elaborate rituals of purification and reconciliation, especially in times when all went wrong and gloom prevailed. Fulcher of Chartres describes one of the trickiest moments in the battle of Dorylaeum (1097) thus:

> What shall I say? Our troops huddled together like sheep in a closed pen, trembling and frightened. It seemed to us that this was happening because of our sins. Shouts went up to heaven of men, women and children, and also of the heathen swooping down on us. We had no hope to live left. Then we decided to beseech God's mercy and to confess our guilt and sin. The Bishop of Le Puy, our patron, was also present with four others, and several priests in white robes, singing and praying. Many people made a rush for them, because they wished to confess their sins before their almost certain death. But then God heard our pleas and took mercy upon us, as He does not take delight in the pomp of noble birth or the clattering of arms but comes to the rescue of people, pure in heart and filled with divine virtues.[24]

It is a story which stands for many. Two things in it should be noted: first that the people in an emergency resorted to the ordinary rituals which the Church provided for such occasions: confession, penitence, the giving of alms, processions. And it was the appointed clergy who was in charge of their enactment. Even a visionary like Peter Bartholomew, the man who discovered the Holy Lance, never contested the authority of the clergy, but rather affirmed it on several occasions, as at the time when he had a vision of Bishop Adhémar, coming down from heaven to tell him to go and see the princes and exhort them to stay united.[25] Another striking feature of the story is the absence of any sense of collective redemption. On the contrary, each crusader had to go to a priest himself to make his own peace with God. That this was the normal routine can be seen in another vision of Peter Bartholomew, in which St. Andrew revealed to him the rules of reconciliation with God: every single person (*unusquisque*) should turn to God and regret his sins and give alms five times or, if he was too poor, pray five Our Fathers because of the five wounds of Our Lord.[26] Although the crusaders fought God's war, the success or defeat of their enterprise depended entirely on the individual behaviour of each participant. Jerusalem would be delivered, but only if the army refrained from sin and fornication and fought with a pure heart. The expedition and its purpose may have been new, even unheard of, yet it took place within the limits set by Church and society, such as they were at the end of the eleventh century.

This might be true but for one exception:the massacre of the Jews in the Rhineland, an unprecedented event, which did, indeed, seem to make a mockery of all moral standards of the time. The general rule had always been that Jews were to be despised and pitied but not to be murdered. So far the most satisfactory explanation for this new and terrible departure from ancient custom has been to highlight the important role which Jews played in Christian apocalyptic phantasies, which in 1096 suddenly became reality. Recently, however, Professor Chazan has shown that one need not invoke apocalyptic feeling to explain the violence against the Jews, but that the decision to murder them was a logical, though distorted, conclusion which could be drawn from the Pope's message to fight Christ's enemies in the Holy Land.[27] He also shows that the massacre was not a spontaneous outburst of popular violence but a carefully orchestrated attack, organised by the official leaders of the German Crusade.[28]

This brings us to the conclusion that an explanation in which the crusade, or even part of it, is seen as an apocalyptic movement of the dissatisfied in the margin of society, approaches the problem from the wrong angle. The crusade was a phenomenon which occupied the centre stage of history and united all Christians from high to low in a common purpose, the deliverance of Jerusalem and the defeat of Christ's enemies. Explanations for its astounding success must be found by focusing on mainline Christianity, not on sectarian behaviour in the margin.

If it is true that the crusaders did not hasten to Jerusalem to witness the end of history, the question is: what kept them going? Professor Prawer pointed out, a few years ago, that from the end of the tenth century onwards Christians began to establish a connection between the earthly city in Palestine and the Heavenly Jerusalem. The spiritual interpretation of the image of Jerusalem, which had been customary in Christianity from its very beginning, made way for a very litteral understanding of Biblical prophecies concerning the Holy City.[29] And it was this new expectation to see heaven on earth in the city of Jerusalem which kept the crowds going in Prawer's interpretation. Now it is certainly true that many pilgrims in the eleventh century did expect to catch a glimpse of the Heavenly, while visiting the earthly Jerusalem. The crusaders themselves when writing to Pope Urban to apprise him of the capture of Antioch expressed the same hope: 'May you finish the journey, which you preached and we started, together with us and open for us the gates to both Jerusalems.'[30] Yet it is not the main motive mentioned in the eyewitness accounts of the crusade, which makes me wonder whether it was the real reason for the success of the Pope's appeal.

Two reasons kept the crusading forces on the move in my opinion. The first was the same that had drawn pilgrims to the Holy Land from the second century on,[31] to see the land 'ubi steterunt pedes eius'[32], and to venerate the relics of Christ. Among those relics two were of paramount importance: first, the Holy Sepulchre itself, the only holy place in Christendom were the absence of the revered person rather than his presence was commemorated. *Iter* or *via S. Sepulcri* is one of the most common names used for the crusade.[33] To visit it after so many years of toil could prove a poignant experience. Fulcher writes: 'When finally we cast our eye on the so desired Holy of Holies, we were filled with an immense joy.'[34] The second relic that drew people to Jerusalem was the True Cross. It was a red cross which distinguished the crusader from other people. Even the defenders of Jerusalem were so aware of its symbolic value that they brandished crosses on the walls of the city, mocking the Christian armies by spitting, even urinating on them.[35] Joyful was the day, therefore, when, some weeks after the capture of Jerusalem, the True Cross, which had mysteriously disappeared, was found again in the house of a native Christian.[36]

Christ's life and death could, of course, be commemorated at home, but only in Palestine could the pilgrim touch the earth and kiss the objects blessed by God during his life on earth. It is hardly conceivable now how strong the need to touch and kiss then was to establish a spiritual bond. When e.g. after days of searching the Holy Lance had finally been found, Raymond of Aguilers became so impatient, because it had taken so long to dig it out, that as soon as he saw its peak protruding from the earth, he jumped into the hole to cover it with kisses.[37] Nowhere but in Jerusalem could a man come so close to Christ's physical presence and relive almost literally the drama of his death and resurrection.[38]

The second reason for the success of the Pope's call was entirely new, to wrest the Holy Places from the hands of the Infidel. The reformers of the eleventh century had taken away the care of sacred from the laity altogether and entrusted it to the hands of the ordained and celibate clergy, thus thwarting the aspirations of many pious laymen.[39] Now the Pope had shown the laity a new way to take part in the Church's sacred mission. The call to wage war on the heathen in the Holy Land also had the effect, of course, that it turned violence outwards and brought peace to Western Europe, as Fulcher does not fail to note in his version of the Pope's speech.[40] But the real reason for the overwhelming response had more to do with the fact that in a reformed Church, where a rigid line had been drawn between the sacred and the secular, the Pope gave a sense of direction to people who wanted to serve God, yet not leave the world for the cloister or the priesthood.[41] In the crusade the old experience of pilgrimage and the new spirit of the Gregorian reform were joined together in a powerful alliance.

As part of this new lay spirituality the image of the Heavenly Jerusalem returns. As said before, there are some indications that even before the crusade pilgrims expected heaven and earth to touch in Jerusalem, but it was not until after the capture of the Holy City that people fully understood what a blessed spot Jerusalem really was and how close to heaven they had been when visiting the Holy Places and touching and kissing the Tomb and the Cross after so many years of hardship.[42] So it was the experience of the crusade itself and not a change of mentality earlier in the century which was responsible for the final reversal of the ancient Christian attitude towards Jerusalem. From now on the Heavenly City was not only foreshadowed by the Church and by its liturgy, but also, and perhaps foremost, by the city in Palestine. Baudry of Bourgueil, a crusade historian of the second generation, gives an excellent illustration of this change of mentality when he stages a priest who preaches a rousing sermon on the night before the final attack: 'From our far lands we have come to this place to pray and to worship the tomb of our God with a kiss. This city has been built after the model of the Heavenly Jerusalem: this city is the form of that to which we aspire.'[43] Albert of Aachen uses even fewer words, he simply calls Jerusalem the gateway to the heavenly fatherland.[44]

The idea that the city of Jerusalem was a gateway to heaven was apparently so attractive that it elicited a flood of protests from monastic circles. The same period in which Jerusalem was thus being exalted, also saw the rise of a new litterary genre in which the cloister was praised as the Heavenly City on earth.[45] This, too, represents a radical change of perspective, as in former days the image of the Heavenly

Jerusalem had always been applied to the whole Church. But as a consequence of the Gregorian Reform, which had split the one Church into two parties, clergy and laity, the name 'Jerusalem' no longer held the same meaning for all Christians. It came to mean one thing to the clergy and another to the laity. Laymen, who needed images and physical contact, should visit Jerusalem, and defend its sacred walls. Thus they could taste the first delights of heaven. Clergymen and monks did not need such stimulation of the senses, they had left the world and entered the forecourts of heaven.[46] According to St. Bernard monks should not journey to the earthly Jerusalem with their feet but to the Heavenly with their hearts.[47] From now on the clergy went one way, the laity another. Fortunately the final destination was still the same for both: the Heavenly Jerusalem 'which is above, which is the mother of us all' (Gal. 4, 26).

---

[1] H. Cowdrey, 'Pope Urban's Preaching of the First Crusade', *History*, 55 (1970), pp. 177-88, and J. Riley-Smith, *The First Crusade and the Idea of Crusading*, London, 1986, pp. 18-25 argue convincingly that Jerusalem and not the liberation of the Eastern Churches was the main purpose of the Crusade in Pope Urban's mind.

[2] P. Alphandéry and A. Dupront, *La Chrétienté et l'idée de croisade*, 2 vols., Paris, 1954-59, I, pp. 57-135.

[3] N. Cohn, *The Pursuit of the Millennium*, London, 2nd ed., 1970, pp. 61-75 and 281-87 for a comparison with totalitarian movements in this century.

[4] R.E. Lerner, 'Medieval Prophecy and Religious Dissent', *Past and Present*, 72 (1976), p. 19.

[5] See the analysis of four eleventh-century prophecies by C. Erdmann, 'Endkaiserglaube und Kreuzzugsgedanke im 11. Jahrhundert', *Zeitschrift für Kirchengeschichte*, 51 (1932), pp. 393-94, 402-03, and also the remarks of P. Classen, 'Eschatologische Ideen und Armutsbewegungen im 11. und 12. Jahrhundert', *Povertà et ricchezza nella spiritualità dei secoli XI e XII, Convegni del centro di studi sulla spiritualità medievale*, vol. 8, Todi, 1969, pp. 131-48. Classen detects eschatological concern in the First Crusade but no apocalyptic tendencies.

[6] B. McGinn, *Visions of the End. Apocalyptic Traditions in the Middle Ages*, New York, 1979, pp. 29-34.

[7] I borrow this distinction from P. Worsley, *The Trumpet Shall Sound. A Study of 'Cargo Cults' in Melanesia*, 2nd ed., New York, 1968, pp. xxxix-xlii. He sharply contrasts millenarian feelings in dissatisfied upper class coteries, which are socially irrelevant but may produce some useful ideas, with apocalyptic mass movements, which rock the boat of civilisation with their violence and ruthless egalitarianism.

[8] Thus e.g. H.E. Mayer, *The Crusades*, 2nd ed., Oxford, 1988, p. 11, and J. Prawer, 'Jerusalem in the Christian and Jewish Perspectives of the Early Middle Ages', *Gli Ebrei nell'alto Medioevo. Settimane di studio del centro italiano di studi sull'alto medioevo*, vol. 26, Spoleto, 1980, pp. 745-50, 781.

[9] See e.g. the words that Christ spoke, according to Albert of Aachen, to Peter the Hermit in a dream to encourage Peter to preach the Crusade: 'Suscitabis corda fidelium ad purganda loca sancta Iherusalem .... Per pericula enim et temptationes varias paradisi portae nunc aperientur vocatis et electis', *Historia Hierosolymitana, Recueil des historiens des croisades, historiens occidentaux (RHC Hocc)*, IV, Paris, 1879, p. 273.

[10] Ekkehard of Aura, *Hierosolymita, RHC Hocc*, V, Paris, 1895, p. 19.

[11] Guibert of Nogent, *Gesta Dei per Francos, RHC Hocc*, IV, pp. 138-39, cf. p. 239.

[12] Alphandéry and Dupront, *Chrétienté*, I, pp. 99-135.

[13] Bryan R. Wilson, *Magic and the Millennium*, London, 1973, pp. 493-94.

[14] Cohn, *Pursuit*, pp. 84-88; Wilson, *Magic*, pp. 307, 309, 349.

[15] Wilson, *Magic*, p. 270; Worsley, *Trumpet*, pp. 248-50, points out that the flouting of ancient taboos is a powerful means of collective integration in these groups.

[16] G. Scholem, *Sabbatai Sevi: The Mystical Messiah*, Princeton, 1973, p. 233-44.

[17] See e.g. the *Gesta Francorum et aliorum Hierosolimitanorum*, ed. R. Hill, Oxford, 1972, pp. 11, 14, 16, 18-19, 23, for a description of the crusaders as Christ's soldiers; the Turks as God's enemies on pp. 22, 32, 40.

[18] *Ibid.*, p. 18.

[19] Thus Petrus Tudebodus, *Historia de Hierosolymitana itinere*, ed. J.H. and L.L. Hill, Paris, 1977, pp. 50, 75, 81. See also H. Cowdrey, 'Martyrdom and the First Crusade', in P.W. Edbury (ed.), *Crusade and Settlement*, Cardiff, 1985, p. 52.

[20] Fulcher of Chartres, *Historia Hierosolymitana*, ed. H. Hagenmeyer, Heidelberg, 1913, p. 203.

[21] Cowdrey, 'Martyrdom', p. 53. Raymond of Aguilers, *Historia Francorum, RHC Hocc*, III, Paris, 1866, p. 300 is jubilant about this new turn in the history of salvation: 'Nova dies, novum gaudium, nova et perpetua laetitia, laboris atque devotionis consummatio, nova verba, nova cantica ab universis exigebat …. In hac die cantavimus officium de Resurrectione, quia in hac die ille qui sua virtute a mortuis resurrexit, per gratiam suam nos resuscitavit.'

[22] *Gesta Francorum*, pp. 56-57; Raymond, *Historia*, p. 256, see also pp. 243-44, 246, 248, 258, 268, 271.

[23] *Gesta Francorum*, pp. 20, 34, 37 ('hoc bellum carnale non est, sed spirituale'); Fulcher, *Historia*, pp. 197, 223, 226-28, 231; Raymond, *Historia*, p. 235, mentions it even in the prologue to his work: 'Exercitus … Dei, etsi pro peccatis flagellum Domini sui sustinuit, pro eiusdem misericordia victor super omnem paganimitatem exstitit.'

[24] Fulcher, *Historia*, pp. 195-97.

[25] Raymond, *Historia*, pp. 262-63, also p. 285 (Peter's ordeal). Several other people had visions of Adhémar, too, see pp. 286-7, 296 (the Bishop ordering penitential processions during the siege of Jerusalem), and p. 300 (he was seen to mount the walls on the day of the capture).

[26] Raymond, *Historia*, p. 258. See also *Gesta Francorum*, pp. 58-59, and Bartulf of Nangis, *Gesta Francorum Iherusalem expugnantium, RHC Hocc*, III, pp. 498-99, 505, where adultery is singled out as a particularly heinous crime, which is all the more interesting, because it shows that the crusaders did not flout sexual taboos, as usually happens in chiliastic movements (Worsley, *Trumpet*, pp. 249-50), but acknowledged the existing rules, even if they did not always observe them.

[27] R. Chazan, *European Jewry and the First Crusade*, Berkeley etc., 1987, pp. 65-84.

[28] *Ibid.*, pp. 63-64.

[29] Prawer, 'Jerusalem', pp. 744-52, 779-82.

[30] *Die Kreuzzugsbriefe aus den Jahren 1088-1100*, ed. H. Hagenmeyer, Innsbruck, 1901, p. 164; a similar double purpose of the journey in a letter of the Patriarch of Jerusalem to the Western Church which contains the appeal: 'Uenite ergo, festinate duplici praemio remunerandi, uidelicet terra uiuentium terraque melle et lacte manante omnique uictuali abundante' (p. 148).

[31] The earliest pilgrim was Melito of Sardes (fl. 160-180), who wanted to see the country 'where these things were preached and done'; E.D. Hunt, *Holy Land Pilgrimage in the Later Roman Empire AD 312-460*, Oxford, 1984, p. 83.

[32] See e.g. Fulcher, *Historia*, pp. 162, 331.

[33] See e.g. Tudebodus, *Historia*, pp. 31-32, 43, 77, 114, 134-35, 141.

[34] Fulcher, *Historia*, p. 331.

[35] Tudebodus, *Historia*, p. 137; Raymond, *Historia*, p. 297; Albert of Aachen, *Historia*, p. 471.

[36] Fulcher, *Historia*, pp. 309-10; Raymond, *Historia*, p. 302.

[37] Raymond, *Historia*, p. 257.

[38] A fine example had been set by Abbot Richard of St. Vannes, who visited Jerusalem in 1026. He spent the Easter night in the Holy Sepulchre: 'Noctem illam pater noster gratia Dei duxit insomnem, Dominum resurgentem adorans, et cum Maria Magdalene in orto mentis, ubi virebant per eum plantaria virtutum, ortolanum Iesum videre desiderans, ut vocaret eum proprio nomine, et se magistrum et Dominum doceret agnoscere, ut factus testis vere resurrectionis eius, in voce fidei annuntiaret fratribus: *Resurrexit Dominus*' (Hugo of Flavigny, *Chronicon*, MGH SS, 8, p. 396).

[39] R.W. Southern, *Western Society and the Church in the Middle Ages*, (Pelican History of the Church, vol. 2), Harmondsworth, 1970, pp. 34-41, on war p. 40.

[40] Fulcher, *Historia*, p. 136.

[41] See e.g. the relief of the Norman knight Tancred, that from now on he could serve God as a warrior, Riley-Smith, *Crusade*, p. 36.

[42] Riley-Smith, *Crusade*, pp. 91-119, has a fine description of the change in crusading ideals resulting from the experience of hardship and final success.

[43] Baudry of Bourgueil, *Historia Jerosolimitana*, *RHC Hocc*, IV, p. 100.

[44] Albert of Aachen, *Historia*, p. 482: 'Iherusalem, quae porta est coelestis patriae.'

[45] Th. Renna, 'The Idea of Jerusalem: Monastic to Scholastic', in E.R. Elder (ed.), *From Cloister to Classroom; Monastic and Scholastic Approaches to the Truth* (Cistercian Studies Series, 90), Kalamazoo, 1986, p. 97. The first author, to my knowledge, who celebrates the cloister as Jerusalem is Jean of Fécamps; see J. Leclercq, 'Une élévation sur les gloires de Jérusalem', *Recherches de science religieuse*, 40 (1952), pp. 330-34.

[46] The distinction between the spiritual insight of the clergy and the literal-mindedness of the laity is wonderfully expressed by Ekkehard of Aura, *Hierosolymita*, pp. 38-39: 'Haec et hujusmodi mille praesagia, licet per anagogen ad illam quae sursum est matrem nostram Jerusalem referantur; tamen infirmioribus membris ab uberibus consolationis praescriptae vel scribendae potatis, pro tanti contemplatione vel participatione gaudii, periculis se tradere etiam historialiter practica discursione exhortantur. Scimus hominem verbi gratia, qui canticum illud *Laetatus sum* cum *alleluia* se in visione fatetur audisse ... ac per hoc in tantum ad eandem peregrinationem animatum, uti nullam spiritus ejus requiem haberet, donec per multas tribulationes corporali praesentia, ubi steterunt pedes Domini pertingens, adoraret.' See for St. Bernard's remarks on the laity's craving of images, *Apologia ad Guillelmum*, XII.28, *Opera omnia*, ed. J. Leclercq and H. Rochais, vol. III, Rome, 1963, pp. 104-05.

[47] G. Constable, 'Monachisme et pélerinage au Moyen Age,' *Revue historique*, 258 (1977), p. 21.

WOMEN MARTYRS IN A REVOLUTIONARY AGE
A COMPARISON OF BOOKS OF MARTYRS

A. Jelsma

I

A comparison of Books of Martyrs is useful, as I hope to prove with the following example. On 16 July 1546 Anne Askewe, 'that most christian martyr', was burned alive with three other martyrs at Smithfield in London, leaving behind her—as John Foxe wrote—'a singular example of Christian constancy for all men to follow'. She had in fact left behind even more than that. Because she wanted to prevent distorted and misleading information about her trial, she had drafted a personal report of her examinations. These accounts were sent to Protestant exiles in Europe. In November 1546, John Bale published her report of the first examination, amplified with a circumstantial comment by his own hand. Three months later the second examination also came out, again interspersed with the comments of Bale, and expanded with an eye-witness account by some Dutch merchants concerning her death. Of these original editions only a few copies remained. In the copies of the second examination some lines were excised. Nobody knows the reason. The editor of the selected works of John Bale, Henry Christmas, has made the suggestion that this had been done to spare the reputation of King Henry's minister, William Paget. There is, however, another possibility.

Without the personal remarks by Bale, the material of both examinations was taken over in the great martyrologies of John Crespin, John Foxe and Adriaan van Haemstede. At the same place where the work of John Bale was mutilated, we find a gap in the books of Crespin and Foxe. Only Van Haemstede offers an addition. This is the more remarkable since he was the only martyrologist who had the habit of abridging his material. His addition concerns the second examination, at the moment of Anne Askewe's interrogation by the Bishop of Winchester, Stephen Gardiner, who criticized her because she, as a woman, had made a study of the Holy Scripture. This had made her lose her head, he supposed. 'Everybody should behave himself in accordance with his destination', he said. 'No more than a pig should be saddled, a woman had to concern herself with the word of God.' Anne laughed. 'Sir', she said, 'why should not a pig bear a saddle, now even an ass bears a bishopsmitre!' The bishop was not amused. It is on this point that the other martyrologists also continue their story. Gardiner threatened her with the death by fire. Her response had a close connection with the discussion about the reading of the Bible by a woman. She said, 'I have searched the whole Scripture, yet I have nowhere found that either Christ or the apostles put someone to death'.[1]

It is still not clear why this dialogue has been curtailed in most martyrologies. The reason cannot be that this passage was too embarrasing for the memory of William Paget, nor even of Bishop Gardiner. The Bishop of Winchester was not highly esteemed in Protestant circles. In the opinion of Calvin—and Crespin was a loyal adherent of the reformer of Geneva—'he surpassed all the devils in that kingdom'.[2] Helen C. White called Gardiner 'Foxe's favourite villain'.[3] I suppose therefore, that it must have been the sharp-witted comment of Anne Askewe, which was considered not fitting for a pious woman. Did her remark perhaps evoke too much the suggestion of radical Anabaptism?[4] However that may be, the example makes clear that there is reason for a careful comparison of Books of Martyrs.

II

Of course, such a comparison cannot be made in all regards. In this article I have confined myself to the image of women martyrs in the Protestant martyrologies of the sixteenth century, and especially the earlier editions of these books. The choice of this subject must be justified. Such an investigation could cause the impression that it should be possible to speak about women in general categories. To women martyrs applies the same principle as to men martyrs: there are no two equal. But there are some reasons for this special inquiry.

1. As were the judges and the executioners, the authors of the martyrologies all were men. In their description of women martyrs they permitted themselves general judgements about the female gender. The martyrologies therefore offer us useful material for an investigation into the image men had formed of women in the sixteenth century. 2. Several authors have recently studied this question. In 1968 Roland H. Bainton published an article about 'John Foxe and the Ladies', which later became a chapter in his tripartite study *Women and the Reformation*. A more profound investigation into the conviction of the women martyrs has been made by Ellen Macek in her article 'The Emergence of a Feminine Spirituality in "The Book of Martyrs"', published in 1988. She confined herself to the book of John Foxe. In 1985 I. van 't Spijker described for

the Dutch situation the position of women in Mennonite martyrologies.[5] It seemed to me an interesting challenge to analyse this material on a broader scale, especially to avoid one-sided conclusions.

For our investigation it will be necessary first, without too many details, to enumerate the relevant martyrologies. In 1552 the orthodox Lutheran minister Ludwig Rabus published in Latin a study about the martyrs of the Old Testament and the early church. Between 1554 and 1558 he produced eight volumes of martyr stories in the German language. The first two volumes deal with the same material as his book of 1552. In 1554 appeared at Geneva the first French edition of a book of martyrs, composed by the Calvinist printer Jean Crespin; a translation of this work in Latin was brought out in 1556.[6] John Foxe, like John Bale an exile on the continent during the reign of Queen Mary, in 1554 published at Strasburg the 'liber primus' of his *Commentarii rerum in ecclesia gestarum*, the beginning of an enterprise which Patrick Collinson, in his study on Archbishop Grindal, characterized as 'the most important of all fruits of the exile'.[7]

The Dutch minister Adriaan van Haemstede wrote his martyrology, while at the same time the magistrates of Antwerp had put the large prize of three hundred Carolusguilders on his head. His work was published in 1559. Three years later the first Mennonite book of martyrs appeared under the title 'The Sacrifice of the Lord'. This collection of martyr acts later has been incorporated by T.J. van Braght in his expanded work 'The Bloody Theatre; Or, Martyrs' Mirror of the Mennonite or Defenceless Christians'.[8]

These books did not all have the same construction. Foxe and Crespin started with the days of John Wycliff. Ludwig Rabus wanted to demonstrate how strongly the Protestant Reformation corresponded with the early church. After his description of the martyrs during the first centuries of the church, he jumped over to the days of John Hus. Adriaan van Haemstede was the first who tried to draft a complete history of persecution, obsessed as he was by the idea, which in another context he more than once expressed, that the true church will always be persecuted. Van Braght later followed his example.

With the exception of the Mennonite martyrologies, all of these authors borrowed their material from each other. Almost all the stories of Crespin were taken over in Van Haemstede's book; Van Haemstede also used some volumes of Rabus and the works of John Bale.[9] In the further elaborated English version of his work, John Foxe not only tried to assemble as many martyr stories as was possible, but also to compose, just as Van Haemstede had done, a complete ecclesiastical history, but now especially for England.[10]

In this superficial survey I have intentionally emphasized the dates of publication. This is of the greatest importance for understanding the motivation behind these works. Reprints in later times, and under other circumstances, were in some regards animated by another urge. This becomes clear by comparing the prefaces and comments in the successive editions. The negative remarks of John Foxe concerning the institutional church and the bishop's office are more in keeping with his experiences under King Henry VIII and Queen Mary than with those under the reign of Queen Elizabeth.[11] It was also not by accident that the first editions of Rabus and Foxe, and the second edition of Crespin, were written in Latin, while reprints in later times, without exception, appeared in the vernacular.

What was the strongest motive behind the first editions of these works? Another question has to be answered first. Why especially did they appear in the period between 1552 and 1562? For the Lutheran territories in Germany this was the humiliating phase of the Interim. After some severe military defeats, Lutheran leaders such as Melanchthon were forced to make excessive concessions, which had evoked vehement indignation amongst the so-called Gnesio-Lutherans, to which group also Ludwig Rabus belonged. In France the position of Protestantism had deteriorated after the death of King Francis I in 1547. His successor King Henry II promised already at the moment of his coronation not only to banish but even to root out Protestant heresy. He did his utmost to fulfill his promise. In the Netherlands the persecution of Sacramentarians and Anabaptists had always been very severe; during the fifties also the Calvinists were pursued. And, last but not least, just in this period the Protestant government of King Edward and his adviser Cranmer was replaced by the Roman Catholic repression under Queen Mary and the cardinals Gardiner and Reginald Pole.

In other words, the Protestant martyrologies appeared in a period of repercussion. The Counter-Reform became an almost irresistible force and the Reformation seemed to be retreating. Protestant martyrologies were published at precisely that moment in history when an armed struggle seemed no longer, or not yet, possible. In this precarious position, Protestant leaders had no other weapon than an appeal to public opinion. They tried to furnish as much information about the cruel repression as they could find, and to disseminate this material on a scale wider than their own country, for which reason they published these works in Latin. The martyrologies were meant as propaganda, in the hope to change the course of history by telling the truth about the unbearable suffering of God's own children.

Only in later times reprints were published in the vernacular, intended for the national public, to keep in memory the great deeds of the powerful warriors of Christ during the hard days. Only then did these books become, as Helen White concluded about the work of Foxe, 'the rationalization of a victory'.[12] The first editions of these martyrologies were guns, the latter a monument.

To make sure that every shot told, the authors of the first editions selected their material carefully. In later editions all the names of martyrs which could be found were assembled. The first editions functioned similarly to the eye-witness accounts in modern times on television, smuggled from South-Africa or from the occupied parts of Palestine: faithful but selected. What Foxe wrote, 'God hath opened the Presse to preach, whose voice the Pope is never able to stop with all the puissance of his triple crown',[13] applies also for his own Book of Martyrs. It is not surprising, that the suffering of the martyrs was depicted with the most shocking details, so that even a gentle character as Foxe could be named 'master of horror'.[14] Because of this motivation the authors of these works pronounced with so much emphasis the punishment of the persecutors by God himself; the miracle of retribution was the only one which Protestants wished to recognize.[15] Against this background it becomes explicable why confessions of faith, written by the martyrs themselves, were treasured up with so much concern. Everyone in the world had to know that under a Roman Catholic government not only disturbers of the social order but also peaceful believers were persecuted and killed.

This framework determined the selection of martyr stories. In principle in the works of Foxe, Rabus, Crespin and Van Haemstede there was no place for Anabaptist martyrs. In these books the victims themselves often criticized, even during painful examinations, the peasants revolt in Germany and the behaviour of the Anabaptists in Munster. Despite their own suffering they agreed with the cruel execution of a man like Michael Servetus in Geneva, if we may believe the authors of these stories. This defensive element we also find in the Mennonite martyrologies. These authors too regularly condemned the disturbance of public order, and what they saw as real heresy.[16]

III

What was the consequence of this motivation behind the martyrologies for the place which could be given to women martyrs and for the way their martyrdom was described? There are two possibilities, as far as I can see. Their suffering could have been accentuated to expose the cruelty of the persecution. In 1559 Thomas Brice published for the first time a Protestant martyrs' calendar, as a replacement for the Roman

Catholic saints' calendar. In his preface he expressly deplored the killing of the humble and the helpless, women, and in particular virgins.[17] But he wrote this already in the phase of victory, with the purpose to smother all remaining sympathy for the Roman Catholic belief.

It is more probable that the share and influence of women in the martyrologies has been minimized. I have reasons for this suggestion. In the oldest editions of the works of Rabus, Crespin, Foxe and Van Haemstede, women formed a small minority. In his description of the first centuries Rabus mentioned many women, but for his own time he confined himself to a few ladies of noble birth, like Argula von Grunbach and Anne Askewe. His description of the martyrdom of the latter was much more curtailed than in the martyrologies of the other authors, and this was contrary to his habit. Typical for his work is that he always copied the complete text of the transmitted material. He only made an exception for one of the few women in his work. He concluded the story of Anne Askewe with the remark that she in a miraculous way had overcome the weakness and vanity of her gender. Perhaps his attitude can be explained by his experiences with independent women. As minister of Strasburg he often took offence at the tolerant behaviour of his colleague's wife Catharine Zell, tolerant even of spiritualists like Caspar Schwenckfeld. In work and writings the two contested each other.[18]

In his original contributions to the history of Dutch martyrs—in other words the material which he had not borrowed from other martyrologies—Adriaan van Haemstede did not mention any women. The same applies for the book of Crespin as for the other martyrologists; none of the women he described actively participated in the dissemination of Protestant principles. Yet this last book deserves special attention with regard to our investigation. His women were indeed not involved in the preaching of the gospel, but they sometimes exhibited a remarkable attribute; in a particular way they could become fascinated by the horrible death by fire. When in 1547 in the French town of Langres some people were sentenced to the stake, it was particularly the women who encouraged their husbands and the other men. One of these women, Jeanne Bailly, compared this death with her marriage. She tried to cheer up her husband with these words: 'My love, in our marriage we were only physically joined together. Please, keep in mind that this was nothing more than a prelude of our future union. On the day of our martyrdom we will be really given in marriage to each other by the Lord Jesus Christ.' This prospect seemed to have heartened her husband.[19] Two years later, on a Saturday, in Orléans, the widow Anne Oudeberte also was sentenced to the fire. On the moment that one of the guards bound her hands together, she exclaimed, 'What a nice wedding ring my husband is giving me! On a Saturday I married my first husband; now it is again on a Saturday that I may be married with my new bridegroom Jesus Christ.'[20] The comparison of the cord around her wrists with a wedding ring illustrates her appreciation of marriage.

There is another reason why the book of Crespin especially demands our attention. In the Latin translation of 1556 the author gives a personal comment when he describes the perseverance of these women. They all went to death with a masculine spirit, 'virilo animo', 'virili constantia', or more masculine than feminine, 'potius virilis quam muliebris'. All these stories were used by Van Haemstede. I have already mentioned that he mostly shortened the original material, but to these typifications he remained faithful. In his book, too, all these women died 'met mannelijke moed', with a masculine spirit.[21] The later French editions of Crespin's work, on the contrary, did not retain these qualifications. With respect to women the author now at best concluded that they were assisted by a more than human force.[22] Why did the author in the French edition of 1570 suppress the qualifications of the Latin edition of 1556? The Latin edition was meant for the intellectual circles of Europe, in other words for men. The French text was intended for people of all ranks, as an encouragement and a comfort for men and women alike. That makes a difference. There is also the possibility that the author in the meantime, between 1556 and 1570, had discovered that his characterization of the masculine spirit of those brave women had been unjustifiable in view of reality, but this explanation seems to me less probable.

Another point in these martyrologies of Crespin deserves our reflection. As we have seen, Protestant Books of Martyrs made a strict selection out of the executed Protestants. Rabus, Crespin, Van Haemstede, and also Foxe, tried to prove for the eyes of public opinion, that people were killed who had nothing in common with real heretics such as the Anabaptists. Crespin emphasized this view by means of an extensive intermezzo about Anabaptist heresy. It is interesting to see what he considered as the climax, the culmination of this heresy. This was, of course, the behaviour of Anabaptists like Jan van Leiden at Munster in 1534 and 1535, but he also detected a dominant influence by women. This opinion is not really astonishing. Such an outlook on women was not new in Western European history. Not only the authors of the notorious *Malleus maleficarum*,[23] but also the sixteenth-century Protestant leaders were in general convinced that women were easier to mislead than men, that they were more accessible for demonical influence, that they fell more easily into heresy.

Philip Hughes, in his study about the Reformation in England, has even suggested that during the reign of Queen Elizabeth the persecution of witches worsened. He saw the growing fear of dangerous women as one of the legacies of the returning exiles. While acknowledging that under Queen Mary Protestants were persecuted, in his opinion these 'bold and hard spirits' did not want anything else, savouring every moment of their defiance.[24] But after the change in government, still according to Hughes, so-called witches had been forced to take over their place of suffering. However that may be, Catholic and Protestant leaders were generally unanimous in their opinion that women should never get the opportunity to become involved in theological issues.

Crespin exhibited the heretical character of Anabaptism, not only in the usual way by relating the course of events at Munster, but also with a story about what had happened at Appenzell, a small town in Switzerland. There a woman had presented herself as the new Christ, the Messiah of women. She had sent out twelve apostles and all the territories of Switzerland had been threatened to become polluted by this plague. But the Protestant magistrates of Bern had rooted out this pestiferous heresy.[25]

What was the source of this story? Had he fabricated it himself? This is not problable. Crespin is usually reliable in his stories. He had to be; his book was intended as a weapon and for that reason attempted to be substantial. And indeed, I have found some of his sources. In his work *In catabaptistarum strophas elenchus* (1527), Ulrich Zwingli offered a detailed description of the Anabaptist movement in the region of St. Gall and Appenzell. Zwingli is, however, not to be totally relied upon, in contrast to Johann Kessler, a saddler from St. Gall, who wrote a chronicle about the history of his town during the years 1525-1539.[26] In this diary Kessler describes the rise of Anabaptism, first in Zurich, and later in St. Gall. The government of this last town was extremely tolerant during this period. Anabaptist preachers often attracted larger audiences than the official ministers of this region. If it is permitted to quote the singer Paul Simon in this article, 'these were the days of miracle and wonder'. Everything seemed possible at that time. Especially women were drawn to the new ideas. Some of them cut short their hair, ashamed that they had ever tried to please other men than Jesus. Other women received prophecies. A young woman, Magdalena Mulleri, described herself to her admirers as 'the way, the truth and the life'. She was often seen in the company of two other women, Barbara Murglen and the maid Frena. After some time the last became the leader of the band. She presented herself as the new Christ, spoke sometimes in a language nobody could understand, and wanted to acquire her twelve apostles. And indeed, she originally came from Appenzell.

The three women started a recruitment campaign. Frena came across a young man, Lienhardt, sitting behind his weaving loom. She ordered him in the name of God to stand up and follow her. 'These were the days of miracle and wonder.' He stood up and followed her. At last they got some hundreds of adherents behind them, wandering through the land, 'singing in the rain'. Bizarre adventures took place. During the winter, compassionate farmers supplied them with food and clothes. They did not really harm anyone. The most important Anabaptist leaders, such as Konrad Grebel and Felix Manz, regularly condemned the behaviour and the assertions of the women. The activities of these women were not considered as typical for Anabaptism. After some time the movement dissolved. Frena came to her senses. She married her disciple Lienhardt. They got a child which they presented for baptism. And it was all over.

Kessler had written down the story of these events because he saw it as a proof of how easily people, who sincerely were seeking the truth, could be mislead. He realised that these occurrences were not typical for Anabaptism in general. Crespin utilized these incidents only as a demonstration of the pestiferous character of Anabaptism. His most convincing argument was the disturbance of the political as well as the social order by the adherents of this heresy. Therefore he characterized the radical Reformation with the stories of Jan van Leiden in Munster and the maid Frena from Appenzell. In this light it is not surprising that in his book of martyrs women could not play an essential role. They were only suited for suffering.

Rabus, Crespin and Van Haemstede wanted to prove with their books that Lutheran and Calvinist martyrs had nothing in common with Anabaptist feelings. One of the consequences was that the women of the Reformation in general had to disappear into the shadows.

If this reasoning is correct, we may expect that Mennonite martyrologies should offer us, in some regards, another picture. And indeed, they do. Instead of the five to ten per cent normally found in other martyrologies, women account for twenty per cent of the martyrs in 'The Sacrifice of the Lord' and even thirty per cent in Van Braght's 'Martyrs' Mirror'.[27]

When Van Braght described the martyrdom of three sisters, he started his story with these words: 'The host of God, which equipped itself for the struggle and the suffering of Jesus Christ did not only consist of men (who sometimes are considered as the stronger sex) but of women as well.'[28] In Mennonite martyrologies women do possess a marvellous knowledge of the Bible. For their relation to God they did not want to stay dependent any longer upon often uneducated priests or even academically trained scholars. Some of these women did achieve a leading role in the Anabaptist movement. In 1549 soldiers made an investigation in the house of a beguine, Elizabeth, in the Frisian capital Leeuwarden. They found a Latin New Testament. 'Now we finally have found the teacher of the group', they exclaimed. Elizabeth was accused of the seduction of a great number of people. She did not deny it. She only refused to mention names.[29]

Moving is the story of Claesken, who was burned at Antwerp in 1559. During the examination her interrogator tried to intimidate her. That theological research had been going on for so many centuries, he asserted, was not without reason. How dared she to suggest that she would be better informed than the holy fathers in the course of 1500 years! Did not her attitude prove her simplicity? Claesken answered, 'I may be stupid in the eyes of men, I am not stupid in my knowledge of the Lord'. Therefore she could no longer stay content with the theology of men. Her husband could not read. She had learned it. Thanks to this lead she had obtained a remarkable self-confidence. By her reading skill she had procured for herself admission to the sources of salvation.[30]

A similar self-consciousness was exhibited by a certain Anneken in the will she had made for her son while in prison at Rotterdam in the year 1539. The testament started with the words, 'Listen, my son, to the teaching of your mother, open your ears for the words of my mouth. See, I am going the way of the prophets, apostles and martyrs, and will drink the chalice they had to drink'.[31]

In 'The Sacrifice of the Lord', the letters between Jeronymus Segers and his wife Lysken, written from prison in Antwerp in 1551, take up a large part of the book. Van Braght completely copied this correspondence in his 'Martyrs' Mirror'. A remarkable detail is that in the later English translation of this work the letters of Lysken were removed. During their separate examinations the interrogator had concluded that Lysken belonged to the most important of the heretics in the town. He reproached her because it was by her influence that her husband stuck to his heretical feelings. He also blamed her for her study of the Bible, which in his opinion was not fitting for a woman. Her task was in the kitchen, not in a book. She had to leave the study of the Holy Scripture to the educated priests.[32]

The husband of Claudine le Vette belonged to the spokesmen of the Anabaptist movement. But often when he was studying in the Bible he asked his wife for advice; she was much better informed than he.[33]

Comparing the material of Mennonite martyrologies with the books of Rabus, Crespin and Van Haemstede, I must conclude that there is a difference, not only in theological views but also in the place which was assigned to women. How are we, in this regard, to judge the work of John Foxe?

In general there has been appreciation for the way he had dealt with women. Comparing John Foxe's *Acts and Monuments* with Bunyan's *Pilgrim's Progress* and the Bible, Roland Bainton concluded: 'All three give a high place to women.' In his opinion, Foxe tells us more about the women of the Reformation in England than does any other source. Ellen Macek affirmed this conclusion regarding Foxe's book: 'His accounts of female Protestants who lacked a voice of their own provide a unique insight into early modern women's religious experience.'[34] I do not want to combat this appreciation, but I wish to append some notes.

After his return to England during the reign of Queen Elizabeth, Foxe did indeed create more space for women in the new editions of his work. He had to do so. The later versions of his work differed from the editions of 1554 and even 1559. Under the new circumstances Protestant leaders definitively tried to win the population for the Reformation. Foxe's book of martyrs attained a new purpose, as Philip Hughes writes: 'The instinct that demanded a Golden Legend was still active and, all unconsciously, Foxe was supplying the need'.[35] I am not sure whether it really happened so unconsciously. Indeed, he vigorously rejected the suggestion that there was anything in common between his book and the Golden Legend so despised by Protestants. But that Foxe was not entirely unaware of the possibility of making an effective substitution becomes apparent in the calendar, very much in the primer fashion, which he prefixed to his book. He did offer a substitute for the rejected Golden Legend, as also Helen White has affirmed.[36] For each day of the year he supplied martyrs to keep in memory, and as the Golden Legend did include many female saints in its calendar, it would have been disgraceful for Protestantism if it could offer only men to keep in recollection.

There is another argument to explain why Foxe made more room for women. In the later editions of his work he wanted to describe as completely as possible the atrocities which society had suffered under the Roman Catholic reaction during the reign of Queen Mary. Therefore he summed up all the names of martyrs that he could gather. Among them were many women. The vast majority of victims belonged to the working classes as the greater part of academically trained Protestants had left the country. Often Foxe did not know anything more about the victims than their names and the places of execution. The percentage of women in the new editions grew indeed, but the number of pages reserved for them remained minimal. It is not always clear what the women he described exactly believed. Not without reason Hughes supposed that some of the martyrs under Queen Mary would also have been executed if King Edward had stayed alive.[37] Consider for example that woman from Exeter. Foxe described her in this way: 'She was as simple a woman to see as any man might behold, of a very little and short stature, somewhat thick, about 54 years of age.' During the examinations she brougt the bishop in despair. Often he uttered the sigh, 'O foolish woman!'. She had left her husband and children and had wandered around in the environment of Exeter. 'Why did you leave them?', the bishop asked. She appealed to the words of Christ, that when an apostle was persecuted in one town he had to flee to another. 'But who persecuted thee', the bishop asked. 'My husband and my children', she answered. They had not listened to her when she had tried to deliver them from their idolatry.[38]

Their urge to completeness could have as consequence that Foxe indeed in the later editions of his work made room for martyrs who would not have been permitted in the earlier martyrologies of Rabus, Crespin or Van Haemstede. This could explain why Foxe, in his description of women's religious experience, took a position between the previously mentioned martyrologies and the Mennonite works. But in one respect he remained on the same level as his Lutheran and Calvinist colleagues. In his book of martyrs, too, women were not allowed to be equally active in teaching as women sometimes could be in Mennonite martyrologies.

IV

A final question remains. Did the position of Lutheran, Reformed or Anglican women differ from that of Anabaptist women not only in the martyrologies but also in reality? I do not think so, at least not during the first half of the century. What Claire Cross wrote in her article 'He-Goats before the Flocks' about English women in the seventeenth century applies, as far as I can see, even more one century earlier. She wrote, 'Many of these women at least partially educated themselves; once they could read, by regular attendance at sermons and exercises and by diligent reading of the Bible and contemporary theological and devotional writers they attained to very considerable biblical learning'.[39]

In the diary of a Dutch chaplain, Christiaan Munters, over the years 1525-1545, we can find an example which reveals how startling this new possibility for women could become in the eyes of men. He noted what had happened in the town of Maastricht. There a woman had met a stranger who wanted to sell her some books. She answered that she could not read. That was no problem, he said. He could teach her. He took her to his home and after some hours she could read. Enriched with this new facility and with some Protestant books she returned to her husband. He asked her where she had stayed so long. 'I have learned to read', she exclaimed, 'I can read everything now!' Her husband paled. Immediately he warned the priest. She confessed what she had done. After the absolution a miracle took place. Thanks to the mercy of God she could no longer read one letter of the alphabet; she was saved.[40]

This incident not only discloses how stormy the process of learning to read sometimes could be, but also to what extent this new possibility could allow women an advantage over their husbands and how threatening this sometimes was for men. It was a development that must have occurred throughout the whole of Europe during the sixteenth century. People with different backgrounds learned to read and got involved in the theological issues of their time on a much wider scale than ever before. Many of these self-taught men and women felt the urge to disseminate what they discovered in the Bible. The frontiers between the different opinions were not always very clear during the first half of the sixteenth century, at least not at the base of society. For the magistrates this must have been an extremely confusing situation. They tried to apply the right names to their religious prisoners: Lollards, Lutherans, Sacramentists, Anabaptists, Spiritualists. Gradually points of recognition became visible, determinating issues being the conception of priesthood, mass and baptism, but also the attitude to the social order, including the relation between men and women.

During the second half of the century, when Roman Catholicism recovered part of its lost territory, the magisterial Reformation looked for means to maintain its position. Books of Martyrs became a weapon in this struggle for survival. Lutheran, Calvinist and Anglican authors tried to prove that in Roman Catholic territories people were persecuted, even though they had no intention to disturb the political or social order. Of course, in these books there was no place for women who were too independent. Thanks to the Anabaptist martyrologies we know somewhat better how intensive the contribution of women, especially in the lower strata of society, must have been. It is not probable that only Mennonite men and women wrote each other letters from prison, but these were not of interest for the other martyrologies, and therefore were not collected, unless in the case of women of noble birth. Women who were too quick-witted, were unprofitable for the image that authors such as Rabus, Crespin, Van Haemstede and Foxe wanted to create.

These concluding remarks bring us back to the beginning, the case of Anne Askewe. I do not think that it has been by accident that her smart remarks were removed from most martyrologies. The metaphor she had used in her discussion with bishop Gardiner had been nothing less than gunpowder. What she really expressed was that in a world where unfitted men could often hold a bishop's see, women had the right, even the obligation, to explain the Word of God. When men defaulted, women should take over their task. If an ass bears a bishop's mitre, a pig has to be saddled with the Word of God.

[1] For the martyrdom of Anne Askewe, see *Select Works of John Bale,* ed. Rev. Henry Christmas, Cambridge, 1849, pp. 137-248; Jean Crespin, *Historie des vrays tesmoins de la verité de l'évangile, qui de leur sang l'ont signée, depuis Jean Hus jusques au temps présent,* Geneva, 1570, f. 164; John Foxe, *Acts and Monuments of Matters Most Special and Memorable, Happening in the Church, with an Universal History of the Same,* 3 vols., London, 1684, II, pp. 483f.; Adriaan van Haemstede, *De geschiedenisse ende den doodt der vromer martelaren, die om het ghetughenisse des Evangeliums haer bloedt ghestort hebben, van den tijden Christi af, totten jaren MDLIX toe, bijeen vergadert op het kortste,* n.p. [probably Emden], 1559, pp. 155-65; Ludwig Rabus, *Historien der heyligen ausserwolten Gottes Zeugen, Bekennern und Martyrern ...,* 8 vols., Strasbourg, 1554-58, III, pp. 184-86.

[2] Patrick Collinson, *Archbishop Grindal 1519-1583. The Struggle for a Reformed Church,* London, 1979, p. 90.

[3] Helen C. White, *Tudor Books of Saints and Martyrs,* Madison, 1963, pp. 152, 153. Foxe himself called Stephen Gardiner when he died, 'A man hated to God and all good men'.

[4] I.B. Horst, *The Radical Brethren. Anabaptism and the English Reformation to 1558,* Nieuwkoop, 1972, pp. 93, 94. John Bale was known for his kind opinion even to Anabaptists.

[5] Roland H. Baiton, 'John Foxe and the Ladies', in Lawrence P. Buck and Jonathan W. Zophy (eds.), *The Social History of the Reformation,* Columbus (Ohio), 1972, pp. 208-22; *idem, Women of the Reformation; in France and England,* 2nd ed., Boston, 1975, pp. 211-229; Ellen Macek, 'The Emergence of a Feminine Spirituality in "The Book of Martyrs"', *Sixteenth Century Journal,* 19, no. 1 (1988), pp. 63-80; I. van 't Spijker, '"Mijn beminde huysvrouwe in de Heere"; Doperse vrouwen in de vroege Reformatie in de Nederlanden', *Doopsgezinde bijdragen,* 11 (1985), pp. 99-108.

[6] J. Crespin, *Acta martyrum, eorum videlicet, qui hoc seculo in Gallia, Germania, Anglia, Flandria, Italia, constans dederunt nomen Evangelio, idque sanguine suo obsignarunt: ab Wicleffo & Husso ad hunc usque diem,* Geneva, 1556.

[7] Collinson, *Archbishop Grindal,* pp. 79, 80. I have used the Latin edition of John Foxe: *Rerum in ecclesia gestarum, quae postremis et periculosis his temporibus evenerunt, maximarumque per Europam persecutionum, ac sanctorum, Dei martyrum, caeterarumque rerum si quae insignioris exempli sint, digesti per regna en nationes commentarii,* Basel, 1559. In contrast with the edition of 1554 this edition especially regards the victims under Queen Mary.

[8] S. Cramer (ed.), *Het offer des Heeren,* in *Bibliotheca Reformatoria Neerlandica,* II, The Hague, 1904; T.J. van Braght, *Het bloedig tooneel, of martelaers spiegel der doops-gesinde of weereloose christenen, die, om 't getuygenis van Jesus haren Salighmaker, geleden hebben, ende gedood zijn, van Christi tijd af, tot desen tijd toe,* 2nd ed., Amsterdam, 1685. For the edicts against heresy in the Netherlands, see J. Meyhoffer, *Le Martyrologe protestante des Pays-Bas 1523-1597,* La Haye, 1907, pp. 5-25.

[9] A.J. Jelsma, *Adriaan van Haemstede en zijn martelaarsboek,* The Hague, 1970, pp. 257-78.

[10] White, *Tudor Books,* p. 141f.

[11] Foxe, *Acts and Monuments* (1684), in 'A Protestation to the Whole Church of England': '... in this History might appear ... the Image of both Churches ... especially of the poor, oppressed and persecuted Church of Christ ... neglected in the World, not regarded in Histories, and almost scarce visibly or known to wordly eyes ....' This presents a picture other than what he wrote in his dedication to Queen Elizabeth.

[12] White, *Tudor Books*, pp. 169f.

[13] Quoted by Perez Zagorin, *Rebels & Rulers 1500-1660*, 2 vols., Cambridge, 1982, I, p. 151. See Collinson, *Archbishop Grindal*, p. 79. About the reliability of the Books of Martyrs, see H.T. Oberman, 'De betrouwbaarheid der martelaarsboeken van Crespin en Van Haemstede', in *Nederlands archief voor kerkgeschiedenis*, Nieuwe reeks, 4 (1907), pp. 74-110, and L.-E. Halkin, 'Les Martyrologes et la critique; Contribution à l'étude du martyrologe protestant des Pays-Bas', in *Mélanges historiques offerts à Mr. J. Meyhoffer*, Lausanne, 1952, pp. 52-73.

[14] White, *Tudor Books*, p. 159. See Ph. Hughes, *The Reformation in England*, 3 vols., London, 1953-54, II, p. 258: '... horror is piled on horror ....' On the kind character of Foxe, see G.R. Elton, 'Persecution and Toleration in the English Reformation', in *Studies in Church History*, vol. 21, *Persecution and Toleration*, Oxford, 1984, pp. 163-87.

[15] Jelsma, *Adriaan van Haemstede*, pp. 246-50. In his epilogue Van Haemstede asks his readers for other examples of executioners who died in an unusual way.

[16] I confine myself to some examples of victims from the Book of Martyrs by Van Haemstede: Peter Spengler, killed in 1525, condemned the peasants revolution; Petrus Bruly, executed in 1545, rejected the second baptism; some French ministers, killed in 1555, agreed with the execution of Servetus. Mennonite martyrs too rejected the disturbance of public order, as had happened in Munster; see F. Pijper, *Martelaarsboeken*, The Hague, 1924, p. 99.

[17] White, *Tudor Books*, p. 134.

[18] Pijper, *Martelaarsboeken*, pp. 121, 122.

[19] Crespin, *Acta martyrum*, pp. 350, 351; *Histoire des tesmoins*, pp. 170, 171.

[20] *Idem, Acta*, pp. 361, 362; *Histoire*, pp. 178, 179.

[21] *Idem, Acta*, pp. 169, 221, 385.

[22] *Idem, Histoire*, pp. 83-85.

[23] For an English edition see the translation by Montague Summers, *Malleus maleficarum*, 2nd ed., London, 1971. The authors were Heinrich Kramer and Jacobus Sprenger.

[24] Hughes, *Reformation*, II, p. 286.

[25] Crespin, *Histoire*, pp. 83-85.

[26] *Quellen zur Geschichte der Taufer in der Schweiz*, vol. II, *Ostschweiz*, ed. H. Fast, Zürich, 1973, pp. 590-632. Ulrich Zwingli, *In catabaptistarum strophas elenchus*, *Corpus reformatorum*, 93 (*Huldreich Zwinglis Sämtliche Werke*, IV, part 1, Rpt. Munich, 1981), pp. 1-196. For the history of the Anabaptists, especially in the region of St. Gall and Appenzell, see Emil Egli, *Die St. Galler Täufer*, Zürich, 1887.

[27] Crespin (1556) described the suffering of 130 men and 8 women, Van Haemstede (1559) 220 men and 16 women, Van Braght (1685) 611 men and 221 women, *Het offer des Heeren* (1904) 20 men and 5 women.

[28] Van Braght, *Het bloedig tooneel*, p. 822.

[29] *Het offer des Heeren*, p. 91.

[30] *Ibid.*, p. 327.

[31] *Ibid.*, p. 70.

[32] *Ibid.*, pp. 136-76.

[33] Van Braght, *Het bloedig tooneel*, pp. 383, 384.

[34] Bainton, *Women of the Reformation*, p. 211; Macek, 'The Emergency', p. 66. See also A.G. Dickens, *The English Reformation*, 4th ed., London, 1968, p. 26: '... the most informative of our sources, the *Acts and Monuments* of John Foxe.'

[35] Hughes, *Reformation*, II, p. 258.

[36] White, *Tudor Books*, p. 136.

[37] Hughes, *Reformation*, II, p. 262; Horst, *The Radical Brethren*, pp. 155, 156. See also W. Haller, *Foxe's Book of Martyrs and the Elect Nation*, London, 1963, pp. 13f.

[38] John Foxe, *Acts and Monuments* (1684), III, pp. 746, 747.

[39] Claire Cross, '"He-Goats before the Flocks": A Note on the Part Played by Women in the Founding of Some Civil War Churches', *Studies in Church History*, vol. 8, *Popular Belief and Practice*, Cambridge, 1984, pp. 195-202.

[40] J. Grauwels (ed.), *Dagboek van gebeurtenissen, opgetekend door Christiaan Munters, 1529-1545*, Assen, 1972, p. 26.

ARMED RESISTANCE AND CALVINISM DURING THE REVOLT OF THE NETHERLANDS

M.E.H.N. Mout

In a fairly recent book on Calvinism in early modern Europe it is argued that Calvinist political theory in France was determined by two factors: fidelity to Calvin's ideas, and unfailing pragmatism. To the eye of the historian these two factors seem more often than not to be at odds with each other, especially during the period of the French Wars of Religion. At first sight Calvin's political thought has the form of a doctrine of non-resistance. There are, it is true, some built-in reservations, but nevertheless this doctrine alone could never have been responsible for the revolutionary ideas about the use of arms by subjects against their legitimate prince which were developed between c. 1560 and 1590. Even if Calvin's political thought were to be combined with the German Lutheran teachings about the right and duty of the so-called inferior magistrates to oppose tyranny or with the notion that a tyrant, having by his tyranny abrogated his own power, was not more than a private citizen and could as such be disobeyed or even punished for his misdeeds, the concoction of ideas was not, at first, powerful enough to ease the Huguenot conscience about the pressing question of armed resistance against the legitimate prince. It needed long and tortuous legal, historical and theological arguments, firmly related to the complex and ever changing political reality of the Wars of Religion, to formulate Calvinist political ideas which were new and revolutionary. The Huguenot pragmatists adapted their propaganda, in which their political ideas were vented, to the needs of the moment. Successively, the problems of religious toleration, the right to resist of the nobles and princes of the blood disguised as 'inferior' magistrates, and the duty of the Huguenots to resist when the kingdom was in danger were discussed. The Massacre of St. Bartholomew (1572) led to the innovative works of the monarchomachs, and was followed, at the end of the century, by a discussion of absolutism and the divine right of kings in a monarchy which could guarantee peace and as much toleration as was inevitable for attaining political harmony.[1]

In roughly the same period covered by the French Wars of Religion, Calvinists in the Netherlands were confronted by comparable problems,

including the question of armed resistance against their legitimate overlord, King Philip II of Spain, during that long series of conflicts which
is now known as the Revolt of the Netherlands. In the course of the Revolt the Dutch Calvinists, like the French, developed a body of political
thought.[2] Were they as faithful to Calvin's political thought as their
French co-religionists and were they also guided by pragmatic approaches to theoretical problems while formulating their own ideas? A
complete answer to these questions would require an elaborate discourse on early modern Dutch political theory in general. In order to
give even a partial answer the attitude of the Dutch Calvinists toward
armed resistance must be examined.

Like the French, the Dutch were able to draw on several different
sources for their ideas on armed resistance. Luther had only very reluc-
tantly and with much prudence formulated thoughts about the right to
resist the lawful government, using legal rather than theological arguments. He, like Calvin, was much more interested in framing a political
theory of good government and good citizenship than in discussing the
limits of obedience and the right to resist. Melanchthon and other Wit-
tenberg theologians developed a more outspoken theory after Luther's
death, especially during the Schmalkaldic War, which called for the
legitimization, both in the legal and the theological sense, of the resistance of the German Protestant princes against the Emperor Charles V.
In 1550-51 Lutheran political thought was rephrased and considerably
altered by the Magdeburg theologians, who defended the right to resist
on religious grounds and based themselves on purely theological, as distinct from legal, arguments. In England questions of obedience and resistance became acute during the reign of Mary Tudor. Bishop John
Ponet wrote his work *A Short Treatise of Politicke Power* (1556) while in
exile in Strasbourg. In this treatise the rights of tyrannicide and resistance are granted to the commonwealth. The case for resistance on religious grounds was strongly put by the Calvinist Christopher Goodman
in *How Superior Powers Ought to Be Obeyed of Their Subjects* (1558). John
Knox wrote his *Appellation* (1558) and other works in the fifties in which
he claims for the body of the people an active right to resist.[3]

The fruits of both German Lutheran and English and Scottish political thought were accessible to the Dutch Calvinists when they had to
find solutions to their own problems in the sixties. It is, however, very
difficult to determine whether and, if so, how they used these theories.
Perhaps it is not unreasonable to think that Calvin's own teachings on
the subject of resistance to the legitimate prince meant more to the
Dutch Calvinists than political ideas of a different provenance.[4]

Calvin developed his political ideas over a number of years in his books, letters and sermons, in direct connection with his theology. It was not, and was probably never meant to be, an entirely consistent system of political thought. Much of it concerned the relations between subject and government. In the preface to the 1535 edition of the *Institutio* Calvin advocated absolute loyalty to the French king. Submission to the civil authorities remained a key note in the following editions of the work, although in matters of religion one was allowed to follow one's conscience. This could lead, in turn, to civil disobedience or passive resistance. Patience was a Christian duty and even tyranny should not be resisted, although in the 1559 Latin edition of the book Calvin stated that a prince who had overstepped the boundaries of his authority had abrogated his own power. This opened the possibility of revolt against such a ruler who had, in fact, stripped himself of his God-given authority and was now no better than any other private evil-doer. The inferior magistrates could, in Calvin's view, intervene and according to his homily on the first book of Samuel (1560) even control the superior magistrates if they exceeded their authority. The term 'inferior magistrates', introduced by Calvin in the course of his otherwise fairly traditional discussion of the role of certain public officers in classical antiquity, was declared to be applicable to contemporary political bodies like the estates. Resistance by them should, however, always have a legitimate foundation and never deteriorate into rebellion. The individual citizen was never given a right to resist, much less to rebel. Only in his homilies on the first and second book of Samuel (1560) did Calvin propose the idea that under certain conditions a private person could offer resistance if it were in the interest of the community.[5]

The impact of Calvin's ideas in France and the use made of them by pragmatic political thinkers in countless famous and influential pamphlets and treatises has often been studied. Quentin Skinner, in his book on early modern political thought, has firmly placed French Calvinist political thought into a general historical context, in which other Calvinists, especially from England and Scotland, also play a major role. Dutch Calvinist political thought in connection with the Revolt of the Netherlands was, as Skinner states, intellectually wholly dependent on the works of the French monarchomachs, who set the tone after the Massacre of St. Bartholomew.[6] Against this it must be said, however, that even earlier, in 1568, the military confrontation with their natural prince had forced the seditious Dutch and especially their leader, William of Orange, to formulate certain political ideas of their own in a number of pamphlets.[7] Even earlier, some Calvinist bodies like church consistories and also a few individuals treated the problem whether armed resistance to the legitimate authorities was permissible. It is impossible to ascertain whether these discussions were, in some way, influenced by contemporary French Calvinist political thought, but it is not improbable.

From about 1550 onwards Dutch Protestants were in contact with Geneva and a number of ministers were trained there in the fifties and early sixties. During the sixties the number of Dutch Protestants with Calvinist leanings rose and the churches came under the influence of French Calvinism. The earliest synods in the Netherlands set their course by the French synodal system of government.[8] The problem of active and armed resistance against a government which had been persecuting heretics since the 1520s became more and more pressing for the Dutch churches in exile and in hiding ('under the cross', as it was called) during the late fifties and the early sixties, when they were confronted with waves of severe repression. The well-known Calvinist minister Petrus Dathenus, noted for his religious ardour, was perhaps among the first to write about the right to resist in his pamphlet *Een christelijcke verantwoordinghe* (A Christian justification), first published in 1559. There he referred to Calvin's inferior magistrates resisting a tyrannical government. Unfortunately the work has only survived in its second edition of 1582, the text of which may have differed significantly from the first.[9]

The Dutch Calvinist historian Van Schelven thought he could detect the influence of Calvin's political ideas in the discussions taking place during the early sixties in some Dutch Protestant churches about the forcible liberation ('effractie' in Dutch) of those who were imprisoned for religious reasons and about some other issues. Is resistance to the government permissible? Are a prison warder and his henchmen or a papal inquisitor representatives of the government? Is a prisoner obliged to explain and defend his faith to authorities whose religion is opposed to his? Is it permissible to take up arms against the Roman Catholics, or to carry arms when attending an illegal Protestant field conventicle? Every one of these questions arose from the acute necessity to define the position of believers who were persecuted by the authorities, but they might have been inspired, too, by the disquieting events in France.

Necessity is not only the mother of invention, but, in this case, also of strife, for instance between the Dutch church in London and the Antwerp synod in 1562. It started with a letter, written by a Dutch minister from the Netherlands to the London consistory about questions of armed resistance and obedience to a government which was persecuting the faithful. The churchmen in Antwerp came to the conclusion that the papal inquisitor and other members of the clergy who were involved in the inquisition were not to be regarded as public officers, and could, therefore, be resisted. Moreover, the government overstepped its power if it harassed people because of their religious views, and in this way forfeited its authority. The forceful liberation of prisoners of conscience was therefore sanctioned by the Antwerp synod of 1562. The London consistory, on the contrary, argued that armed resistance against the government was never permissible and that inquisitors, being public officers, should be obeyed. God, they said, would bless only nonviolent action. The result of the exchange of opinions between a Dutch church in comparably safe and quiet exile in London and the representatives of Dutch churches 'under the cross' battered by persecution in Antwerp was a quarrel, in which the Antwerp synod had to repudiate the notion that it was no better than the adherents of the late Thomas Müntzer. The question of armed resistance remained unresolved, and even in London there was at least one member of the Dutch church who was of the opinion that an individual was allowed to resist the government in order to save a suffering co-religionist.[10] In this discussion no participant ever quoted sources, so one can only guess whether the quarrelling Dutch believers were really basing their views on Calvin's own writings—the *Institutio* had been translated into Dutch in 1560 and leading ministers had clearly been familiar with the work before.[11] It is also quite possible, of course, that they drew on other contemporary works on the relation between government and subject by Ponet, Goodman or Knox or perhaps Theodore Beza's *De haereticis a civili magistratu puniendis* (1554).

A few years after these discussions took place in Dutch Calvinist circles came the troubled times of 1566, the year of the iconoclast movement and of growing opposition to the government. At that moment, the right of resistance became a central issue for all those who opposed the government and they were by no means only Calvinists. In many places reformed Protestants had taken up the habit to attend field conventicles while carrying arms, and armed adherents of 'the new religion' had often been instrumental in removing and destroying images from the churches during the iconoclast movement.[12] The Prince of Orange, who in 1566 was still nominally a Catholic, asked several German Protestant princes for political advice on the situation in the Netherlands. The subject of the right of resistance was touched upon in a memorandum for Orange's envoy Ludwig von Wittgenstein who was instructed to ask the rulers of Hesse and Saxony whether it was permissible for the Netherlands to resist their overlord 'because of the true religion' and, if it were permissible, how and to what extent it should be done.[13] The Calvinist nobleman Nicolas de Hames, an ardent supporter of the Compromise—the league of the lesser nobility (1566)—, asked the then still Lutheran brother of the Prince of Orange, Lodewijk van Nassau, to give his opinion and if possible send him a treatise on the reasons for which the inferior magistrates could take up arms when the superior authority behaved like a tyrant or was 'asleep', i.e. idle and indolent. De Hames' letter is a rare proof of the possible use of writings on political theory by active politicians. Lodewijk van Nassau in turn requested 'consilia' from his elder brother Jan—also still a Lutheran at the time—about the problem of armed resistance to public officers who tried to stop Protestant preaching.[14] Soon the burning question appeared to be whether the turbulent events of 1566 meant that the stage had now been set for intervention by inferior magistrates according to Calvin's precepts. At the end of the year 1566, when there was still much public unrest although the iconoclast movement had come to an end, the possibility of government action against the Protestants loomed large. In December 1566 the Dutch Protestant consistories asked themselves whether it was permissible that 'part of the vassals (i.e. the nobles of the Compromise) together with part of the subjects in the Netherlands would take up arms against a government in case it infringed the privileges and resorted to injustice and open violence'. The answer was in the affirmative, provided sufficient means could be found to carry out the operation. By sufficient means the consistories meant a leader or leaders, money and people. They considered the Prince of Orange to be a suitable leader provided he promised to protect the reformed religion and to accept six Protestant nobles as his councillors as well as six merchants who would be responsible for financial matters. If Orange were not available, Horne and Brederode, or either of them, would do as well.[15] Evidently the consistories thought that answering the question of armed resistance must, inevitably, involve the planning of a revolt. Representatives of several consistories attended the conference of the rebellious nobility in St. Truyen (St. Trond) in July 1566, where in principle the decision to take up arms against the king was reached.[16]

In 1567 Philip II sent his new governor the Duke of Alva to the Netherlands. This initiated a period of severe repression and the anxieties of the Dutch Protestants are reflected in the pamphlets they wrote. In one of them, the *Conseil sacré d'un gentilhomme françois aux églises de Flandre*,[17] Philip II is depicted as a tyrant against whom armed resistance is a mere act of self-defence. In the following year, 1568, William of Orange and his supporters started their military campaign against the government, which was accompanied by an avalanche of pamphlets in defence of their revolt. Armed resistance to the legitimate ruler was now no longer limited to the freeing of the odd prisoner or skirmishes over field conventicles, the use of churches for Protestant worship or the breaking of images. Now government and rebels were openly at war and

Calvin's maxim that tyranny has to be endured and not fought, was not of much use to those who wanted to justify their rebellion. This becomes quite clear from the *Advys aengaende den twist in de Nederduysche kercke tot London in Engellandt* (Memorandum about the quarrel in the Dutch church at London in England) written in 1568 by Philips Marnix van St. Aldegonde, a close collaborator of the Prince of Orange. After the military confrontation between rebels and government had started, the members of the Dutch church in London were still divided on the question of armed resistance. In his memorandum Marnix defended a limited right to resist tyranny, but not every member of the London church was convinced, as is clear from a reply of its consistory to Orange who had solicited help for his military campaign. The consistory stated that the Prince of Orange had no right to resist the King, much less to make war on him and to try to seize power in the Netherlands. If this policy were carried through, the Londoners predicted ruin for the Netherlands and dishonour for Orange.[18] In the early seventies some members of the London church still refused to give money for the Revolt for reasons of conscience. The rebels, they argued, were violating the right of the legitimate ruler, although their intentions may have been pure. 'But', they said, 'it is not enough that the cause is just, the means should also be right.'[19]

A special problem was the defence of religion as a reason for armed resistance. In 1567 Marnix tried to justify the actions of the Dutch nobles against the king, the field conventicles and the iconoclast movement in his *Vraye narration et apologie des choses passées au Pays-Bas, touchant le fait de la religion*. He was following Calvin when he stated that submission to tyranny was always preferable to rebellion, but that civil disobedience for the sake of religion was permissible. Religion in itself could never be a ground for armed resistance, but persecution of Protestants was contrary to the privileges which had to be defended, as the Prince of Orange said in 1568. As long as the leaders of the revolt tried to win over Catholics and other non-Calvinists to their cause, it appeared to be most unwise to treat religion as a reason for armed resistance.[20]

What the adherents of the revolt wanted and needed was a political theory in which the right to resist tyranny, if necessary by armed struggle, was incorporated. Inspiration for this could be found either in the German Empire, where lawyers had formulated the right to defend the country against rulers who violated the privileges,[21] or in France, where two of Calvin's closest followers, Beza and Hotman, if not Calvin himself, were openly supporting the Huguenot struggle against the Guises who, in their view, held the young Francis II prisoner and were responsible for the troubles in France.[22]. The Dutch rebels followed the

German example in introducing the concept of 'patria' ('fatherland') into their political thinking. Especially in the circles of Calvinist exiles after 1567 loyalty to their country was dissociated from loyalty to the king and at the same time associated with allegiance to the 'true religion'. In pamphlets and political correspondence the Prince of Orange stressed his heroic defence of this 'fatherland'.[23] Religion was not treated as a main cause for resistance, although Orange was presented in certain pamphlets as a defender of the true faith.[24] French Huguenot reasoning taught the Dutch rebels to pretend that they were rising against the evil servants of a good king, not against the king himself. The tyrannical rule in the Netherlands was Alva's, not King Philip's doing, as in France the Guises were responsible for tyranny, not the king, who was still under age. In this way the revolt could be presented as a less serious matter because it left the rights of the legitimate ruler intact.[25]

During the decade before the Massacre of St. Bartholomew (1572) French Calvinist political thinking moved from a discussion on the right to resist tyranny to the conviction that this was not so much a right as a duty.[26] In the Netherlands the change was more sudden. In the fateful year 1568 the Prince of Orange and his advisers, among them Calvinists such as the minister Hubert Languet and the lawyer Jacob van Wesembeke, wrote pamphlets in support of the Revolt.[27] Their tenor was simple: not only the Prince of Orange, the nobility and the estates had a duty to resist Alva's tyranny, but also the ordinary subjects were obliged to defend the privileges and customs of the country:

> Therefore, my seigniors, brethren and companions ... recognise the truth, take a firm stand for the maintenance of your own welfare, resist your oppressors with all your might, help by all means those who exert themselves to pull you out of this miserable servitude.[28]

Even foreigners, so Orange and his advisers maintained in 1568, had the duty 'to help resist such terrible tyranny'.[29] This idea was put into practice during a later stage of the Revolt when during the late seventies and the early eighties foreign princes such as the Archduke Matthias of Austria or the French Duke of Anjou were called in to act as governors of the country. In 1580 a staunch Calvinist like Christiani, secretary to Jan van Nassau, positively recommended to create Anjou, who was a Catholic, 'prince et seigneur' of the Netherlands, and to accept his help in the rebellion.[30] A year earlier an anonymous writer had argued:

> If he [i.e. Anjou] were a Tatar, a Samaritan or a Russian, or even a Turk, we have to accept what comes from God, in so far as he can come to our rescue and is willing to protect and sustain our privileges, rights, liberties and religion unless we want to rebel and protest against God.[31]

In the early seventies the Prince of Orange sent a lengthy memorandum to Queen Elizabeth I, in the hope of enlisting her help, in which he depicts himself as an inferior magistrate who has the right to defend himself and his subjects against a tyrannical superior magistrate, the King of Spain. On this occasion Orange clearly did not want to appear as an adherent of radical Calvinist political thought. He did keep, however, to Calvin's general views about the possible intervention of inferior magistrates in case government had deteriorated into tyranny.[32]

More warlike was the Latin treatise written in 1571 by Henricus Geldorpius, a Calvinist schoolman, which contained a plan of campaign for the Prince of Orange and belligerent exhortations addressed to him and to the Dutch in general. Geldorpius put God firmly on the side of the rebels and incited them to armed resistance:

> Not every hesitation signifies caution; often it is mere cowardice; and not every gentleness is a virtue, for often it represents a willingness to tolerate faults, and a refusal to inflict upon the godless the extreme punishment they deserve. Unless we desire to be moles, we should realise that the approbation of the Christian nations, who though not involved applaud us and abhor the tyrant, as well as the support we find in this country, the tyrant's indolence, the small number of mercenaries and the fact that the whole fatherland is embittered by the execrable torments we suffer because of the blood lust and immorality of the enemy, by requisitioning and pillage, incite us to take revenge and clearly show us that we should not faint-heartedly delay to seek the help God is willing to render us.[33]

The author solicited Orange's approval of his work and hoped to get it published at his expense. It is understandable, however, that the Prince was not willing to have this forceful language printed under his aegis. The prudence which Geldorpius abhorred was at that moment the hub of Orange's policy and therefore the pamphlet was published only in 1574.[34]

After 1572, when the centre of the Revolt had shifted to the northern Netherlands, belligerent prose in propagandist pamphlets produced by the rebels had become the rule, not the exception. Armed resistance was now accepted as a matter of course, and did not need to be supported by apologetic writings any more. Doubtless the Massacre of St. Bartholomew also influenced the rebels' attitude to the use of arms. As Orange wrote to Marnix van St. Aldegonde while the latter was imprisoned by the enemy:

> Memory of the massacre in France too, which happened in spite of a peace so solemnly sworn, cannot be effaced from our hearts and teaches us where to place our trust. We cannot forget that it took place a long time after the war, in time of peace and even during a wedding-feast. We should truly

consider what would in all probability be in store for us, with our country still full of soldiers and especially Spanish soldiers.[35]

When the States General had to reply to mediatory proposals put to them by the Emperor Rudolf II in 1578, they mentioned the question of armed resistance, but presented it as a natural reaction to the king's tyranny:

> As the king decided to ruin the men who so far rendered him allegiance, obedience and gallant service and still are doing so and promise to do so in future and as he deprived them of their hope of a peaceful settlement, what remains to these poor people but to have recourse to what both divine and secular right allows in such matters, what nature commands, what reason prescribes and law permits, that is, to taking up arms and providing for their prosperity and safety by all means that present themselves and staving off the great dangers which threaten them?[36]

The discussion about the right to use arms against the lawful ruler was now closed; what remained, was the need to justify the Revolt, especially to prospective allies outside the Netherlands and to those within the Netherlands who still supported the Spanish king. At the end of the seventies Dutch political thought came under the influence of the Scottish Calvinists and the French monarchomachs.[37] Pamphlets were published which maintained that it was the duty of the government to establish the true religion and, if this was not done, the subject had the duty to resist, if need be by arms. These ideas, however, were never adopted by the leaders of the Revolt, who preferred a more subtle approach and would not proclaim the rebellion to be 'religionis ergo'.[38]

In Dutch Calvinist circles ideas about armed resistance appear to have been determined by the course of events, such as the beginning of the military campaign in 1568 which led to a sudden sharpening of the arguments with which the Revolt was justified. When it was found suitable, however, the edge was taken off, as the Prince of Orange did when he wrote to Queen Elizabeth I in the early seventies. In the late seventies, when the polarization of the Revolt had reached such a stage that reconciliation between the warring parties seemed to be a very remote possibility, the duty to resist was stressed by the States General and in by several pamphlet writers. Although traces of Calvin's political thought are certainly found in Dutch theories of resistance during the first stage of the Revolt (until 1572), a much greater part was played by pragmatism, which the situation had forced on the rebels.[39]

[1] M. Yardeni, 'French Calvinist Political Thought, 1534-1715', in M. Prestwich (ed.), *International Calvinism 1541-1715*, Oxford, 1985, pp. 315-26.

[2] M.E.H.N. Mout, 'Van arm vaderland tot eendrachtige republiek. De rol van politieke theorieën in de Nederlandse Opstand', *Bijdragen en mededelingen betreffende de geschiedenis der Nederlanden*, 101 (1986), pp. 345-65. The valuable dissertation of Martin van Gelderen, *The Political Thought of the Dutch Revolt (1555-1590)*, unpublished Ph.D Thesis, European University Institute, Florence, 1988, is now in print. I wish to thank the author for presenting me with his thesis while it was still in manuscript.

[3] Q. Skinner, *The Foundations of Modern Political Thought*, II, Cambridge etc., 1978; E. Wolgast, *Die Religionsfrage als Problem des Widerstandsrechts im 16. Jahrhundert*, Sitzungsberichte der Heidelberger Akademie der Wissenschaften, Philosophisch-Historische Klasse, 1980, 9. Abhandlung, Heidelberg, 1980.

[4] M.E.H.N. Mout, *Plakkaat van Verlatinge 1581*, The Hague, 1979.

[5] Calvin, *Institutio*, chap. 16; Yardeni, 'French Calvinist Political Thought'; Skinner, *The Foundations of Modern Political Thought*, II, pp. 302-48; W. Nijenhuis, 'De grenzen der burgerlijke ongehoorzaamheid in Calvijns laatstbekende preken: ontwikkeling van zijn opvattingen aangaande het verzetsrecht', in *Historisch bewogen. Opstellen over de radicale reformatie in de 16e en 17e eeuw* (Festschrift A.F. Mellink), Groningen, 1984, pp. 67-99.

[6] Skinner, *The Foundations of Modern Political Thought*, II, pp. 210, 215, 337-38; for a critical approach to Skinner's treatment of Dutch political thought cf. E.H. Kossmann, 'Popular Sovereignty at the Beginning of the Dutch Ancien Regime', in *The Low Countries History Yearbook*, 14 (1981), pp. 1-28; Mout, 'Van arm vaderland tot eendrachtige republiek', pp. 347-49.

[7] Cf. Mout, 'Van arm vaderland tot eendrachtige republiek' and M. van Gelderen's forthcoming book on the political thought of the Dutch Revolt (cf. note 2).

[8] A. Duke, 'The Ambivalent Face of Calvinism in the Netherlands, 1561-1618', in M. Prestwich (ed.), *International Calvinism*, pp. 109-26. Cf. also P.M. Crew, *Calvinist Preaching and Iconoclasm in the Netherlands, 1544-1569*, Cambridge, 1978; W. Nijenhuis, 'Variants within Dutch Calvinism in the Sixteenth Century', in *The Low Countries History Yearbook*, 12 (1979), pp. 48-64.

[9] Peeter Dathenum, *Een christelijcke verantwoordinghe op die disputacie, ghehouden binnen Audenarde ...*, 2nd ed., Antwerpen, 1582. Cf. also Van Gelderen, *The Political Thought of the Dutch Revolt*, pp. 99-100.

[10] A.A. van Schelven, 'Het begin van het gewapend verzet tegen Spanje in de 16e-eeuwsche Nederlanden', *Handelingen en mededelingen van de Maatschappij der Nederlandsche Letterkunde te Leiden over het jaar 1914-1915*, Leiden, 1915, pp. 126-56; A.A. van Schelven (ed.), *Kerkeraads-Protocollen der Nederduitsche vluchtelingenkerk te London 1560-1568*, Amsterdam, 1921, pp. 321-23, 354, 357, 386; A. Jelsma, 'The "Weakness of Conscience" in the Reformed Movement in the Netherlands: The Attitude of the Dutch Reformation to the Use of Violence Between 1562 and 1572', in W.J. Sheils (ed.), *Studies in Church History*, vol. 20, *The Church and War*, Oxford, 1984, pp. 217-29.

[11] Duke, 'The Ambivalent Face of Calvinism in the Netherlands', pp. 120-21.

[12] J. Scheerder, *De beeldenstorm*, 2nd ed., Haarlem, 1974.

[13] G. Groen van Prinsterer (ed.), *Archives ou correspondance inédite de la Maison d'Orange Nassau*, 1e série, II, Leiden, 1835, pp. 288-93, 300 (16 September 1566).

[14] *Ibid.*, p. 214 (16 August 1566).

[15] A.C.J. de Vrankrijker, *De motiveering van onzen Opstand. De theorieën van het verzet der Nederlandsche opstandelingen tegen Spanje in de jaren 1565-1581*, 2nd ed., Utrecht, 1979, p. 71; R.C. Bakhuizen van den Brink, *Studiën en schetsen over de vaderlandsche geschiedenis en letteren*, I, Amsterdam, 1863, pp. 519-20.

[16] A.A. van Schelven, *Willem van Oranje. Een boek ter gedachtenis van idealen en teleurstellingen*, Haarlem, 1933, pp. 118-20.

[17] [Gervais Barbier?], *Conseil sacré d'un gentilhomme françois aux églises de Flandre, qui peut servir d'un humble exhortation à l'excellence des trésillustres princes protestans du sainct empire, et d'advertissement certain aux seigneurs des pais bas*, Antwerp, 1567.

[18] Philips van Marnix van St. Aldegonde, *Godsdienstige en kerkelijke geschriften*, I, ed. J.J. van Toorenbergen, The Hague, 1871, pp. 135-82; J.H. Hessels (ed.), *Ecclesiae Londino-Batavae Archivum*, vol. II, *Epistulae et tractatus*, Cambridge, 1889, p. 304.

[19] R. Fruin, 'De Nederlandsche ballingen in Engeland betrokken in den opstand hunner landgenoten tegen Spanje. 1568-1570', *Bijdragen voor vaderlandsche geschiedenis en oudheidkunde*, 3e reeks, 6 (1892), p. 70.

[20] Mout, *Plakkaat van Verlatinge 1581*, pp. 34-35.

[21] K. Wolzendorff, *Staatsrecht und Naturrecht in der Lehre vom Widerstandsrecht des Volkes gegen rechtswidrige Ausübung der Staatsgewalt*, Breslau, 1916; Wolgast, *Die Religionsfrage als Problem des Widerstandsrechts*, pp. 25-27; Mout, 'Van arm vaderland tot eendrachtige republiek', p. 352. Cf. also R. Vierhaus (ed.), *Herrschaftsverträge, Wahlkapitulationen, Fundamentalgesetze*, Göttingen, 1977.

[22] Yardeni, 'French Calvinist Political Thought', pp. 318-19.

[23] A. Duke, 'From King and Country to King or Country? Loyalty and Treason in the Revolt of the Netherlands', *Transactions of the Royal Historical Society*, 5th Series, 32 (1982), p. 126; Mout, 'Van arm vaderland tot eendrachtige republiek', pp. 354-55; G. Schmidt, 'Des Prinzen Vaterland? Wilhelm I. von Oranien (1533-1584) zwischen Reich, deutscher Nation und den Niederlanden', in R. Melville a.o. (eds)., *Deutschland und Europa in der Neuzeit. Festschrift für Karl Otmar Freiherr von Aretin zum 65. Geburtstag*, Stuttgart, 1988, pp. 223-27.

[24] K.W. Swart, 'Wat bewoog Willem van Oranje de strijd tegen de Spaanse overheersing aan te binden?', *Bijdragen en mededelingen betreffende de geschiedenis der Nederlanden*, 99 (1984), pp. 564-66.

[25] Mout, 'Van arm vaderland tot eendrachtige republiek', p. 352

[26] Yardeni, 'French Calvinist Political Thought', pp. 319-20.

[27] M.E.H.N. Mout, 'Het intellectuele milieu van Willem van Oranje', *Bijdragen en mededelingen betreffende de geschiedenis der Nederlanden*, 99 (1984), pp. 615-17.

[28] E.H. Kossmann and A.F. Mellink (eds.), *Texts Concerning the Revolt of the Netherlands*, Cambridge, 1974, p. 88: *Fidelle exhortation aux inhabitans du pais bas, contre les vains et faux espoirs dont leurs oppresseurs les font amuser*, 1568.

[29] M.G. Schenk (ed.), *Verantwoordinge, verklaringhe ende waerschowinghe*, Amsterdam, 1933, p. 125.

[30] Groen van Prinsterer (ed.), *Archives*, 1e série, VII, p. 467.

[31] *Eersame goede mannen, het is nu hooch tijt dat ghij lieden eenmael besluyt oft ghy het Spaensch iock wilt teenemael aflegghen ofte niet*, 1579.

[32] De Vrankrijker, *De motiveering van onzen Opstand*, pp. 97-99; Mout, 'Het intellectuele milieu van Willem van Oranje', p. 618.

[33] Kossmann and Mellink (eds.), *Texts Concerning the Revolt of the Netherlands*, p. 89: Henricus Geldorpius, *Belgicae liberandae ab Hispanis hypodeixis*, 1574.

[34] R. Fruin, 'Nederland in 1571', in *idem, Verspreide Geschriften*, II, The Hague, 1900, pp. 170-74.

[35] Kossmann and Mellink (eds.), *Texts Concerning the Revolt of the Netherlands*, pp. 111-12: Orange to Marnix van St. Aldegonde, Delft, 28 November 1573.

[36] *Ibid.*, pp. 151-52: *Antwoorde van de generale Staten van de Nederlanden op de propositie ghedaen van weghen de Keyserlijcke Maiesteyt ...*, 1578.

[37] Mout, 'Van arm vaderland tot eendrachtige republiek', p. 359.

[38] Mout, *Plakkaat van Verlatinge 1581*, pp. 34-35; Mout, 'Van arm vaderland tot eendrachtige republiek', p. 355.

[39] For the role of pragmatism in Dutch political thought, cf. also Mout, 'Van arm vaderland tot eendrachtige republiek', pp. 364-65.

RESISTANCE AND REVOLUTION IN SIXTEENTH-CENTURY THOUGHT: THE CASE OF CHRISTOPHER GOODMAN

Jane E.A. Dawson

One Sunday morning in 1557 the English exiles in Geneva gathered as usual for worship in their church of Marie la Nove. They heard a forceful sermon from Christopher Goodman, one of their ministers, in which he called for the violent overthrow of England's Queen, Mary Tudor. The congregation heartily approved of Goodman's justification of active resistance and some of them even pressed him to expand his sermon into a book so that its important message could be heard in England and throughout the rest of Europe. Goodman took their advice and *How Superior Powers Ought to Be Obeyed* was published in Geneva on the first day of the new year (1558).[1] He was not the first to challenge the doctrine of non-resistance which had been upheld so strongly in England and was one of the central tenets of Protestantism. The pressure of circumstance had forced the Protestants to re-examine their political ideas first in the Holy Roman Empire at the time of the Schmalkaldic Wars, then in England at the accession of Queen Mary, the Roman Catholic ruler and subsequently in France and the Netherlands.[2] Even in comparison with other sixteenth-century resistance theories Goodman's ideas were profoundly shocking. He alarmed his contemporaries in two ways, by being willing to advocate popular resistance to a ruler and by deriving his theories directly and explicitly from Scripture. This willingness to flout the established conventions of Protestant thought ensured that Goodman moved beyond the justification of resistance to the advocacy of revolution and he produced some of the most radical political ideas of the century.

It was no accident that Goodman's revolutionary ideas were first expounded in a sermon for he viewed his theory of resistance as an extension of his biblical exegesis. His assertion of biblical support for his ideas upset his Protestant contemporaries as much as the doctrines themselves. As 'Sola Scriptura' was at the heart of the Protestant position it made a biblically based theory impossible to ignore. Goodman used the Bible in two different ways to justify his political ideas. In the first place he offered a new interpretation of the key texts which had supported the established doctrine of obedience and non-resistance. By attacking its

biblical base he challenged the doctrine directly and was the only sixteenth-century resistance theorist to do so openly. Secondly, Goodman
employed a specifically biblical concept, the covenant, and used it as the
basis for a new vision of politics.

If he were to refute the prevailing sixteenth-century doctrine of obedience Goodman had to challenge the interpretation of certain key New
Testament texts. Luther had revolutionized political thought by putting
the Bible back into the centre of theorising and discussion, and in so
doing had abandoned most of the established late medieval traditions.[3]
He had reinstated Romans 13 as the most crucial text and it had become
the centrepiece of the doctrine of non-resistance, supporting the twin
propositions that all rulers were divinely ordained and that active resistance to a monarch was never justified. Passive resistance could be permitted in the event of a ruler ordering an action which contravened
God's commandments. As it was never permissible to disobey or ignore
a divine command, the subject must refuse to obey his ruler and then
suffer passively whatever punishment he was given. In such an instance
Luther and the other Protestant writers appealed to the famous passage
in Acts when the Apostles Peter and John declared, 'We ought to obey
God rather than men'.[4] This allowed them to make the critical distinction between total obedience to a temporal ruler in all his commands,
godly and ungodly, and the idea of non-resistance. It provided a vital
conscience clause which preserved the moral and religious integrity of
the Protestant while ensuring that this did not lead to violent resistance
or threaten the social and political order.

That conscience clause had achieved even greater prominence in the
persecution which the English Protestants faced under Mary. It was the
sole justification for their refusal to obey the new religious laws which
had been carefully and constitutionally enacted by England's Parliament. Ultimately, it underpinned the validity of their martyrdom and
so it had a deep emotional significance particularly for the English.[5]
Goodman first directed his fire upon this conscience clause. He took as
the text for his original sermon the incident recorded in Acts when Peter
and John defied the Sanhedrin and insisted that obedience to God always comes before obedience to man. In his new interpretation of this
passage Goodman quite simply redefined the meaning of 'obedience to
God'. He turned obedience from a passive acceptance into an active and
aggressive action. To do this he broadened the scope of obedience by
adopting a new definition. It now included 'doing the contrary', a doctrine which was of considerable significance in his political thought. By
it Goodman meant that all God's commands contained a positive in-
junction which must be obeyed, even if the original command were

phrased in a negative way. Full obedience to God required not only abstaining from the thing forbidden but also actively doing the opposite of the forbidden thing. As Goodman explained, 'God is not fullie obeyed, when we will not do the ungodlie commandements of men, except also we apply ourselves with all diligence to do the contrary'.[6] For example, the seventh commandment with its express command not to commit adultery, carried with it the positive corollary to make a happy and faithfull marriage.

> We learne by the commandements of God, that so oft as he forbiddeth any thing which he wolde not to be done, in the self same, he commandeth us the contrarie, as for example: Thou shalt not murther, steale, commit adultrie, or beare false wittnes. It is not ynough to abstaine frome these thinges, neither is God therin fullie obeyed, except we do the contrarie ... that is, to save, preserve, and defende, as well the goodes as the persones of our brethren and neighbours.[7]

Full and true obedience to God required a positive turning towards Him and the active implementation of His Will in the world.[8] The idea that God's commands extended beyond their negative prohibitions did not originate with Goodman. In his interpretation of the Ten Commandments Calvin had used the same basic idea. He explained in his precise and measured style,

> So in each of the commandments we must first look to the matter of which it treats, and then consider its end, until we discover what it properly is that the Lawgiver declares to be pleasing or displeasing to him. Only we must reason from the precept to its contrary in this way: If this pleases God, its opposite displeases; if that displeases, its opposite pleases: if God commands this, he forbids the opposite; if he forbids that, he commands the opposite.

Calvin explained that the Commandments were a positive commendation of virtue and more than just the censure of vice. He continued,

> We maintain that it goes farther, and means opposite duties and positive acts. Hence the commandment 'Thou shalt not kill', the generality of men will merely consider as an injunction to abstain from all injury, and all wish to inflict injury. I hold that it moreover means, that we are to aid our neighbour's life by every means in our power.[9]

Goodman made devastating polemical use of this uncontroversial principle. He made the general point that all obedience to God should be active and that obeying God and following His Will required the implementation of the positive aspects of all the Commandments. He then focussed upon the particular question of false worship and idolatry condemned in the first table of the Commandments. He began by pointing out that if a ruler were to command the worship of idols, then the Christian must disobey and under no circumstances pollute himself with such idolatrous worship. This was the conventional position and had been vigorously promoted by the English Protestants in face of the reintroduction of Catholicism by Queen Mary.[10] Goodman went farther by insisting that not obeying an ungodly command was insufficient and could not constitute complete obedience to God. He asserted that in addition to a staunch refusal to participate in or to countenance Catholic worship (which was idolatry in Protestant eyes), the English Protestants should also actively oppose that idolatry and resist the ungodly commands and those who were wicked enough to advocate idolatrous practices. The Protestants in England should not simply refuse to attend Mass and meekly suffer the consequences—imprisonment and eventual martyrdom—but were instead to try to destroy Catholic worship and overthrow the Catholic monarch and her idolatrous regime. The precise nature of the resistance was not spelt out by Goodman at this stage in his book but he commended the example from the Apocrypha of Mattathias who had slain those who came to worship and smashed the altar.[11]

This was what Goodman meant when he called upon his fellow countrymen to 'do the contrary' of the ungodly commands of Mary. The idea of the contrary with its insistence upon the positive demands of all divine commands was a very simple and rather crude device to undermine the doctrine of non-resistance. At a stroke it removed the normal option of passive disobedience to a ruler who commanded something against the laws of God. The conscience clause was an essential component of the doctrine of non-resistance but it was also its most vulnerable point. That doctrine had always been open to just such a simple redefinition of the obedience owed to God as Goodman provided. The view that all obedience was active and that resistance to a ruler was merely obedience to the higher authority of God Himself had a straightforward appeal particularly to the English Protestants who were facing persecution for their beliefs. It matched the new atmosphere which was already noticeable at the martyrdoms in England. The mood had changed from silent and passive suffering for the faith to an act of triumphant defiance against the Catholic authorities.[12]

If Goodman used his idea of the contrary as a blunt instrument to batter down the doctrine of non-resistance, then his treatment of the other key text was more subtle and proved to be more significant. The whole edifice of the theory of political obedience was supported by Romans 13. Luther had returned that chapter to the centre of political discussion and it had been enthusiastically adopted by the apologists of Henry's Royal Supremacy, becoming the main plank in the English 'cult of authority'. The most frequently cited verses were the first five of the chapter which in the Geneva Bible run,

> 1. Let everie soule be subiect unto the higher powers: for there is no power but of God: and the powers that be, are ordeined of God.
> 2. Whosoever therefore resisteth ye power, resisteth the ordinance of God: and they that resist, shal receive to them selves iudgement.
> 3. For princes are not be feared for good workes, but for evil. Wilt you then be without fear of the power? do wel: so shalt thou have praise of the same.
> 4. For he is the minister of God for thy wealth: but if thou do evil, feare: for he beareth not the sworde for noght: for he is the minister of God to take vengeance on him that doeth evil.
> 5. Wherefore ye must be subiect, not because of wrath onely, but also for conscience sake.

The preface of John Hooper's *Annotations on Romans XIII* (1551) illustrates the central place this text held in English and Continental Protestant thought.[13] Hooper told the ministers of his diocese of Gloucester that in this chapter St. Paul had explained the whole of the Second Table of the Commandments containing the political, social and moral duties of the Christian man. He instructed them to teach the people in their care the message of this chapter every week.[14] There was nothing particularly unusual in Hooper's exposition nor in the need he felt, particularly after the rebellions of 1549, to bolster the obedience of the people.[15] He set out, as the majority of Protestant writers since Luther had before him, the basic deduction from verse 2 that 'the office of a magistrate is the ordinance of God'. The very possession of political power in itself indicated divine ordination no matter whether the ruler were good or bad.

> Let the king and magistrate be as wicked as can be devised and thought, yet is his office and place the ordinance and appointment of God, and therefore to be obeyed.

The second fundamental deduction was that resistance was never justified: 'subjects may not, nor upon pain of eternal damnation, ought not, by force nor violence to resist the officer of his higher power.' To resist a ruler was to resist and disobey God.[16]

These two basic assumptions became the starting-point for Protestant political discussions and the text of Romans 13 was supported by a long tail of further Scriptural citations. Together they constituted an extremely difficult barrier for all Protestant resistance theorists to surmount. The way most theorists chose to circumvent this obstacle was to emphasize that all powers, inferior as well as superior, received their authority from God. The inferior magistrates within a kingdom or an empire had a dual status as both rulers and subjects. In certain cir-

cumstances their duty to act as rulers overrode their obedience as subjects and they could resist the superior magistrate without violating the
basic tenet of obedience. In this way the family of 'inferior magistrate'
theories could bypass the text of Romans 13 rather than deny it. This
had the added advantage of reinforcing the duty of obedience required
from those without political authority, the common people. They were
still not permitted to resist under any circumstances.[17]

Goodman refused any such compromise and directly challenged the
interpretation of Romans 13.[18] He cut the Gordian knot which had baf-
fled his contemporaries by quite simply denying the basic assumption
that all powers were ordained by God. He shifted attention away from
the 'powers that be' and he dismissed the view that the actual possession
of political power was the only method of identifying those to whom
obedience was due. Instead he focussed upon the phrase 'ordained of
God'. He argued that to be ordained of God implied that a ruler had to
be acceptable to God. By this method Goodman was able to switch the
discussion from the possession of political power to the way a ruler used
his power. Goodman was certain that not all rulers were ordained of
God. Some rulers flagrantly broke divine laws and it was inconceivable
that they could have God's approval for such behaviour. These men
were obviously not ordained of God and so obedience was not owed to
them. It was therefore possible to resist these rulers without resisting
God and his laws. No penalty would be incurred by resisting a tyrant
because obedience was not owed to a tyrant as he could not be divinely
ordained.

> All men are bownd to obey such Magistrates, whome God hathe ordeyned
> over us lawfully according to his worde, which rule in his feare according
> to their office ... For he [God] never ordeyned anie lawes to approve, but
> to reprove and punishe tyrantes, idolaters, papistes and oppressors. Then
> when they are suche, they are not Gods ordinance. And in disobeying and
> resisting such, we do not resiste Gods ordinance, but Satan.[19]

By denying that anyone who possessed political authority had divine
sanction Goodman unequivocally broke away from the mainstream of
Protestant political thinking. He was then able to re-introduce the idea
of judging a ruler by his actions rather than by the simple fact of possessing political power. He could employ the fundamental medieval distinction between a king and tyrant and so use the wealth of ideas and
theories evolved in the Middle Ages for dealing with a tyrant.[20] This
position also permitted Goodman himself to advance a resistance theory
without strings. In his book Goodman offered a complete reinterpreta-
tion of the key texts of the Protestant doctrine of non-resistance. His
treatment destroyed the theory at its very root, the biblical base. Good-

man had swept away the religious duty of obedience and replaced it by a religious duty of resistance.

Having destroyed the doctrine of non-resistance with biblical weapons Goodman also used the Bible to construct his new vision of politics. Goodman's distinctive and highly original contribution to six-teenth-century thought is to be found in this positive development of the biblical concept of the covenant.[21] The political life of the people of God was to be understood through the Old Testament concept of God's cove-nant with Israel. Goodman deliberately used an Old Testament model rather than a New Testament one because he wished to discuss the Christian political community and not the Christian church.

Goodman asserted that God had made His Will known for the gov-ernment of a Christian community in the model of the Mosaic cove-nant.[22] It was applicable to all ages, Christian as well as Jewish, because God had revealed His Will directly to Moses on Mount Sinai. God had spoken without intermediaries so there could be no distortion or misun-derstanding of the divine Will. He had given His Law and covenant to Moses and this direct and complete revelation was preserved for Chris-tian societies in the Pentateuch. It was waiting in the Bible to instruct any Christian nation which sought to enter into a special relationship with God and become His people. As Goodman explained,

> This example [Mosaic covenant] ought never to departe from the eyes of all such as are, or woulde be Gods people. Wherein as in a most clere glasse it dothe appeare how they are bownd to God, what God requireth of them, and what they have promised to him.[23]

The basic requirement of the covenant was obedience to the Law of God. When a political community accepted the special relationship with God embodied in the covenant they thereby agreed to uphold the moral and judicial aspects of the Mosaic Law. The ceremonial parts of that Law had been abrogated by the coming of Christ and were not binding upon Christians, but the rest of the Law remained in force. 'God hath charged thee beinge one of his people, with the same Lawes (the Cere-monies except) wherwithe he charged his people Israel before.'[24] A political community became the people of God when they openly and publicly adopted the true religion of God, by which Goodman meant his own strict interpretation of Protestantism. They accepted a communal and public commitment to the Mosaic covenant and Law. In the Chris-tian era this opportunity was open to all reformed states and was not restricted by any form of racial exclusiveness as in the Jewish kingdoms of the Old Testament.[25] Goodman thought that, in addition to the com-munal acceptance of the covenant by the whole nation, each individual also entered the covenant personally. At baptism every Christian promised to obey, maintain and defend the Law of God. This promise was an absolute one and did not depend for its fulfullment upon the actions of the rest of the community. The obligation each Christian made was to uphold the Law of God in his own life and to ensure that its precepts were observed by the rest of the community.[26]

Both individual and community were under the same obligation to maintain a public standard of conformity to the Divine Law. Goodman stressed that this was a matter of external behaviour and had nothing to do with inner conviction or faith. This public adherence to the Law of God throughout the entire political community was the key to the whole covenant relationship. If the Law were upheld then the covenant was healthy, if it were neglected or broken with impunity then the covenant was threatened. The community's attitude towards the Law and the covenant could be assessed most easily by its willingness to punish those who broke the Law. The community must keep itself pure by punishing lawbreakers. The punishment of transgression was the external sign of the maintenance of the covenant and the health of the relationship between God and His people.

In Goodman's view the proper execution of punishment was absolutely essential and the vital demonstration of the fulfillment of the covenant obligation. Consequently, that punishment must be executed at all costs so that the Law and the covenant were preserved. This was why he had insisted that the covenant obligation was individual as well as communal. The responsibility to punish lawbreakers was normally held by the whole community and vested in its rulers. However, in Goodman's theory, that communal obligation was paralleled by an individual obligation to see that transgression was punished. Because of his personal covenant promise each and every member of the political community had the right and the duty to uphold the Law and the covenant not only for himself but also for the whole people. Goodman could then argue that if the community through its magistrates and rulers had failed in their duty to punish lawbreakers and so defend the covenant, then the people themselves must ensure that the punishment was executed and the covenant upheld.

The act of punishment and the fact that it was accomplished were of far greater importance to Goodman than the hand which performed the deed. He was quite prepared to permit any and every individual, including all those who held no political authority at all, to punish, if and when the need arose. The covenant obligation was of overriding importance and must be fulfilled. When the magistrates neglected their central duty, then the common people should take over that duty. The paramount requirement was to keep the community pure and within the covenant.

> If the Magistrates would whollye despice and betraye the iustice and Lawes of God, you which are subiectes with them shall be condemned except you mayntayne and defend the same Lawes agaynst them ... for this hath God required of you, and this have you promised unto him not under condition (if the Rulers will) but without all exceptions.[27]

This stance led Goodman to some very revolutionary conclusions. In the sixteenth century the right to punish was referred to as wielding the sword of justice and was regarded as the key attribute of political power. Goodman was advocating that every individual was capable of wielding the sword of justice, even the common people who held no political office or public authority whatsoever. For him the need to maintain the covenant with its execution of the Law superseded all considerations of social and political order or degree. Goodman did concede that the idea might appear subversive:

> And thoghe it appeare at the firste sight a great disordre, that the people shulde take unto them the punishment of transgression, yet, when the Magistrates and other officers cease to do their dutie, they are as it were, without officers, yea, worse then if they had none at all, and then God geveth the sworde in to the peoples hande, and he himself is become immediately their head.[28]

Not surprisingly, the idea that the common people could take the sword of justice into their own hands sent shock waves around Europe.[29] Goodman was even willing to take his theory one stage further and explained that as well as taking over the function of the magistrates, the common people could also punish the magistrates themselves when they became tyrants.

> It is all one to be without a Ruler, and to have such as will not rule in Gods feare. Yea it is much better to be destitut altogether, then to have a tyrant and murtherer. For then are they nomore publik persons, contemning their publik auctoritie in usinge it agaynst the Lawes, but are to be taken of all men, as private persones, and so examyned and punished.[30]

The reference to treating the magistrate as a private person links the right of punishment with one of Goodman's other arguments for resistance, the private law theory which he adapted from the earlier Lutheran resistance theories.[31] This position also connects the covenant obligation with Goodman's redefinition of Romans 13. A magistrate was only a lawful magistrate and one to whom obedience was owed when he ruled 'in God's fear'. If the magistrate ceased to rule in this manner then Goodman indicated that he need no longer be obeyed. In such circumstances it was better to be without a magistrate than to have one who abused his public authority.

Goodman's theory of the people of God based upon the biblical concept of the covenant shocked his comtemporaries. They were deeply worried both because he advocated popular revolution and because his justifications were rooted in the Bible, the supreme authority for all Protestants. It was very difficult to dismiss Goodman as an Anabaptist extremist because he belonged so obviously to the mainstream of the magisterial reformation and was a friend of Calvin, Beza, Vermigli and Bullinger as well as being a leading light of the English church.[32]

Goodman's ideas about resistance led straight to revolution both in the modern sense of the term and in the medieval and early modern understanding of a return to a lost condition in the past. His biblically based theories called for a new type of political system and its achievement in a swift and violent transformation. But they also strove to restore a perfect model from the past, the Mosaic covenant revealed by God and preserved in the Old Testament.[33] Goodman's prophetic cry was both forward to, and back to, the covenant. Among the theories which the Protestants produced in the sixteenth century, the Lutherans, the Dutch and the Huguenots dealt with the problem of resistance in a more comprehensive and effective way than Goodman. But few were as revolutionary as Goodman with his call for popular and active resistance by the whole people of God.

---

[1] *How Superior Powers Oght to Be Obeyd of their Subiects: and Wherin They May Lawfully by God's Worde Be Disobeyed and Resisted,* Geneva, 1558 (hereinafter *HSP*); Preface by William Whittingham, pp. 4-5.

[2] For a general discussion of sixteenth-century resistance theories, see Q. Skinner, *The Foundations of Modern Political Thought,* Cambridge, 1978, vol. II.

[3] W.D.J. Cargill-Thompson, *The Political Thought of Martin Luther,* Brighton, 1984, pp. 7-8, 93, 173.

[4] Acts 4 v. 19 and 5 v. 29.

[5] J. Shakespeare, 'Plague and Punishment', in P. Lake and M. Dowling (eds.), *Protestantism and the National Church in Sixteenth-Century England,* London, 1987, pp. 103-23.

[6] *HSP,* pp. 64 and 15-20, 42-48.

[7] *HSP,* pp. 69-70; Goodman also used the story of Daniel, pp. 70-73.

[8] This whole approach is explained in J.S. Coolidge, *The Pauline Renaissance in England,* Oxford, 1970, pp. 1-22.

[9] J. Calvin, *The Institutes of the Christian Religion,* II.8.8-9; trans. H. Beveridge, Calvin Translation Society, Edinburgh, 1845, I, pp. 437-38.

[10] For example, M. Coverdale, 'An Exhortation to the Carrying of Christ's Cross', in *Remains,* ed. G. Pearson, Cambridge, 1846, pp. 227-78; and J. Bradford, *Writings,* ed. A. Townsend, Cambridge, 1853, pp. 34-253.

[11] *HSP,* 75-77; the story of Joshua, pp. 77-81.

[12] This new mood was also reflected in the acceptance of resistance ideas among all of the Marian exiles; see G. Bowler, 'Marian Protestants and the Idea of Violent Resistance to Tyranny', in *Protestantism and the National Church,* pp. 124-43.

[13] J. Hooper, *Later Writings,* ed. C. Nevinson, Cambridge, 1852, pp. 93-116.

[14] Hooper's Preface to the Dean, Chancellor and all other clergy in the diocese of Gloucester, *ibid.,* pp. 95-98.

[15] For example, Cranmer's treatises at the time of the 1549 rebellion, in *Miscellaneous Writings and Letters*, ed. J. Cox, Cambridge, 1846, pp. 163-202.

[16] Hooper, *Later Writings*, pp. 103-15.

[17] R. Benert, *Inferior Magistrates in Sixteenth-Century Political and Legal Thought*, Ph.D. thesis, University of Minnesota, 1967. Later radical theorists still emphasized the people's duty of obedience based upon Romans 13, for example, Beza and the author of the *Vindiciae*, in *Constitutionalism and Resistance in the Sixteenth Century*, ed. J. Franklin, New York, 1969, pp. 109-10, 144-45.

[18] *HSP*, chap. 9 deals with objections from the New Testament.

[19] *HSP*, pp. 109-10.

[20] *The Cambridge History of Medieval Political Thought*, ed. J. Burns, Cambridge, 1988; Skinner, *Foundations*, vol. I.

[21] D. Danner, 'Christopher Goodman and the English Protestant Tradition of Civil Disobedience', *Sixteenth Century Journal*, 8 (1977), pp. 60-73. For a fuller exposition of the religious duty of resistance and the covenant ideas, see J. Dawson, *Christopher Goodman and British Protestant Thought* (forthcoming).

[22] For a recent discussion of the vast subject of the importance of the Mosaic covenant, see M. McGiffert, 'From Moses to Adam: The Making of the Covenant of Works', *Sixteenth Century Journal*, 19 (1988), pp. 131-55.

[23] *HSP*, pp. 164-65.

[24] *HSP*, p. 168. On the recent literature concerning the third use of the Law, see M. Johnson, 'Calvin's Handling of the Third Use of the Law and Its Problems', in *Calviniana*, ed. R. Schnucker (Sixteenth Century Essays and Studies, X), Kirksville (Missouri), 1988, pp. 33-50.

[25] Cf. P. Collinson, *The Birthpangs of Protestant England*, London, 1988, chap. 1

[26] *HSP*, p. 170.

[27] *HSP*, pp. 180-81.

[28] *HSP*, p. 185.

[29] Calvin and Beza both sought to distance themselves from Goodman and his friend and colleague John Knox and their embarassing books; Calvin to Cecil, 29 January 1559; Beza to Bullinger, 3 September 1566, *Zurich Letters*, ed. H. Robinson, Cambridge, 1842-45, I, p. 131, II, pp. 34-36, 131. Goodman was forced into hiding on his return to England in 1559, *ibid.*, I, pp. 19-20.

[30] *HSP*, pp. 187-88.

[31] Skinner, *Foundations*, II, pp. 223, 227; E. Hildebrandt, 'The Magdeburg Bekenntnis as a Possible Link between German and English Resistance Theories in the Sixteenth Century', *Archiv für Reformationsgeschichte*, 71 (1980), pp. 227-53.

[32] Goodman insisted that he had consulted these eminent figures on the subject of resistance before he had published the book; Goodman to Peter Martyr Vermigli, 20 August 1558, *Original Letters Relative to the English Reformation*, ed. H. Robinson, Cambridge, 1846-47, pp. 768-71. For Goodman's career see J. Dawson, *The Early Career of Christopher Goodman and His Place in the Development of English Protestant Thought*, Ph.D. thesis, University of Durham, 1978.

[33] For a general discussion of the idea of restitution, see J.C. Spalding, 'Restitution as a Normative Factor for Puritan Dissent', *Journal of the American Academy of Religion*, 44 (1976), pp. 47-63.

THE EXILE CHURCHES DURING THE *WONDERJAAR*

A. Pettegree

One of the best eyewitness accounts of the turbulent events of 1566 was written by an Englishman, an agent of the merchant and financial manager Sir Thomas Gresham named Richard Clough. Clough reported with growing fascination the political ruptions of early summer, the hedgepreaching, and finally the iconoclasm. 'We have had this night past', he wrote from Antwerp on 21 August, 'a marvellous stir, all the churches and chapels and houses of religion utterly defaced, and no kind of thing left whole within them.'[1] Clough's account of that dramatic night catches the sense of wonderment and disbelief that must have been experienced by most of the thousands who stood and looked on as the iconoclasts went about their work. Wandering into the church of Our Lady, Clough found a brilliant and shocking spectacle, 'above ten thousand torches burning, and such a noise as if heaven and earth had got together, with falling of images and beating down of costly works, such sort that the spoil was so great that a man could not well pass through the church. So that, in fine, I can not write you in ten sheets of paper the strange sight I saw there, organs and all destroyed.' In one night twenty-five or thirty churches were ransacked, and yet in the chaos Clough found a strange appearance of order: for all was done 'with so few folks that it is to be wondered at'.

> For when they entered into some houses of religion, I could not perceive ... more than ten or twelve that spoiled, all being boys and rascals: but there were many in the church lookers on, or as some thought, setters on.

The contrast between the apparently wanton destruction and purposeful, almost orderly manner in which it was accomplished was one which struck many observers of the events in Antwerp and elsewhere. And it was this contrast above all that has fuelled debate as to the causes and prime movers of the destruction. Almost before the rubble had been collected the battery of charge and counter-charge had begun, with the ruling powers and catholic observers condemning the Reformed ministers, and the ministers seeking to distance themselves from responsibility. Historians, too, have found no real consensus as to the real causes of the iconoclasm, with the respective contributions of religious agitation and political discontent set against the underlying economic and social tensions of these difficult years.[2] This essay will be concerned with the explicitly religious component of the events of 1566, and in particular the involvement of the Calvinist exile communities.

The exile churches are justly recognised as the cradles of Dutch Calvinism. During the decades before 1566, it was largely the achievement of the churches in exile, at London and Norwich in England, and in Germany at Emden and Wesel, that the Dutch evangelical movement had survived the persecution of the 1540s and 1550s and latterly begun to take on coherent shape as an organised Reformed church. These secure and well-organised churches abroad provided the small secret communities within the Netherlands with every kind of help, sending ministers and books, and offering advice on theological questions and church building. It remains to be seen how far these relationships established over the previous decade might influence the course of events in the Netherlands in 1566. What role could the exile churches play during this year of helter-skelter growth and wondrous change? Most crucially, were the exile churches in London and Emden able to maintain any sort of control over the emerging churches in the Netherlands, either directly or through the many ministers and laymen who hurried back to take part in the events in their homelands?

The crisis of 1566 in the Netherlands, for all that it was a long time preparing, in fact blew up very quickly in the spring and summer of 1566. From the time that the regent, Margaret of Parma, made public the King's letter of November 1565, making clear that there would be no change of policy with respect to the prosecution of heresy, some sort of confrontation with the disaffected nobility seemed inevitable.[3] In April 1566 these opposition forces, the great magnates on the one side and a band of lesser or Confederate nobles on the other, extracted from Margaret a crucial concession: a moderation of the heresy laws pending regulation of the religious situation by the Estates General and subject to Philip's final approval.[4] Tentative and provisional though the Moderation was, it was immediately seen as a major reversal of policy, both by the political opposition and the evangelicals who promised to be the immediate beneficiaries of any relaxation in the heresy laws. Over the next couple of months the small evangelical communities in the Netherlands began to emerge from their secret meeting places, culminating in the first open-air sermons, the hedge-preachings, in May and June.

The effect of these political events was also felt abroad, in the exile churches. One consequence of the Moderation was to persuade many of those who had taken refuge abroad that it was now safe to return. On 10 May the church at Emden decreed a day of fasting and prayer for, amongst other things, the progress of the Gospel in the Netherlands, 'that it may not be impeded in this change for the better'.[5] Individual members of the church, meanwhile, hastened to set their affairs in order so that they could return to their former homes.[6] The official reaction in London is not known, since, frustratingly, the consistory minutes for these years have disappeared; but from England, too, large numbers of exiles were reported to be crossing over to Flanders and Brabant to swell the numbers of the evangelical congregations.[7] Among them were a number of ministers, who together with colleagues already active in Antwerp and the Flanders Westkwartier, now took the crucial step of preaching in the open. The first public sermon in Flanders was preached by Sebastian Matte, who had just then come over from England, as had several others who preached in the Westkwartier during the course of the year. Another minister, Jacob Pontfort, came back from Emden to preach in his home town of Ypres.[8]

From this point events began to move with a frightening pace. The first open preaching in the woods outside Antwerp took place on 22 May in the presence of a crowd of about two hundred. By the end of June, just four weeks later, crowds of five thousand were reported at Antwerp and the preaching had spread across the whole of the southern provinces. Alarmed at this wholly unintended consequence of her concession, the Regent Margaret tried in vain to exercise some restraint, but the only effect of orders banning the sermons was to encourage the Reformed to go out to their sermons fully armed.[9] By July government officials in the south were reporting alarming rumours that some sort of violent outbreak was in the offing, possibly an attack on monasteries and priests, all too plausible given the evident confidence and organisation of the Reformed.[10] Even so the iconoclasm when it came took the authorities by surprise, not least for the rapidity with which it spread across the provinces, and the efficiency of its execution. Starting with an attack on the St. Laurence monastery at Steenvoorde on 10 August, the church-breaking spread swiftly through the industrial villages of the Westkwartier and the towns of the south. The destruction of the churches of Antwerp on 20 August produced a new chain reaction through the towns of northern Flanders, Brabant and Holland, so that by the time order was restored few major centres of population remained unscathed.

An examination of the iconoclasm is obviously central to any analysis of the role of the Reformed congregations during the Wonderyear, and indeed of the part played by exiles in organising or perpetrating the attack. More than one well-informed contemporary voiced the suspicion that the whole episode had been carefully planned in advance, and there were enough utterances by some of the ministers to give credence to this view. Thus the minister Cornille de la Zenne was reported to have said, addressing a crowd near Lille in June, 'that the time was not yet ripe (for the destruction of idolatry), but he would tell them when the hour had come, and that he hoped that it would be quite soon.'[11] Against this the Calvinist leadership were subsequently quick to distance themselves from responsibility for the destruction, particularly when the disastrous political effects of the image-breaking became apparent. Their public protestations and later apologetic writings carry less conviction, however, for their failure to provide any plausible alternative explanation of the violence. Marnix de St. Aldegonde, in his *True Narrative and Apology for What Happened in the Year 1566*, was reduced to ascribing responsibility to Catholic priests acting as *agents provocateurs* and to a motley group of women, children and 'men without authority', aided and abetted by Divine Providence: 'for certainly, considering the facts in all their detail, it is easy to see that God himself intervened to lead the whole action and carry it out, and men cannot resist God's power.'[12]

Marnix's words reflect very clearly the ambivalence felt within the Reformed movement towards the forcible destruction of images, an ambivalence which emerges equally strongly from the most detailed modern examination of the role of Calvinist ministers in the troubles, Phyllis Mack Crew's *Calvinist Preaching and Iconoclasm in the Netherlands*. Crew examines the ministers' actions during and after the image-breaking, and then seeks to identify the roots of their behaviour in, amongst other factors, their experience in exile: 'in fact, the only experience which the ministers seem to have had in common was that of flight; almost every minister had spent some time as a religious refugee ... in the years before the Troubles.'[13] Unfortunately there seems to be nothing in this common experience of exile to explain why ministers should have behaved so differently in 1566, certainly not why some should have become 'moderates' and some 'radicals' in Crew's terminology.[14] Crew's work also raises the more fundamental question of whether the ministers truly were the controlling force behind the destruction of images. The fact that the image-breaking took a different course in different parts of the Netherlands, or even in neighbouring towns in the same locality, suggests that the patterns which Crew identifies for Flanders did not necessarily pertain elsewhere. Before offering any generalisations about the responsibilty of the Calvinist leadership, either locally or abroad, it will be necessary to observe the image-breaking over a rather wider field. Following Scheerder, it is possible to distinguish three distinct phases to the violence: the first attacks in the Flanders Westkwartier being followed by a wave of violence in the large towns of the Scheldt region around Antwerp, which in turn set off a final wave north of the great rivers.[15] In each case initial similarities mask a subtle difference in the pattern of events.

The attack on the St. Laurence monastery at Steenvoorde which began the iconoclasm in Flanders was followed three days later by an assault on the St. Anthony house at Belle. From there the image breaking spread very quickly through the region. Hazebroeck and Hondschoote suffered on the 15th, Ieper the following day. By the end of the month few villages in the region had escaped unscathed, and the image breaking had spread well beyond the Westkwartier: south to Tournai and Valenciennes, north to Antwerp.[16] At first sight events in this first phase seem most likely to support theories of prior organisation by the Calvinist communities abroad. The iconoclasm in the Westkwartier was initiated by two ministers who had recently returned from England, Sebastian Matte and Jacob Buzère, both of whom had trained in the refugee church at London. After the attacks at Steenvoorde and Belle the two went their separate ways, Matte to organise further destruction in the district around Ieper, Buzère preaching at Hazebroeck and elsewhere. Many of those who travelled with them were also recently returned exiles from England.[17]

Even here, however, it is necessary to exercise a degree of caution, before attributing to the exile churches in England responsibility for initiating the religious violence in Flanders. For, firstly, it is important to make a distinction between these ministers who had been in exile and the exile churches themselves. Opinions in London were sharply divided on the issue of how far it was legitimate to defy the authority of the state power. This was an issue which had first emerged in 1561-62 in relation to armed preaching and breaking open prisons to free arrested reformers, and it would erupt once more after 1566 when the minister Godfried van Winghen denounced the iconoclasm from the pulpit of the Dutch church.[18] Although the London consistory minutes for 1566 do not survive, it is likely that opinions then were as divided as they had been in the earlier debate, when the respected minister Peter Delenus had expressed forthright opposition to any armed resistance, and had succeeded in holding to this line against the contrary opinion of the Antwerp church and a significant dissenting minority in England. It should be noted that the core of the radical group, who moved between England and Flanders in 1562-63 and made clear their disenchantment with the attitude of the London hierarchy, included a number of ministers who would reappear as leaders of the iconoclasm in 1566: Pieter Hazard, Gilles de Queeckere, and both Matte and Buzère.[19] These and others out of sympathy with the London leadership tended to graduate

to Sandwich on the Kent coast, a largely artisan community closely at-
tuned to events in Flanders and broadly sympathetic to radical action.
The exile communities were thus themselves divided in their attitudes
towards the image-breaking. The divisions within the London church in
particular greatly diminished the extent to which it could play an effective directing role within the Netherlands, in 1566 or for some time
thereafter.[20]

There is, too, a second reason for rejecting too simple an explanation
of the iconoclasm in the Westkwartier. For while the ministers with their
peripatetic bands of returned exiles played an important role in the destruction, the part played by local men must also not be overlooked. In
Hazebroeck, it was a rich citizen of the town, the silk merchant Jehan
Braems, who led the attack on the churches. He was also suspected of
having paid those who carried out the image-breaking. In Hondschoote
the iconoclasm was largely the work of local men, as was also the case
in Armentières.[21] The pattern that emerges is one where in larger towns
and villages the initiative was taken by and large by local evangelicals,
while in smaller places where the new doctrines had not as yet made
much of an impact it was outsiders who were responsible.

The role of local laymen was again an important factor as the iconoclasm moved north from Flanders to the major towns of the Scheldt
region. The crucial trigger of this second phase of the image-breaking
was the attack on the churches in Antwerp on 20 August.[22] From here,
the destruction spread quickly through the other major cities of the region: Ghent and Breda on the 22nd, Mechelen and Turnhout the next
day, and then, as news of events in Antwerp spread, across the great rivers into Holland and Zealand. A rather different pattern was at work in
these places. Rather than roving bands of iconoclasts, here the destruction was organised by and large in the towns themselves, and from there
spread to the surrounding villages. But the crucial question remains:
who was responsible for the image-breaking? The local Reformed
leadership? Or was it, as they were later inclined to claim, a largely
spontaneous outbreak perpetrated by vagabonds and urchins?

It is important to note that in many of these towns the Reformed had
some sort of presence before 1566. In Antwerp organised churches had
existed for at least ten years, with two French and Dutch-speaking congregations, a consistory and resident ministers.[23] This was the exception
for in few other places had it proved possible to introduce a formal
church structure; even so in Bruges, Ghent and a number of smaller
places some sort of congregation was definitely in existence by 1565.[24]
Initially these congregations were almost entirely dependent on the exile
churches for their survival. Ministers despatched to serve them passed

back and forth at frequent intervals to minimise the dangers attendent on prolonged residence in one place. But with the onset of the political crisis in the Netherlands in 1565-66, these previously small, tight-knit communities underwent a significant change, one that has profound implications for an investigation of the events of 1566. For as the persecution relaxed, new sympathisers began to emerge and join themselves to the congregations, among them a significant number from the towns' higher social echelons. The congregations adapted themselves to these changed circumstances, either organising formally for the first time, or in some cases electing a new consistory incorporating these new supporters to replace the old artisan core of the years of persecution. In both Bruges and Ghent a striking feature of the Reformed communities which emerged during 1566 was the high social status of the known members of the consistory.[25]

The support of men of this sort, merchants, advocates and local officials, was of crucial importance to the progress made by the Reformed communities during the spring and summer of 1566. It was also highly significant in explaining the rapid spread of the image-breaking. Crew has concentrated on the role of the ministers, but it seems that in many towns it was prominent laymen who provided the guiding hand behind the attacks on the churches. In Antwerp observers noted the contrast between the highly charged atmosphere in the days before the iconoclasm, when the traditional procession for the Feast of the Assumption was heckled by bystanders, and the clinical efficiency with which, on 20 August, the churches were despoiled.[26] 'This thing was done so quiet and still', as Clough remarked, in some places by groups of no more than ten or a dozen, though thousands came out on the streets to see the spectacle. Although the ministers were later to deny their complicity, the evidence seems overwhelming that the iconoclasm at Antwerp was carefully planned by leading members of the Reformed community and carried out under their supervision by men of lower social status, many of whom were hired and paid.[27]

Elsewhere it was a similar story. At Ghent the iconoclasm was planned at a meeting in the house of Lieven Onghena, whose brother Jan was despatched to confer with Jan Dierickx, an advocate and member of the consistory. Most of the iconoclasts were local men, reinforced by a few from Antwerp.[28] At Ghent the ministers definitely opposed the iconoclasm and urged caution, but others were not so fastidious: the iconoclasm at Tournai on 23 August took place in the presence and apparently with the support of the ministers.[29] Often, though, it was leading Calvinist laymen who took the initiative, as at Valenciennes and Den Bosch, where the iconoclasm was led by members of the consistory.[30] In other towns the real leaders remained in the shadows, setting on men of lower status to do the work: this was the case in both Mechelen and Breda, where after the iconoclasm a delegation of rich Calvinists intervented to warn the magistrates against punitive action against those who had perpetrated the destruction.[31]

Two further features of this phase of the iconoclasm are worthy of comment. Firstly it is striking how often an attack on the churches followed immediately after the arrival of news of the destruction in Antwerp. Sometimes this was the result of communication between the Reformed communities in the towns concerned, but elsewhere just the report of events in the metropolis was enough to set off the church-breaking: a reflection perhaps of Antwerp's increasingly dominant role in the life of the provinces.[32] A second common feature was the extremely tentative response of the local authorities, faced with what was often an extremely small, if determined band of assailants. Sometimes the magistrates did attempt to intervene, as in Den Bosch, where they succeeded in raising enough of a guard to protect some of the precious objects in the cathedral. But elsewhere the towns capitulated with astonishing speed, often confining their activity to an attempt to have the images carried to places of safety before the iconoclasm began.[33]

Why, on the whole, was there so little resistance? That it was by no means impossible to stand out against the tide was demonstrated in Bruges, a town with a substantial and active Reformed community. But despite pressure, both from within and from neighbouring Antwerp and Ghent, the magistrates here succeeded in facing down the local Calvinists by prompt action, shutting up the churches for their own protection, raising troops and carefully controlling who came through the city gates. As a result iconoclasm was avoided altogether, and the Reformed prevented from ever possessing a church within the city.[34] Why then did the authorities elsewhere make such a poor showing? Here the conclusions of Deyon and Lottin, who in their study of the iconoclasm in the French-speaking provinces of the south lay stress on the general political uncertainty as a cause of this widespread official paralysis, certainly command respect.[35] Everywhere the government seemed to be in retreat; faced with this, the ambivalent behaviour of the great magnates and an absence of clear instructions, magistrates were naturally reluctant to take a firm stance in such a fluid and fast-changing political situation. The Calvinists, it must be said, showed considerable skill in the way in which they exploited this general climate of uncertainty. In Flanders it was widely believed that the removal of images enjoyed the support of the magnates, prompting a number of ministers to exhibit spurious documents apparently emanating from Egmont whom they claimed had authorised the destruction.[36] Adopting the same strategy, Lieven Onghena appeared before the local magistrates at Ghent with what he declared was a letter of authorisation to remove images. Without further ado the high bailiff gave permission for the images to be removed.[37]

It seems barely credibly that the magistrates would capitulate so easily. Sometimes, it is true, the representations of the Calvinist spokesmen were reinforced by public demonstrations of a more threatening nature, but often it seems that the magistrates had not the heart to resist. The fact that a number of local officials were themselves sympathetic to the Reformed did not help their cause. At Lier the schout stood by laughing as the iconoclasts, his servants among them, set about the destruction of the churches.[38] At Eindhoven it was the Burgomaster who opened the doors of the church for public preaching, and the local minister who led the iconoclasm in the presence of a nobleman, the Drossart of Kranendonk.[39] This example sums up neatly the different forces at work: while it was undoubtedly the case that a sermon preached by the minister often gave the signal for the iconoclasm to begin, the precise form it took depended as much on the response of the magistrates and the religious balance of forces locally.

Turning finally to the third phase of the iconoclasm in Holland and the north, a number of these same factors are again recognisable. But the pattern of events did differ in some respects, reflecting the different path taken by the Reformation in the years before 1566. In the northern provinces, farther away from the prying eye of central government, religious tensions were much less acute. Prosecutions for heresy were comparatively rare, and seldom pursued to a conclusion: no-one had been executed in Amsterdam since 1553, and a similar situation had pertained in Rotterdam since 1558, when three anabaptists were rescued from the stake by a sympathetic crowd.[40]

Several commentators have remarked on the astonishing openness with which unorthodox opinions might be expressed in the decades before the Revolt. Even when an individual went too far, as for instance when Frans Jacobsz wrote to the chapter at Den Briel that he wished to have his child baptised 'in the manner that Christ instituted baptism', the town authorities were extremely reluctant to take action. Despite an investigation that revealed him in possession of Lutheran books, Frans got off with a warning and paying the costs of the investigation.[41] In this sort of climate it was far easier than in the south for a critical layman, or indeed priest, to remain unmolested within the old Church. Men like Huibert Duifhuis of Rotterdam or Adriaan Jansz of IJsselmonde, who taught evangelical doctrines more or less openly in his parish for many years, are not untypical figures in the north in the two decades before the Troubles.[42] In 1566 a high proportion of those who preached evangelical doctrines in Holland were not returning exiles, but men who had remained at their posts all along and now declared themselves for the reform: a marked, and highly significant contrast from the situation in Flanders.

The north was the particular sphere of influence of Emden, the exile community established in nearby East Friesland. In the decade before 1566 the church in Emden had established contact with a small number of Reformed cells in Holland and the north: we know of groups in Brill, Alkmaar, Amsterdam, and of fairly frequent contacts with Groningen.[43] But the situation was not without its frustrations for the exiles. Given the degree of lassitude permitted within the old Church, it was much more difficult to persuade sympathisers to abandon their old allegiance and join the conventicles.[44] According to Brandt there were only two ministers active in Holland before the outbreak of the Troubles in 1566.[45]

In view of this it is not surprising that the impetus for the organisation of public worship in Holland came, not from Emden, but from the echo of events in the south. And it was not until 8 July that a group of the principal members of the Amsterdam Reformed community met together and decided, in consultation with the minister Jan Arentsz, to emulate their brethren in Flanders and Brabant by organising a public sermon in the fields outside the town. Arentsz's sermon, preached near Hoorn on 14 July, evoked a strong response, and a second sermon near Haarlem the following week by Peter Gabriel attracted a crowd that may have numbered as many as five thousand.[46] The rapid spread of the preaching was though impeded by the acute shortage of preachers, and at some point it was resolved to appeal to Emden to help remedy the deficiency. The leaders of the congregation at Amsterdam wrote to Cornelis Cooltuyn, now minister at Emden but a native of Alkmaar, explaining the problem, and it was through his agency that a dozen or more ministers made their way from East Friesland to serve congregations in Holland.[47]

The trigger for the iconoclasm was, as in so many towns in the south, news of the attack on churches in Antwerp. On 23 August merchants and travellers arriving in Amsterdam gathered in the market and began to relate to bystanders what they had seen. They were able to authenticate their narrative with fragments of broken altars which they had brought with them.[48] An attack on the Oude Kerk followed almost immediately. On this occasion the magistrates succeeded in dispersing the crowd, but the following day iconoclasts began breaking up the churches in Delft, and incidents followed in most of the principal towns of the province: in The Hague on 25th, Leiden and Den Briel on the 26th. The churches in Utrecht were also attacked on the 25th, and the other northern provinces did not escape unscathed: on 6 September the churches were cleansed in Leeuwarden, and ten days later in Groningen.

The search for patterns reveals some interesting similarities, but also some differences, from events in the south. In several towns (The Hague, Leiden, Den Briel for example) the iconoclasm followed immediately after the preaching of a sermon by a Reformed minister; but that is not to say that these sermons in any real sense 'caused' the iconoclasm. In Holland, more even than in the south, the guiding hands behind the removal of images seem to have been those of leading evangelical laymen. In Delft the iconoclasm was directed by Adriaan Menninck, a member of the town's business elite, who then went over to assist the breaking of images in The Hague.[49] At Den Briel the assault on the churches was led by the schout, Eeuwout Cornelisz, Willem Willemsz, an apothecary, and a carpenter, Gilles Jacobsz. In Leiden, where the destruction was particularly fierce, the breakers worked under the direction of members of the local nobility, Jacob Oom and Arent van Duivenvoorde.[50]

The ferocity of the assault in Leiden was somewhat exceptional; elsewhere in Holland the movement was remarkably orderly. In Den Briel the schout called out the town guard to protect the iconoclasts. In The Hague, in a situation with echoes of Ghent, the leaders of the Reformed congregation appealed to the President of the Court for men to assist them in their task, claiming to possess a letter of authorisation. Although no such letter was actually produced, the president put twelve men at their disposal, each of whom was paid seven stuivers for his day's work.[51]

This is a far cry from the wanton destruction and pillage which Catholics had feared earlier in the summer, and offers a clear indication of the character of the movement in the north. Scheerder argues in the conclusion to his survey of the iconoclasm that the primary motivation of the movement was clearly religious. With autumn coming on the Reformed needed to force the issue; but where they could secure an accommodation without violence they were usually happy to do so. It is interesting in this connection to note that in Utrecht the destruction was confined to the four parish and two monastic churches, while the richest of all, the Cathedral, was left untouched. Was this, as Scheerder has argued, because the Reformed wanted above all to force the Council to make over a church for their services, and they were aware that the magistrates had no jurisdiction over the Cathedral?[52] Certainly in a number of towns where the council were prepared to accommodate the congregation, iconoclasm was avoided altogether. Rotterdam was one example where a combination of firm action and flexibility on the part of the magistrates succeeded in preserving the peace, and in both Leeuwarden and Groningen the Reformed took possession of the churches with little wanton destruction.[53]

How far then can these generalisations be made to apply to the south, in Flanders and Brabant, where events certainly took a more tumultuous course? Here, where the religious atmosphere had been poisoned by decades of persecution, the destruction was more frenzied, more indiscriminate, and accompanied by frequent open manifestations of contempt and hostility towards the old church. In places the destruction certainly provided an outlet for social strains that had little to do with religion; and it is worth remarking in this connection that in the one place in the north where the churches were plundered as well as cleansed, Leiden, there is evidence of an unusual degree of social dislocation and poverty among the broad mass of the population. But even in the south the element of popular riot and wanton destruction may not have been as pronounced as contemporary reports seem to imply. There are a number of observations that may be made in this connection. Firstly, it is not surprising that governors, magistrates and chroniclers would emphasise the element of popular tumult, since this was what men like Egmont would find most striking. But it was also the case that there were some, the town councils for instance, who had their own interest in playing up the suggestion of popular disturbance, not least to excuse the weakness of their own response. Thirdly, it is hardly surprising that it should have been men of low social status who, by and large, actually carried out the iconoclasm. Church-breaking was, after all, hard physical labour. But often enough, as we have seen, they were paid for their work by the men who stood behind them. Shrewd observers like Clough were struck not by the tumult, but by the purposeful calm which characterised events in Antwerp. The same was true elsewhere: subsequent investigation has revealed that the organisation of the iconoclasm was tighter than eye-witnesses had indicated, and the religious motivation stronger: 'under the appearance of impulsiveness a clear plan was at work.'[54]

The account offered here has certainly laid more stress than is customary on the involvement in the iconoclasm of the Reformed hierarchy. In town after town later enquiries showed up the leading roles played by men who would shortly take their places as members of the Reformed consistory, even if the consistory was at this point not formed.[55] What then of the dichotomy proposed by Crew between radicals and moderates? Did this reflect genuine theological divisions within the evangelical movement? It is certainly true that a number of the most prominent ministers active in the Netherlands, De Brès, Taffin and Junius for example, opposed the attack on the churches and counselled caution. They did so because they believed that only the authorities could give the order, or perhaps because, more far-sighted politically, they foresaw the disastrous cousequences of the iconoclasm on the support of their erstwhile allies, the nobility.[56] Some of the leaders of the exile churches shared these misgivings, but they were in a position to view events in the Netherlands with a degree of detachment. The Dutch ministers who had spent time ministering to the secret congregations during the time of persecution did not on the whole show the same forbearance: the principal ministers of the Antwerp church, Van der Heyden, Moded and Wybo, all supported the iconoclasm.[57] But it is worth making the point that such disagreement as there was, concerned means rather than ends. There was no disagreement that images were idolatrous, and that their removal was necessary before the Reformed took possession of the churches.

Here one approaches the crucial contribution of the exile churches to events within the Netherlands during 1566. As far as day to day events were concerned, the exile churches were seldom in a position to intervene directly. Once the exiles had returned to their former homes, the organisational role played by the churches abroad quickly passed to the communities within the Netherlands. The directing hand behind the hedge-preaching and iconoclasm was not the exile churches, but the leading ministers and laymen of the emerging congregations in the Netherlands. But why, particularly in the case of the laity, was hostility towards images so profound, and indeed, so universal? Here the exile churches had made a decisive contribution to forming the climate of opinion within the Dutch evangelical movement that emerged with such explosive force in 1566.

Most of the leading ministers active in the Netherlands in 1566 had spent time in the exile congregations, and many had received their first religious training there. Their sermons would be one conduit for the churches' teaching; another was printed literature. In the decade before the Dutch Revolt large quantities of Reformed literature were imported into the Netherlands from the exile towns. The centre of this Reformed exile printing was Emden, in East Friesland. Between 1554, when the presses were first set up, and 1566, Emden printers turned out a considerable quantity of religious polemical works, in addition to the bibles, catechisms and psalm editions for the use of the secret communities. Many of these works expressed anti-image sentiments. William

Gnapheus's *Mirror and Consolation of the Sick*, a new edition of which appeared at Emden in 1557, provides one example. Gnapheus viewed all images as suspect:

> Even greater blindness is that we seek consolation, help and support from some saints, which we say we honour here on earth in their wooden statues. In doing so we break God's first commandment, which forbids all strange gods and the making of any likenesses or statues.[58]

An important category of literature expressing criticisms of this sort were the plays of the Chambers of Rhetoric, a number of which received wide publicity through Emden reprints. Although not specifically Calvinist or Reformed, the tone adopted towards traditional Catholic practices and beliefs is well illustrated by an extract from the play entitled *A Good Comedy with Three Characters, a Priest, a Weaver and a Sexton* (Emden, 1565). In this play the weaver, called 'Gospel understood', represents the evangelical position against 'self-will', a priest, and 'worldly man', a verger. He argues that images lead the ordinary man into superstition, and that any attempt to represent God's divinity by material substances is blasphemy:

> For my own sake, they may as well remain,
> But I complain about many an innocent person
> Who serves honours and prays to them like a child
> To such things my soul is a mortal enemy ...
> Will you then attempt to represent the incomprehensibly vast godhead,
> With wood, stone, silver or golden figures?
> That way you will blaspheme against the godly majesty.[59]

Rederijker literature was important, because the people voicing and reading such sentiments were members of the towns' natural elites, men who might normally be expected to respect the law. But in the event members of the Chambers of Rhetoric took a prominent part in the iconoclasm in several towns. In Ghent the leader of the iconoclasm, Jan Onghena, was a prominent rederijker, while at Leiden members of the local Chamber of Rhetoric suspended an image across the Breestraat, and whirled it in front of passers-by. At Den Briel the rederijkers met at the town hall and performed a mock trial of the image of St. Roche, which was then ceremonially burned.[60]

At the other end of the social scale, anabaptists were equally outspoken in their hostility to images. This is clearly expressed in a song in the song-book attached to the anabaptist martyrology, the *Offer des Heeren*. The Emden authorities would not allow anabaptist books to be printed in the town, but they did not prevent publication of a number of works by the German spiritualist writer Sebastian Franck, such as the *Chronica*, which includes a trenchant denunciation of catholic sacramental practice and image worship.[61] It is not necessary to multiply examples further: the essential point is that the evangelicals who took up arms against images in 1566 could draw on a deep and broad-ranging tradition of hostility to catholic practice, from the scathing wit of the rhetoricians to the forthright condemnation of the Heidelberg catechism.[62] If the exile churches cannot be credited as a controlling influence over the actual events of 1566, their part in creating the underlying atmosphere of hostility to Catholic practice must not be under-estimated.

In the early months of 1566 large quantities of books were being brought into the Netherlands, and Emden books were much in demand.[63] Eye-witness accounts reported booksellers driving out from the towns to set up their stalls in the corners of fields where the preachings took place; the psalms which the crowds sang were Utenhove's metrical versions published in successive editions at Emden.[64] But even here, in the area where the exile communities had made their most profound contribution to the movement, 1566 witnessed a subtle change in the relationship. The sudden upsurge of protestantism in the Netherlands, first with the hedge-preaching, then with the establishment of authorised congregations, created a vast demand for printed books which the exile presses alone could not satisfy. Emden was too far away to react with the necessary speed to the pace of change. A couple of examples will suffice to illustrate the point. In May 1566 the Regent Margaret of Parma wrote to the magistrates of Bruges to warn them against a seditious pamphlet circulating in Brussels which denounced the Moderation as a trick. It was scarcely possible that this book could have been printed in Emden since the Moderation had been published barely a fortnight previously, and in fact none of the explicitly political literature published during the year emanated from the Emden presses.[65] Later in the summer it was reported that the ministers preaching at Ghent were distributing to those who attended their sermons books claiming the authority of the church fathers for their preaching. These pamphlets, apparently written in response to objections raised against them, must again have been printed locally.[66] It was one of the great advantages of the printing press that it was technically an extremely flexible medium. By the end of the year the Reformed were printing most of the literature they needed within the Netherlands. At Christmas the minister Gerobulus, writing from Delft, promised to send to his colleague at Den Briel a Confession of Faith and some psalms printed there: both, incidentally, reprints of works previously published in Emden.[67]

In the same way that the exile presses were very largely superceded during the course of 1566, so it was in the movement as a whole. The directing hand which the exile congregations had exercised in the previous decade passed to those better placed to react to fast moving events, notably the influential Antwerp church. Here were gathered some of the most senior and experienced ministers, who, together with the consistory, itself made up of rich and influential figures in the world of commerce and politics, exercised a sort of informal primacy over the Reformed churches, taking the initiative in the organisation of synods, negotiations with allies among the nobility and the collection of the three million guilder request.[68] The situation in the Netherlands was in some ways analagous to that in France, in the relationship between Geneva and the French Calvinist movement. When the French Calvinist church was in its infancy, Geneva had played a vital role, providing ministers for the new congregations, advising on organisation and publishing books for clandestine importation. But with the developing political crisis in France after 1559, the French churches began to manifest a new independence. The Paris church, in particular, emerged as a powerful influence, and the French churches generally demonstrated in the years before the outbreak of war a militancy which left Calvin troubled and uneasy.[69] So it was in the Netherlands. In the decade after 1555, a decade of severe persecution, the exile churches provided the Dutch church with a vital lifeline. But as the political crisis in the Netherlands opened up a new prospect, it was local churches who were best placed to seize the moment. For the exile churches the speed with which events moved in the summer of 1566 made it virtually impossible to exercise any real measure of control over the movement.

The events of the Wonderyear can thus be said to have revealed both the strengths and limitations of the relationship between the exile movement and the Reformation in the Netherlands. Its principal role was to lay the basis, to provide the building materials for the evangelical movement to flourish in 1566. This was not confined to polemical literature: the importance of the organisational structures established by the exile congregations should also be recognised. The elders and deacons of the churches established in the Netherlands during 1566 played as important a role as the ministers, raising money for the maintenance of their congregations, and later for more seditious purposes, as the pains taken by the Council of Troubles to identify former consistory members bear witness.[70] This organisational efficiency owed everything to the preparation of the churches in exile. But it meant also that the mother churches abroad were superceded all the more quickly in 1566.

That is not to say, however, that with 1566 the usefulness of the exile congregations was at an end. Rather, with the collapse of the movement in the Netherlands in 1567 the exile churches came once more into their own. Many thousands, including many who had committed themselves openly to the movement for the first time in 1566, sought safety in exile. London, Emden, Wesel and Frankenthal were soon once more full to overflowing. A new phase of the revolt was begun. Once more the exiles were left to organise, to agitate, and to pray for better days.

[1] Letter printed in J.M.B.C. Kervyn de Lettenhove (ed.), *Relations politiques des Pays-Bas et de l'Angleterre, sous le règne de Philippe II*, 11 vols., Brussels, 1882-1900, IV, pp. 337-39.

[2] O.J. de Jong, *Beeldenstorm in de Nederlanden*, Groningen, 1964; M. Dierickx, 'Beeldenstorm in de Nederlanden in 1566', *Streven*, 19 (1966), pp. 1040-48; J. Scheerder, *De Beeldenstorm*, 2nd ed., Haarlem, 1974. E. Kuttner, *Het Hongerjaar 1566*, Amsterdam, 1949, argues for the importance of short-term economic factors. See also H. van der Wee, 'The Economy as a Factor in the Beginning of the Revolt of the Netherlands', *Acta historiae Neerlandicae*, 5 (1971), pp. 52-67.

[3] A good summary of the political prelude is Geoffrey Parker, *The Dutch Revolt*, London, 1977, pp. 41-67. The second volume of F. Rachfahl, *Wilhelm von Oranien und die Niederländische Aufstand*, 3 vols., The Hague, 1906-24, gives a detailed account of the same period.

[4] Parker, *Dutch Revolt*, pp. 68-72.

[5] Emden, Archiv der evangelische reformierte Gemeinde, Kerkeraadsprotocollen (hereafter Emden KP), 10 May 1566.

[6] Bernard Hagedorn, *Ostfrieslands Handel und Schiffahrt im 16. Jahrhundert*, Berlin, 1910, I, pp. 206-07.

[7] *Correspondance du Cardinal de Granvelle*, ed. E. Poullet, 12 vols., Brussels, 1877-96, I, pp. 231, 253, 325. *Correspondance de Marguerite d'Autriche*, ed. Baron de Reiffenberg, Brussels, 1842, p. 26. Rachfahl, *Wilhelm von Orangien*, II, pp. 637-38.

[8] Marcel Backhouse, 'Hagepreken in het Vlaamse Westkwartier (mei-december 1566)', *De Franse Nederlanden*, 1984, pp. 131-35.

[9] Clough to Gresham, 10 July 1566. *Relations politiques*, IV, p. 314.

[10] S. Deyon and A. Lottin, *Les casseurs de l'été 1566. L'iconoclasme dans la Nord de la France*, Paris, 1981, pp. 149ff.

[11] Letter from Rassinghien to Margaret of Parma, 30 June 1566. Quoted in Deyon and Lottin, *Casseurs*, p. 215.

[12] *Philips van Marnix van St. Aldegonde: Godsdienstige en kerkelijke geschriften*, ed. J.J. van Toorenenbergen, 3 vols., The Hague, 1871-91, I, pp. 98-101, 109-10 (translation taken from E.H. Kossmann and A.F. Mellink, *Texts Concerning the Revolt of the Netherlands*, Cambridge, 1974, pp. 78-81).

[13] P.M. Crew, *Calvinist Preaching and Iconoclasm in the Netherlands, 1544-1569*, Cambridge, 1978, p. 41.

[14] *Ibid.*, p. 49. These categories are necessarily somewhat arbitrary, since few of the ministers spoke out clearly on the issue. Crew classifies ministers who preached before an incident of iconoclasm as radical, but ministers who preached after may be radical or moderate.

[15] Scheerder, *Beeldenstorm*, p. 18.

[16] *Ibid.*, pp. 19-35. See also M. Backhouse, *Beeldenstorm en Bosgeuzen in het Westkwartier (1566-1568)*, Kortrijk, 1971.

[17] Scheerder, *Beeldenstorm*, l.c. On Matte and Buzère see J. Decavele, *De dageraad van de reformatie in Vlaanderen*, 2 vols., Brussels, 1975, I, pp. 402-04. *Kerkeraads-protocollen der Nederduitsche vluchtelingen-kerk te Londen, 1560-1563*, ed. A.A. van Schelven (Werken van het Historisch Genootschap, 3rd series, 43 [1921]), pp. 35, 78, etc. P.C. Molhuysen and P.J. Blok (eds.), *Nieuw Nederlandsch biographisch woordenboek*, 10 vols., Leiden, 1911-37, III, p. 179 (Buzère).

[18] A.A. van Schelven, 'Het begin van het gewapend verzet tegen Spanje in de 16-eeuwsche Nederlanden', *Handelingen en mededeelingen van de Maatschappij der Nederlandsche Letterkunde te Leiden*, (1914-15), pp. 126-41. Decavele, *Dageraad*, I, pp. 416-26. A. Pettegree, *Foreign Protestant Communities in Sixteenth-Century London*, Oxford, 1986, pp. 239-50.

[19] J. Decavele, *Dageraad*, I, pp. 403, 409, 416ff. *Idem*, 'Jan Hendrickx en het Calvinisme in Vlaanderen (1560-1564)', *Handelingen van het Genootschap Société d'Émulation te Brugge*, 106 (1969), pp. 17-32.

[20] Pettegree, *Foreign Protestant Communities*, pp. 252-53. On the radical character of the community at Sandwich the work of Marcel Backhouse is authoritative.

[21] Scheerder, *Beeldenstorm*, pp. 21-2, 35, 108.

[22] *Ibid.*, pp. 35-41. Robert van Roosbroeck, *Het Wonderjaar te Antwerpen, 1566-1567*, Antwerp, 1930, pp. 23-40.

[23] Pettegree, 'The Exile Churches and the Churches "Under the Cross": Antwerp and Emden during the Dutch Revolt', *Journal of Ecclesiastical History*, 38 (1987), pp. 187-209. A.J. Jelsma, *Adriaan van Haemstede en zijn Martelaarsboek*, The Hague, 1970, pp. 18-81.

[24] Decavele, *Dageraad*, I, pp. 330-35, 345-54, 433-34.

[25] V. Fris, 'Notes pour servir a l'histoire des iconoclastes et des calvinistes à Gand de 1566 à 1568', *Handelingen der Maatschappij van Geschied- en Oudheidkunde te Gent*, 9 (1909), pp. 105-141. M. Delmotte, 'Het Calvinisme in de verschillende bevolkingslagen te Gent (1566-1567)', *Tijdschrift voor geschiedenis*, 76 (1963), pp. 145-76. A.C. de Schrevel, *Troubles religieux du XVIe siècle au quartier de Bruges, 1566-1568*, Bruges, 1894. See also L. Vandamme, 'Calvinisme in het Brugse koopmansmilieu: het consistorielid Godefroot Slabbaert', in *Brugge in de Geuzentijd*, Brugge, 1982, pp. 123-34.

[26] Clough to Gresham, 21 August, KL, IV, pp. 338-39. C.G. Brandt, *Historie der Reformatie*, Amsterdam, 1671, I, pp. 341-46 (English translation, *History of the Reformation in the Netherlands*, London, 1720, I, pp. 192-94).

[27] Three or seven stuivers depending on whether they were adults or youths. Scheerder, *Beeldenstorm*, p. 40. Cf. Roosbroeck, *Wonderjaar te Antwerpen*, pp. 32-39.

[28] Brandt, *History*, I, pp. 197-98.

[29] Scheerder, *Beeldenstorm*, p. 48.

[30] *Ibid.*, pp. 52, 65.

[31] *Ibid.*, pp. 61, 64-65. A.J.M. Beenakker, *Breda in de eerste storm van de Opstand*, Tilburg, 1971, pp. 70-84.

[32] As for instance in Ghent, Breda, Den Bosch and Middelburg. At Ghent, pipes from the shattered organ at Antwerp were paraded through the town. Brandt, *History*, I, p. 198. Scheerder, *Beeldenstorm*, pp. 63-65, 71. Men from Antwerp were present at the church-breaking in Breda and Lier, while in Axel and Hulst the iconoclasm took place according to a plan hatched in the metropolis. Brandt, *History*, I, p. 197. Beenakker, *Breda*, p. 69; J. Decavele, 'De reformatorische beweging te Axel en Hulst (1556-1566)', *Bijdragen voor de geschiedenis der Nederlanden*, 22 (1968-69), pp. 15-19.

[33] Scheerder, *Beeldenstorm*, p. 66.

[34] Schrevel, *Troubles religieux*, pp. 32-65.

[35] Deyon and Lottin, *Casseurs*, pp. 165-72.

[36] *Ibid.*, pp. 156-57.

[37] Brandt, *History*, I, p. 198. Fris, 'Calvinistes à Gand', pp. 61-71.

[38] Scheerder, *Beeldenstorm*, p. 42.

[39] *Ibid.*, pp. 67-68.

[40] H. ten Boom, *De reformatie in Rotterdam, 1530-1585*, Dieren, 1987 (Hollandse Historische Reeks, 7), pp. 93-95.

[41] W. Troost and J.J. Woltjer, 'Brielle in Hervormingstijd', *Bijdragen en mededelingen betreffende de geschiedenis der Nederlanden*, 87 (1972), p. 324. See also, J.J. Woltjer, *Friesland in hervormingstijd*, Leiden, 1962, esp. pp. 90-104.

[42] Ten Boom, *Rotterdam*, pp. 98-110 (Duifhuis), 88, 117 (Jansz).

[43] From Emden KP; e.g. 28-4 and 27-7-1558 (Amsterdam, Alkmaar), 20-6-1558, 6-2 and 2-3-1559 (Groningen), 18-3-1559, 9-4-1565 (Brill).

[44] Woltjer, *Friesland*, pp. 90-104.

[45] Brandt, *History*, I, p. 178.

[46] *Ibid.*, I, pp. 178-79. For a survey of the movement in the north see A.C. Duke and D.H.A. Kolff, 'The Time of Troubles in the County of Holland, 1566-1567', *Tijdschrift voor geschiedenis*, 82 (1969), pp. 316-37.

[47] Brandt, *History*, I, p. 187.

[48] *Ibid.*, I, p. 199. Scheerder, *Beeldenstorm*, pp. 79-81.

[49] D. Hoek, 'Adriaan Menninck, beeldenstormer en watergeus', *Zuid-Hollandse studien*, 8 (1959), pp. 100-25. See also J. Smit, 'Hagepreeken en beeldenstorm te Delft, 1566-1567', *Bijdragen en mededeelingen van het Historisch Genootschap*, 45 (1924), pp. 206-50.

[50] Scheerder, pp. 72-73, 78-79. Troost and Woltjer, 'Brielle in hervormingstijd', pp. 326-28. D.H.A. Kolff, 'Libertatis Ergo. De beroerten binnen Leiden in de jaren 1566 en 1567', *Jaarboekje voor geschiedenis en oudheidkunde van Leiden*, 58 (1966), pp. 118-48.

[51] Brandt, *History*, I, pp. 201-02. J. Smit, *Den Haag in den geusentijd*, The Hague, 1922, pp. 38ff.

[52] Scheerder, *Beeldenstorm*, pp. 84-85. Brandt, *History*, I, pp. 202-03. J.C.J. Kleijntjens and J.W.C. van Campen, 'Bescheiden betreffende den beeldenstorm van 1566 in de stad Utrecht', *Bijdragen en mededeelingen van het Historisch Genootschap*, 53 (1932), pp. 63-245.

[53] Ten Boom, *Reformatie in Rotterdam*, pp. 110-16. Woltjer, *Friesland in hervormingstijd*, pp. 150-55.

[54] O.J. de Jong on Utrecht, quoted in Scheerder, *Beeldenstorm*, p. 85.

[55] Jacob Marcus, *Sententien en indagingen van het Hertog van Alva, uitsproken en geslagen in zynen Bloedtraet*, Amsterdam, 1735, cites numerous such cases.

[56] E. Braekman, *Guy de Brès: Sa vie*, Brussels, 1962. On de Brès's political activities see L.A. van Langeraad, *Guido de Bray. Zijn leven en werken*, Zierikzee, 1884, Appendix A. On Taffin, see C. Boer, *Hofpredikers van Prins Willem van Oranje*, The Hague, 1952, pp. 19-30.

[57] Crew, *Calvinist Preaching*, p. 49.

[58] K. Moxey, 'Image Criticism in the Netherlands before the Iconoclasm of 1566', *Nederlands archief voor kerkgeschiedenis*, 57 (1976-77), p. 150. On Emden printing, Pettegree, 'Antwerp and Emden', pp. 196-99.

[59] Moxey, 'Image Criticism', pp. 151-52.

[60] *Ibid.*, p. 156.

[61] S. Franck, *Chronica, tytboeck en gheschiet bibel ...*, [Emden, Gailliart], 1558, part 3, pp. 145-54.

[62] Heidelberg Catechism, questions 94-99. 'Q: But may not pictures be tolerated in churches in place of books for the unlearned? A: No, for we must not try to be wiser than God who does not want his people to be taught by means of lifeless idols, but through the living preaching of his Word.' A.C. Cochrane, *Reformed Confessions of the Sixteenth Century*, London, 1966, pp. 324-25. Cf. Calvin, *Institutes*, ed. J.T.McNeill (Library of Christian Classics, 20-21 [1956]), pp. 99-112. On Protestant hostility to images see most recently Carlos Eire, *War against the Idols*, Cambridge, 1986.

[63] Schrevel, *Troubles religieux*, p. 334 (sentence of banishment against Cornille de Neckere for having sold Emden books in Bruges). J. Decavele, 'Enkele gegevens betreffende de relaties tussen het drukkerscentum Emden en het gebied Gent-Oudenaarde tijdens het Wonderjaar', in *Liber Amicorum Dr. J. Scheerder*, Louvain, 1987, pp. 17-28.

[64] Fris, 'Calvinistes a Gand', p. 28. Marcus van Vaernewyck, *Van die beroerlicke tijden in die Nederlanden*, ed. F. van der Haeghen, 5 vols., Ghent, 1872-81, I, p. 52. Howard Slenk, 'Jan Utenhove's Psalms in the Low Countries', *Nederlands archief voor kerkgeschiedenis*, 49 (1968-69), pp. 155-68.

[65] Schrevel, *Troubles religieux*, p. 122. In fact the culprit was an Antwerp printer, Gilles Coppens van Diest. Paul Valkema Blouw, 'Gilles Coppens van Diest als ondergronds drukker, 1566-67', and Willem Heijting, 'Protestantse confessies in het Wonderjaar 1566', in *Het oude en het nieuwe boek. Liber amicorum H.D.L. Vervliet*, Kapellen, 1988, pp. 129-63.

[66] Van Vaernewyck, *Beroerlicke tijden*, I, p. 287.

[67] 'Kerkelijke Herinneringen uit het Jaar 1566 en volg.', *Kerkhistorisch archief*, 1 (1857), pp. 429-30; 2 (1859), p. 253. The printer of these books was Harman Schinckel. See H. de la Fontaine Verwey, 'Meester Harman Schinckel, een Delftse boekdrukker van de 16e eeuw', *Oud Delft*, 3 (1964), pp. 5-78.

[68] A.A. van Schelven, 'Het verzoekschrift der 3.000.000 goudguldens, October 1566', *Bijdragen voor vaderlandsche geschiedenis en oudheidkunde*, 6e reeks, 9 (1930), pp. 1-40. J. Scheerder, 'Eenige nieuwe bijzonderheden betreffende het 3.000.000 goudguldens rekwest (1566)', *Miscellanea historica in honorem Leonis van der Essen* 2 vols., Brussels, 1947, pp. 559-66. Roosbroeck, *Wonderjaar te Antwerpen*, pp. 151-69, 209 ff. L. van der Essen, 'Les progrès du Luthéranisme et du Calvinisme dans le monde commercial d'Anvers', *Vierteljahrschrift für Sozial- und Wirtschaftsgeschichte*, 12 (1914), p. 220 ff.

[69] R.M. Kingdon, *Geneva and the Coming of the Wars of Religion in France, 1555-1563*, Geneva, 1956. Menna Prestwich, 'Calvinism in France, 1555-1629', in *idem* (ed.), *International Calvinism*, Oxford, 1985, pp. 85-86.

[70] Marcus, *Sententien en indagingen, passim*.

'ENGLAND'S WARS OF RELIGION'? RELIGIOUS CONFLICT AND THE ENGLISH CIVIL WARS

I.M. Green

In this paper, two concepts will be discussed with particular reference to the English civil wars: the relationship between the church and revolution, and the nature of a 'war of religion'. We need to look at the first because of a significant change in the way that historians have portrayed the leaders of the episcopalian church of the 1630s. Until the 1960s, historians tended to see those leaders as reactionaries who were anxious to restore their power as priests and royal advisers and to recover alienated wealth. By 1640 their conservative opinions and high-handed methods were held to have provoked a furious reaction which, together with other discontents, led to revolution, in the sense of a violent overthrowing of the existing political and ecclesiastical system. During the 1970s, however, an alternative view gained hold: the doctrinal, liturgical and other changes made by the leaders of the Caroline church were thought to have represented such a radical departure from the norm that they had the effect of driving their critics into carrying out a *counter*-revolution in the 1640s in order to protect the pattern of belief and worship that had prevailed during the reigns of Elizabeth and James I. We also need to look at the concept of a religious war because during the 1980s, the events of the 1640s have increasingly been depicted as 'England's Wars of Religion', a choice of term designed not only to highlight the divisiveness of religious issues in the 1640s, but also to modify existing accounts of the period, including those which saw revolutionary elements at work in it.[1]

The term 'revolutionary' has in fact been applied to the events of the mid-seventeenth century in at least three different ways during the last hundred and sixty years, though for our purposes the first two applications—the 'Puritan Revolution' and the 'English Revolution'—can be bracketed together in that they both portray the leaders of the early Stuart church as a conservative body who provoked strong and eventually violent opposition by their backward-looking policies. One of these usages dates from the second half of the nineteenth century, when the monumental labours of Samuel Rawson Gardiner convinced him that there had been not just a civil war or a rebellion but a revolution, what he dubbed 'the Puritan Revolution' in that he thought that a leading part in the fight against an absolutist king and a persecuting church had been taken by that group of ardent, reformist Protestants referred to at the time as 'Puritans': 'Puritanism not only formed the strength of the opposition to Charles, but the strength of England itself.'[2] Gardiner's was the first study of the period based solidly on the major sources available, and the soundness of his judgments on many individual events is not in question. Moreover, any explanation of the events of the period 1640-1660 must take into account the faith of a man like Oliver Cromwell, a distant relation of Gardiner whom he admired not only as a committed Puritan but also for putting the 'revolution' back on course after the wavering of 1647-53. Unfortunately, Gardiner never defined 'Puritanism' precisely, and tended to assume that since most Puritans were parliamentarians, all parliamentarians were Puritans which was far from true. His broader analysis of the period was also strongly coloured by concerns which were more typical of the nineteenth century than of the seventeenth, in particular the rise of parliamentary democracy and religious toleration. Great events must have great causes, so Gardiner was predisposed to finding mounting tension between aggressive church leaders and a vocal opposition committed to further reform of the church.[3]

In the mid-twentieth century Gardiner's general thesis came under attack from historians like Christopher Hill and Brian Manning who put forward a Marxian or Marxist thesis, and revived the term 'English Revolution' first aired by Guizot and Engels in the previous century. For Hill the instigators of this revolution were members of a rising bourgeoisie of progressive gentry, capitalist merchants and professional men who were anxious to remove the economic restraints of a 'feudal' régime, though he makes it clear that there was potential for a popular revolution within the revolution. For Manning economic change and class tension were also crucial, though he sees the initiative as coming from lower social strata than Hill.[4] Both historians, however, feel that Puritanism made an important contribution to the challenging of the conservative attitudes of king and church, though they depict this less in doctrinal terms than as a source of legitimation for those elements in society which were anxious to overthrow a privileged and paternalistic establishment. Like Gardiner, these historians have a point worth making about the ecclesiastical history of the period: there were all sorts of ways in which the words or actions of church leaders could have provoked opposition on financial or political as much as theological grounds; and as Dr. Hill in particular has shown, there could be a subtle interaction of doctrinal and social or political pressures in the minds of many radical English Protestants.[5] But many historians, at least on this side of the Atlantic, do feel that the Marxist interpretation is as guilty of a teleological concern with social change as Gardiner's was with liberty;[6] and from our immediate point of view, the problem is that the history of the church before 1640 has again been approached with the presupposition that there was a growing confrontation between rival groups whose identity and aims can be best established by reading the conflicts of the 1640s back into the 1630s or beyond.

From the late 1960s to the early 1980s, many of the ideas of Gardiner and Hill were attacked, in particular by a group of historians who have come to be known as the 'revisionists'. Their prime interest was the political history of the early Stuart period. Where previous accounts had stressed conflict—absolutist kings versus freedom-loving Englishmen, or feudal élite versus progressive bourgeoisie—the revisionists pointed to the large amount of cooperation and consensus between king and people. Where the older view of parliament was of an institution that was rising in confidence and strength, with a coherent opposition party sharing common principles and aims, the revisionists detected hesitation or confusion, and attributed much of the trouble in parliament to faction-fighting between courtiers.[7] As a result, the reasons for the political crisis of the early 1640s should not automatically be sought in the clashes between crown and parliament in the period 1604-29; the breakdown of 1640-42 was probably brought about as much, if not more, by shorter-term difficulties aggravated by structural weaknesses in the machinery of government and by Charles' problems in governing three contrasting kingdoms at the same time.[8] One might have expected that the 'revisionists' would also have called into question older assumptions about mounting tension in the early Stuart church; but this is not quite what has happened. One wing of the revisionists, including Conrad Russell and Nicholas Tyacke, has indeed challenged previous accounts, but in such a way as to come close to substituting a new pair of violently opposed parties for the old one. In their view the religious conflicts of the late 1620s and the 1630s stemmed largely from the rise to power of a small group of anti-Calvinists or 'Arminians' as they later came to be called. Under Elizabeth and James, it is suggested, the predestinarian teaching of Calvin and Beza had become dominant, and provided an ideological bond between on the one hand those conformists who (perhaps with some reservations) accepted the structure, discipline and liturgy of the Elizabethan church, and on the other those Puritans who still hankered after further reform and found it impossible to conform in full. But when the Arminians began to challenge Calvinism, and even worse tried to silence it once they were given power by Charles I in the later 1620s, the relative calm of the Jacobean period was broken. The Arminians tried to blacken their opponents' reputation by alleging that those who held Calvinist views wished to modify the existing church along Puritan lines. This forced those Calvinists who were staunch supporters of a moderate episcopalian church to reconsider their position. According to this view, it was the new Arminian leadership which initiated a doctrinal and liturgical revolution, and it was the moderate episcopalian, Calvinist majority, together with the Puritans who had almost given up all hope of reform, which staged a counter-revolution in the early 1640s.[9]

Today we seem to be entering a post-revisionist era in which, while the justice of much of the revisionist case is accepted, some of its boldest assertions are being challenged.[10] But even before this reaction began, there had been criticism of its analysis of the ecclesiastical situation. In fact, another wing of the revisionists, led by Kevin Sharpe and Peter White, had already expressed doubts about the severity of divisions within the early Stuart church. The greatest weakness of the Russell-Tyacke thesis, it was suggested, was that it created an entity called Arminianism which did not exist in England. The ubiquity of the term can be explained by the strength of contemporary fears of Catholicism and by the way in which 'Arminianism' was equated with 'popery' by the most determined anti-Catholics of the day. Thus the label tells us much more about the attitudes of those who invented and used it than it does about the ideas of those who were supposed to have become Arminians.[11]

It is certainly far from easy to define what is meant by Calvinism or Arminianism in an English context. English theologians were influenced by the writings of a number of continental reformers, and though Calvin's work had achieved a wide respect in England by the 1570s or '80s this did not mean that his teaching was followed slavishly. Moreover, after his death subtle but important changes were made to his teaching in Geneva, France, the Netherlands and Scotland, and in England too. Indeed, the work of Kendall and Jensen on the doctrine of assurance, of Lake on church government and of Tyacke himself on the atonement suggests that there were substantial differences of opinion among Calvin's most ardent admirers in England, greater differences than among comparable groups of admirers in Scotland or on the continent.[12]

Even if we play down the differences and suggest that after 1600 the distinctive feature of English Calvinism was a measure of agreement on double predestination, Calvinist hegemony in England is still open to question. The idea seems to have arisen through a concentration on two areas of contemporary religious life—theological debate in the universities, and the teaching found in printed works—at the expense of others. Certainly academics at Oxford and Cambridge seem to have fallen out over predestination (and over other matters—they were a quarrelsome breed); but how many of their students took part in or understood that debate is unknown. The majority of ordinands did not study theology as part of their undergraduate career; and even 'godly' colleges like Sidney Sussex, Cambridge and Magdalen, Oxford, did not produce anti-Arminian clones.[13] As for printed works, predestination figured largely in some types of publication, such as the polemical treatise and the technical guide on how to tell if one was elect; but in the majority of religious publications such as bibles and aids to bible study, prayer books and devotional works, and religious verse and music, predestinarian teaching was not a central feature or was altogether absent (the significance of the Geneva Bible in this respect has probably been exaggerated).[14] Instead, if one looks at the most frequently reproduced works, including the official formularies prepared under the influence of Luther, Zwingli, Bucer, Bullinger and others besides Calvin, one finds a form of Protestantism that has much to say about the evils of popery, about redemption through Christ and about trying to lead a better life, but relatively little about indefectible grace or the practical syllogism.[15] Predestinarianism might have been injected into parish life in fairly large doses by such means as preaching and catechizing, but once again we cannot be sure: some admirers of Calvin, such as Cartwright and Perkins, thought predestination should be taught widely, while others like Archbishop Whitgift and James I thought this unwise. Our knowledge of the typical sermon—as opposed to the more polished set-piece which got into print—is distressingly small, but there are indications that many sermons expounded the essentials of the faith (as expressed in the official formularies) or commemorated the church's festivals rather than the finer points of the *ordo salutis*.[16] As for catechisms, it is true that some of the most frequently reprinted forms, such as Nowell's and More's, were overtly predestinarian, but these were relatively advanced works, and the form of catechism in most common use—that of 1549, revised in 1604—not only lacked predestinarian teaching but contained phrases which some strict Calvinists found objectionable.[17] There was much more to the Protestantism of the English church than double predestination, and it seems odd to isolate this particular doctrine as its definitive benchmark or ideological cement.

What of the other half of the equation: the rise of 'Arminianism'? By the early 1640s no less than four different meanings of the term can be found. The first suggested that an Arminian was someone who opposed Calvinist teaching on predestination ('Calvinist' by this stage denoting the views of Beza, the Heidelberg theologians and William Perkins). This label might be applied to some academics in England if it meant that they had derived their ideas from Arminius, but on the whole English critics of Calvinist teaching seem to have derived their ideas from English, German or patristic sources rather than the Dutch theologian.[18] That having been said, there *were* parallels between the predestinarian disputes in England and Holland, not least in that in both countries the dispute would probably have remained largely academic if it had not been sucked into political strife and in so doing lost much of its original identity. In 1630 a leading academic remarked that not one in a hundred clergy and not one in a thousand laymen understood the Arminian controversy;[19] and for all Dr. Tyacke's enquiries I am not sure if this estimate was far wrong.

A comparison with Holland is also useful for the second usage—the allegation that Arminians were secretly in league with the papacy and the Habsburgs. In the tense atmosphere that prevailed in Holland during the twelve years' truce with Spain and in England during the 1620s, it was easy to argue that those who were not totally committed to an anti-Catholic crusade must be against it. If anything, the reverse was true, in that in both countries a number of those branded as 'Arminians' were notable for their anti-Catholic writings. But the careful distinctions they drew in their work, for example in saying that the Pope might not be the Antichrist referred to in the first epistle of St. John, were not well received by those who saw everything in dualistic terms of good and evil. The so-called 'Arminians' were, however, not alone: both James and Charles also rejected an over-simple view of the European situation, and bridled at the thought of having their foreign policy dictated to them by a vocal section of their subjects.[20]

A third charge against the English 'Arminians' was that they put greater stress on the sacraments as channels of grace. In Holland, there is no evidence that Arminius or his followers were sacramentalists, and in England the evidence consists not of a clear set of theological statements but a mixture of allegations from hostile sources and deductions drawn from the remarks of a small number of individual churchmen.[21] There *were* attempts to standardize the physical setting for the administration of the Lord's Supper and a conscious attempt to halt the trend towards an ever-wider definition of iconoclasm. But it is again the case that anti-Arminian allegations have been given much greater credence than the testimony of the accused, who insisted that the rails erected at the east end were meant to prevent the communion table from being sat upon or otherwise abused. If these men rejected the indecent bareness of Geneva as well as the superstitious gaudiness of Rome, this did not mean that they had ceased to believe in justification by faith; if they sought to restore the Christocentric emphasis that high Calvinism put at risk, this did not make them Anglo-Catholics.[22]

The fourth allegation was that Arminians wished to exalt both royal and priestly authority over that of parliament and the law. Again this does not seem to have been the case in Holland, where the followers of Arminius leant towards those politicians who could protect them from the hostility of the hard-line Calvinists and towards toleration rather than high clerical claims.[23] In England, moreover, it was only partly true, for until the 1620s, as Johann Sommerville has shown recently, there appears to have been a consensus among churchmen, whether strict predestinarian or not, on the powers of the king and of the church.[24] It was only in the late 1620s and the '30s that differences of political theory emerged between some (not all) of those who held differing views on predestination, as prominent non-Calvinists like Neile and Laud stood out by their *continued* defence of the claims of strong royal and ecclesiastical power at a time when other people were becoming unsettled by the growing criticism of both. Significantly the burden of the charges against Laud in the early 1640s would be political and constitutional rather than theological.[25] In short, there does not seem to be enough to substantiate the idea of a coherent Armininan movement that derived a revolutionary set of political and ecclesiastical imperatives from an anti-Calvinist theology. And if there was neither a coherent Arminian movement nor a homogeneous Calvinist one, how much weight can we give to the idea that the rise of 'Arminianism' led to a redrawing of the religious battle-lines in the period prior to the civil war?

The idea of an 'Arminian Revolution' has served to alert us to the nature and divisiveness of a theological debate that had not received much attention in previous accounts (though the religious tensions of the 1620s and '30s can perhaps more plausibly be viewed as the result of a complex interaction between a number of groups). We should also be grateful to Professor Russell and Dr. Tyacke for stressing that the opposition to Archbishop Laud was drawn not just from the old reformist Puritans but also from many moderate episcopalians, men who were sufficiently worried by the allegations of growing Catholic influence at court and of 'popish' developments in the church to reconsider their rejection of the Puritans' demands. (Again this insight may need qualifying: some bishops who were admirers of Calvin like Thomas Morton either acquiesced in or did not openly oppose Laud's policies, while opposition to Laud could be based on personal rivalry as much as theological grounds, as in the case of Bishop Williams.[26]) But in at least two respects the Russell-Tyacke thesis is very similar to the older accounts that it claims to be replacing: first, in its readiness to see the church history of the period as being dominated by a growing confrontation between rival groups; and secondly in its willingness to state that one of those groups was challenging the *status quo* and the other defending it.

These conclusions seem to me to underestimate two other features of the period: the amount of doctrinal common ground among English Protestants, especially against the teachings of Rome; and the many positive achievements of the early Stuart church. Indeed, a case can be made for saying that a number of developments reached a peak between 1600 and 1640: the quality of the pastoral care exercised by the bishops, the influence of the church courts on morality, the educational qualifications and moral standards of the parish clergy, the quantity and quality of new catechisms, and the number of pocket-sized bibles and prayer books being sold for personal use in the 1620s and '30s.[27] Furthermore, in so far as there *was* conflict, it seems unnecessary as well as unwise to take sides by arguing that one side was rocking the boat more than the other. As strong a case can be made for viewing the aggression of the Puritans or of the hard-line Calvinists of the 1580s and '90s as a cause of the episcopal reaction under Bancroft and Laud as the other way round; and it is far from easy to decide if one side was more revolutionary than the other on the basis of contemporary usage, since all parties habitually appealed to the bible or to past practice as justification for their actions.

The weakness of the Russell-Tyacke thesis stems from the same root as that of the older ideas of a 'Puritan Revolution' or an 'English Revolution': the risk of distortion brought about by viewing the period before 1640 in the light of the dramatic events of the 1640s. Some of the events of the early 1640s, such as the passage of the Triennial Act of 1641, were striking and unexpected departures from the normal path of English politics. A strong case can also be made for judging the king's trial and execution, the abolition of the House of Lords, and the declaration of a republic, to be such a drastic and unprecedented series of moves as to warrant (by twentieth-century usage) the term 'revolutionary', though it may be added that most of the men who made that 'revolution' had become convinced of the need for it only months beforehand, and that they then spent much of the next decade trying to undo at least part of their handiwork.[28] But the risks of distortion brought about by applying the term 'revolution' to the events of 1640-42 or of 1648-49 or to both are so great that even historians who have freed themselves from the teleological concerns of earlier generations may in the end fall prey to the temptation of being the ones who have found the key that will unlock the mysteries of the 1640s. A revolution has to have revolutionaries, so the incentive is to seek proto-revolutionaries in the preceding period, not to weigh the many quiet achievements of the early Stuart era against its weaknesses and tensions, but to look at the articulate minorities who took part in the controversies of the day. Of course, there were many connections between the disputes and discontents of the 1630s and those of the 1640s, but in the case of the church in particular, as long as we continue to view the period 1603-40 as a prelude to revolution instead of the tail-end of the first century of English Protestantism,[29] we are likely to emerge with potentially misleading stereotypes such as 'Puritan' and 'Anglican' or 'Calvinist' and 'Arminian' rather than the more complex realities—and the more confident mood and creative aspects—of early Stuart Protestantism.

This brings us neatly to our second main concept, that of a war of religion. Six years ago John Morrill suggested that historians had been so busy trying to integrate events in Britain into the General Crisis of the seventeenth century, or so busy seeking parallels between the English Revolution and the French and Russian Revolutions, that they had missed an obvious point: 'The English civil war was not the first European revolution: it was the last of the wars of religion.'[30] In two essays which are a foretaste of a major study yet to appear, Dr. Morrill argues that in the early 1640s there was a much stronger perception of ecclesiastical misgovernment than in previous decades: whereas before it had been thought to be a handful of leading clerics, by 1641 it was thought to be a whole army of priests forcing 'popish' innovations on the nation. The reasons for this stronger perception lay, first, in the evidence of clerical misconduct that M.P.s thought they had uncovered in 1640 and 1641, and, secondly, in the fears of 'popish' plots which were greatly increased by rumours and by the apocalyptic language of some of the clergy who were selected to preach before them. As a result, the members of the lower house decided to assume greater powers over the clergy, the church courts and the parishes. However, the taking of these powers not only upset conservatives but also began to alienate many moderates who saw the tactics of the House of Commons—and the radical support it was attracting from outside—as a potentially greater threat than popery. It was at this point, in 1641, that two sides began to emerge, based on different solutions to the problem of church government and worship. There had been other sources of disagreement between king and people, other perceptions of misgovernment, says Morrill, but to some extent during 1640 and early 1641 these issues had been resolved, or by their nature they did not lead to militancy in the way that the more difficult religious problem did. There were, he says, 'no constitutional militants', only religious ones; it was the 'ideological dynamism' of religious feeling which drove opposed minorities to use force, and which forced the majority in the middle to make reluctant choices.[31] In these and other ways there were direct parallels between events in England and later sixteenth-century France and Holland and early seventeenth-century Germany. Dr. Morrill does have another string to his bow—the idea that in late 1641 and 1642 some members of the peerage tried to reassert their power in the absence of a clear or acceptable lead from Charles— but the new book is provisionally entitled *England's Wars of Religion*. Moreover, a growing number of other historians, including Anthony Fletcher and Patrick Collinson, have adopted this label in recent years, though usually with more reservations than Morrill.[32]

There are some overlaps between Morrill's case and that of Russell and Tyacke: Morrill also doubts the value of a socio-economic interpretation of the wars, and he is on record as saying that Charles I's greatest mistake was to ally himself with a party in the church that was abhorrent to the majority of English Protestants.[33] But the chronological focus of the two is clearly different: Russell and Tyacke have stressed certain developments before 1640, while Morrill is currently highlighting developments within the early 1640s; and Tyacke and perhaps Russell seem to see one element in the church as being revolutionary and another as counter-revolutionary, whereas in Morrill's view there were minorities on *both* sides who combined a measure of conservatism (in that both wanted to return to their own particular vision of the past) with an element of ideological dynamism (in their determination to fight if necessary to protect that vision).[34] Morrill also consciously substitutes the more neutral term 'wars' for the problematic 'revolution'.

Nevertheless, it does seem a little odd to choose the adjective 'religious' to qualify the term 'war', in that elsewhere the notion of religious wars seems to be falling out of use. Today the suggestion that the French civil wars or the revolt of the Netherlands were essentially 'wars of religion' would perhaps find few supporters. The trend seems to be against explanations which focus on a particular factor, on the ground, as Professor Kossmann put it recently, that on closer examination they mostly turn out to be 'not only inadequate but pointless'.[35] So before English historians rush forward to nominate the English civil wars for membership of a club that other members seem to be leaving, it might be pertinent to ask what membership entails.

If we stand back far enough, the three longest-serving members of the club—the French civil wars of the late sixteenth century, the Dutch Revolt and the Thirty Years' War—do seem to display some common characteristics. In each case there was a crisis of law and order which exposed the administrative and financial problems of the central government; there was discontent among sections of the propertied élite, which were prepared to use the government's moment of weakness to pursue sectional interests of a fairly conventional kind; and there was also a measure of economic slump and social discontent among the middling and lower orders. By itself this combination of circumstances was not unique, but if we leave out the crusades as a special case, and ignore the odd medieval rising or two, what *was* new was the adoption of religious nonconformity by a section of the propertied élite. Moreover, when a rival section of that élite supported religious orthodoxy and the opposing groups became involved in alliances with middling and sometimes even popular elements at home and co-religionists abroad, the possibility of extended conflict became strong. In each case, the longer the war went on, the less clear-cut became the role of religious rivalry, due partly to political developments at home and abroad, and partly to the brutalizing effect of the fighting itself. Nevertheless the role played by religious differences in provoking the initial conflict, in legitimizing its continuance and in keeping together unlikely groups of men may, as Professor Collinson has suggested, warrant the use of a label like 'religious war' to mark these conflicts out from other ones.[36] There may, in fact, be a case for saying that in early modern Europe the nature of religious commitment and the type of Christianity taught was sufficiently different from that of the Middle Ages or the late modern period to justify the use of a different set of terms for that period.

On closer inspection, however, the three founding members of the club are not so alike, especially as far as their origins are concerned. The French troubles of the later sixteenth century seem to stem less from the rise of religious dissent than from political circumstances: the premature death of Henry II, which left a much strengthened but not problem-free monarchy in the hands of young princes who could not hold the reins of power effectively, and the existence of selfish noble factions vying for power and patronage. We can also now see that both the Catholicism of sixteenth-century France and the reform movements in the French cities possessed a more complex character than was once thought.[37] In the 1560s religious divisions may have made a bad situation worse, but cannot be said to have been the main cause of the crisis.

In the Netherlands, we have a very different situation: a series of provinces, some only recently and partially integrated into the whole, each different in its social structure and economy, but all trying to come to terms with a ruling dynasty that was based hundreds of miles away and had vast interests beyond the Low Countries. We also have a more complex pattern of religious development than in France, with Erasmian humanism, Lutheranism, Anabaptism, and different varieties of

Reformed thought all more vigorously established by the 1550s; and we have a set of government measures against heresy which raised all sorts of constitutional and legal principles as well as practical problems of enforcement.[38] Not surprisingly given this greater complexity, trouble when it broke out did not do so neatly: the revolts of 1566, 1572 and 1576 were different in their character and personnel, and although there was a certain amount of common ground or overlap in the issues raised or in the language used to explain and defend resistance, the revolts often seem to resemble a number of characters in search of an author. This is not meant in a disparaging sense, rather that many principles or institutions seem to have crystallized during rather than before the revolts, for example the nature of Dutch liberties, the concept of 'bons patriotes', the organization of a Calvinist church, and so on.[39] Two groups may have said they knew what the fighting was all about: the very small minority of hard-line reformers, who saw it as a campaign for purity of religion, to set up the New Israel; and the ultra-loyal greater nobility of the South, who retained an unshakeable commitment to the prince and an unswerving attachment to the church—for them heresy and insubordination posed greater threats to the *status quo* than Spanish policies. But for the majority of Netherlanders in between, moderate Catholics and moderate Protestants, the political and religious situation may have seemed less clear-cut and would remain so for some time. As far as the origins of the revolt are concerned, it is doubtful if Calvinism was sufficiently politicized or sufficiently strong to have united the rebels against Spain; and thereafter it may have been as much a source of division as of strength.[40]

In one sense the Thirty Years' War is the most avowedly religious of the three: religious conflict went back nearly a century, and was being reinforced by the confrontation between resurgent Catholicism and an entrenched Protestantism. Moreover, in Germany even before the fighting began there were military alliances built on confessional lines and co-religionaries abroad waiting to help if necessary; and in the persons of the Emperor and the militant Calvinists of the Palatinate, there were (as in the Netherlands) two elements which saw the situation in stark terms of the need to consolidate their own ecclesiastical position before the other side made that impossible. But it is open to question whether the German Lutherans were as committed to fighting for their faith as their Swedish counterparts, or whether princes like Maximilian of Bavaria were as loyal to the cause of Catholicism as was the Emperor. Furthermore, the political situation in central Europe was even more complex than in the Low Countries: not only were there different types of state in conflict as Professor Polisensky has indicated, but also a be-

wildering variety of political, doctrinal and social tensions. In this situation it is very hard for us to separate the political rivalry of men like
Ferdinand II and the Elector Palatine from their religious antagonisms;
and many of the lesser princes and states caught up in their contest were
probably under no illusion as to just how high the political and social as
well as the ecclesiastical stakes were for them too.[41]

However, to talk like this is to some extent to play the game according
to the rules laid down by those historians in the nineteenth and early
twentieth centuries who cultivated the idea of 'wars of religion'; all we
may be doing is replacing their perceptions by a more secular view of
ourselves and the past. A more serious objection to the concept is to
suggest that over the last half century, especially through the influence
of those members of the *Annales* school who became interested in *menta-
lités*, it has become increasingly difficult to isolate a sphere of belief or
action that can be meaningfully labelled 'religious' in the traditional
sense. Research into popular culture and popular religion and into the
early phases of the Reformation and Counter-Reformation has identified
non-Christian as well as Christian elements in the contemporary
worldview, and has also revealed the social or political functions of
many doctrines and ceremonies.[42] One could add work done on the
mental world of individual members of the literate élite or on subjects
which today might pass for secular, such as political theory, literature
or the visual arts, but which in the early modern world often began and
ended with God.[43] In my own work on elementary religious instruction,
I have found it artificial to try to separate the ability to read and write
from the acquisition of Christian vocabulary and concepts, or to distinguish too rigidly between the classical ethics of humanist education and
the Christian moralism of official formularies. Christian words and ideas
were so much a part of the air that people breathed that it is often almost
impossible to isolate some aspects of behaviour as 'religious' and reject
others as 'secular'. Indeed, one leading scholar has called into question
our use of a whole string of words like 'religion', 'society', 'holiness',
'church', 'communion', on the grounds that their meaning not only was
changing between 1400 and 1700, but also in some cases has been redefined within the last hundred years.[44]

Even if historians today could agree on terminology, this does not
solve our problem, for we still have to ask what the men and women of
early modern Europe meant by the terms they used. Did they understand these terms in the way that the contemporary church meant them
to be understood, or in the way that we do today? Or, as in the case of
the miller Menocchio or the vintner Hans Keil, did some contemporaries read very different meanings into the words or concepts used

than those intended?[45] Another problem is whether contemporaries understood Christian teaching literally or metaphorically. In seventeenth-century England, we can find many individuals or groups citing scriptural precedents for vigorous action, urging people to fight the good fight, to put on the armour provided by God, to set up a New Jerusalem or to go on crusade against the Antichrist. But while some people clearly took these calls to action literally, others, very close in doctrine and ecclesiology, equally clearly took them to be matters on which the magistrate rather than the private citizen should take the lead or to be metaphors of internal, spiritual strife.[46] This brings us to a further problem: once a war had started, how far were the continued bloodshed and destruction the result of religious imperatives, and how far were they due to military imperatives of the 'kill or be killed' variety, imperatives which could override the normal rules about life and property?[47] But perhaps enough has been said to explain why in practical and semantic terms the term 'war of religion' has become problematic.

Turning back to the Morrill thesis, our first problem is to establish what we mean by 'religious'. Doctrinal and liturgical matters and wider ecclesiastical issues such as tithes and discipline, of course, but what about phenomena such as anti-clericalism, anti-Catholicism or millenarianism which were often composites of a number of feelings and perceptions, not all of them 'religious' in a conventional sense? Do we also include what is often referred to today as 'social control', in so far as the church may have played an active if perhaps unpopular part in exerting it?[48] The sources available also pose problems of interpretation: how far was a contemporary's use of biblical language deliberate and informed? how far were labels such as 'Puritan' or 'papist' applied maliciously? and how much weight can we put on allegations which may have been orchestrated or which no longer exist, such as most of those eight hundred petitions against the parish clergy of which Dr. Morrill makes much?

According to Morrill, the perception of religious misgovernment in the crucial years 1640-42 was more intense than other perceptions of misgovernment, and the language then used to denounce those churchmen who had supported Charles in the 1630s was more militant than that used to condemn his lay supporters.[49] But can one divide these perceptions into watertight compartments as a basis for comparison? How far could the king's critics separate fear of 'popery' or of Laudianism from fear of royal absolutism, since by 1640 king and archbishop were so mutually supportive? And how far would the king's supporters separate their dislike of attacks on a divinely appointed monarch and an established church from their concern at the unconstitutional way in

which those attacks were being pursued?[50] As for the language of denunciation, this was often taken from the bible, but that work has much
more to say against idolatry and false prophets than illegal taxes or arbitrary courts. It was also perhaps considered tactically unwise in 1641
or 1642 to use the anathemas against unjust kings which were available
in the bible, and it was easier for the parliamentary managers and their
country gentry, lawyer and burgess supporters to attack a relatively soft
target like the clergy than to prosecute members of their own ranks who
had also played a part in implementing royal policies in the 1630s. The
attack on the clergy was carried out in the name of reformation, but
there is more than a whiff of opportunism about it and a distinct odour
of anti-clericalism, which had been a recurrent feature of English social
history for two or three centuries, if not longer.[51]

There are further problems if we try to define what the two sides stood
for at the start of the fighting in August 1642. The parliamentarian side,
says Morrill, derived its impetus from the desire for a 'religious renewal', a 'godly reformation'. But the reformation to which these men
were committed seems to be definable only in negative terms: it was
anti-Catholic, anti-'Arminian', anti-Laudian, and to some extent anti-
episcopal and anti-Prayer Book. The parliamentarian side had no
agreed alternative church structure or liturgy, such as existed when hostilities began in France in 1562 or in Germany in 1618; there was not
even (at that date) a call for toleration of different structures as there
had been in the Netherlands.[52] In the absence of an agreed goal for that
renewal it is hard to gauge its appeal or the level of commitment to it.
This is more than a debating point, for there are examples of men who
were hostile to popery and Laudianism but who apparently did not feel
constrained to take up arms for the parliament;[53] and these men need to
be set alongside both those well-known zealots who felt that it was their
religious duty to fight—and win—a war and those who apparently
agreed to fight with some reluctance or in the hope that an honourable
draw might result.[54]

As for the king's supporters in August 1642, many of them may have
seen the issue as one of authority: certain sections of the population had
rebelled against their king, and had to be stopped. In fighting for the
king they were also fighting for the old church, but the main purpose
was to defend and reassert the king's control of church and state. The
crux was not Laudianism itself but the manner in which it had been attacked in parliament in the early 1640s and the extra-parliamentary
support which that attack had received, two circumstances which led
them to fear that what was intended was a democratic church in which
each congregation would elect its minister and help to discipline the

flock. Fears of political turmoil and perhaps of social levelling too were inextricably tied in with ecclesiastical concerns among those who sought to put down the parliamentarian rebellion.[55] The difference is visible in the catechism prepared for the soldiers in the king's army in 1645, as a riposte to a similar catechism prepared for the parliamentarian army in 1644. Both catechisms reassured soldiers that if they died fighting they would win a martyr's crown, but whereas the parliamentarian form said that the war was being fought to save the king from a 'popish malignant company' and to save the laws and liberties of England and the true Protestant religion, the royalist one said that the war was being fought to defend the rightful authority of the king against rebels and to recover what had been unjustly taken from him. Rebellion was a great sin, and only Jesuits and Puritans taught subjects to resist their king.[56] However, it must be added that there were many who supported the king's stance but did not feel impelled to fight for it, so that again one needs to seek additional reasons why some episcopalians (like some 'Puritans') were prepared to fight, while others were not.[57]

Assessment of the two sides' motives needs to be supplemented by consideration of the attitudes of the many who tried to remain neutral. The 'weapons of the church were prayers and tears' said one Essex minister who helped to organize a petition for peace in (allegedly Puritan) Essex in the winter of 1642-43; it was eventually signed by eighty ministers. A minister in Lancashire said that the king was his father and parliament his mother, and it was his duty to reconcile them rather than take sides.[58] Indeed, it seems likely that contemporaries, whether neutral or actively committed to one side, were motivated not by one predominant concern, but by a variety of overlapping or even conflicting attitudes and interests, the exact combination of which varied not only from group to group but also from individual to individual, as Ivan Roots suggested in a very wise and unjustly neglected essay.[59]

Over-simple characterizations of the wars are also weakened by the fact that the longer the fighting went on the more complex the issues became. At the start of the first war, for example, one could say that there were two or three main religious standpoints: Laudian, moderate episcopalian, and reformist; but six years later by the start of the second war there were several: three or four kinds of Presbyterian, a range of Independents and a growing variety of sects as well as a strong episcopalian rump. In 1642 one of the main issues was whether the state church would continue to be episcopalian; by 1648 it was doubtful if the state church would survive, or if a statement of Christian belief could be agreed among the warring Protestants.[60] Parallel or interwoven with these changes in doctrine and ecclesiology went changes in political perception. By late 1648, the more cautious elements in the parliamentarian camp were anxious to put Charles back into power with some political restrictions and a Genevan-style church, while the more radical elements, including many congregationalists and sectaries, were prepared to execute Charles I as a 'man of blood' against whom the Lord had witnessed in battle. The victory went to the group which had the support of the army, and by March 1649 a 'godly' republic had been set up.[61]

Does the strength of the godly in this new republic mean that England's civil wars had after all been 'wars of religion'? To a certain extent one could say that it does, for without the fear of Catholicism exploited by John Pym or the absolute conviction of the need to fight the Lord's battles felt by men like Oliver Cromwell, parliament would quite possibly not have been able to raise a large force, let alone win two wars. The struggle was a religious war in the limited sense that some of those on one side often spoke and acted as if it was[62] (though this raises the question of whether the zealots in the French, Dutch and German conflicts were also to be found mainly on one side). However, if one tries to pin down what it was that made some parliamentarians so determined, it is very hard to do so. Anti-Catholicism was an amalgam of fears—political, social and racial as well as 'religious'—and was not a monopoly of those who fought for parliament.[63] A sense of being one of the elect and a belief in divine providence were probably important for many individuals, but did not necessarily make men fight, let alone fight for parliament, as the careers of Calvinist episcopalians like Morton and Ussher show.[64] Millenarianism was certainly significant too, but again was not a Puritan monopoly, and in its potentially most explosive form did not take proper hold until after the wars had started. Moreover, as the years passed and the new dawn did not break in the form expected, interpretations of Daniel and the Revelation of St. John became so diffuse that they began to lose their power to rouse and to unite.[65] As for the desire for religious toleration which became a key issue in the later 1640s, this meant different things to different groups and initially was as much about forms of government or about which group would obtain power as it was about religious ideals.[66]

By examining teachings which stressed the need to guard against the wiles of the Antichrist we may come close to a 'war of religion' in the sense that such teaching may, by the early 1640s, have had an unsettling effect on the political or social perceptions of a large number of people. It may, for a time, have made them feel a sense of crisis, but it did not necessarily make them want to get up and fight. In providentialism, on the other hand, we may be dealing with a particular form of Christian teaching which, for some key figures, was of paramount importance and produced not just a sense of unease but a much more aggressive pattern of behaviour. But there are still so many unanswered questions about English millenarianism in the 1640s that we cannot be sure how many people were affected by it or for how long, and we have so few spiritual biographies of the protagonists in the civil war that we cannot be sure in what ways providential beliefs may have interacted with other ideas or interests in determining their behaviour.[67]

Like the events in late sixteenth-century France and Holland and early seventeenth-century Germany, the English civil wars were probably due as much to constitutional conflicts and to personal antagonisms, social ambitions and mutual misunderstandings as to differences over doctrine, liturgy or ecclesiology.[68] But as Professor Kossmann indicated, historians might be better advised to devote less time to looking for the causes of wars and more to looking at specific aspects of the period with an open mind as to what might turn up.[69] It would not be hard to draw up a list of suitable topics: a series of studies of village communities during the 1630s and early '40s to try to detect how far the king's ecclesiastical politics had filtered down into them, and with what results; a comparative study of urban and rural faith and religious practice before 1640; a comparison of the religious motivation of the individual with that of the group; a survey of the use of biblical imagery before and after 1640, to assess the frequency with which more aggressive images such as Christ cleansing the temple or urging his followers to leave their families appeared; a comparison of the relative importance of Old and New Testament texts in justifying the use of force in and after 1642; and further study of the tensions between military imperatives and the normal standards of Christian behaviour. In short, we need to think and to find out far more about the nature of people's faith before we are dogmatic about its effects on their behaviour.

[1] For a fuller account of the historiography, see R.C. Richardson, *The Debate on the English Revolution Revisited*, London, 1988. I am grateful to Dr Martin Ingram and the members of the Exeter colloquium for their comments on this paper.

[2] S.R. Gardiner, *History of the Great Civil War 1642-49*, London, 1893-94, I, p. 9; and idem, *History of England from the Accession of James I to the Outbreak of the Civil War*, London, 1884, and *History of the Commonwealth to the Protectorate*, London, 1897-1903.

[3] Richardson, *Debate*, pp. 82-86; Gardiner's conclusions are criticized in M.G. Finlayson, *Historians, Puritanism and the English Revolution*, Toronto, 1983, pp. 17-18, 24-27, 62-67, and J.P. Kenyon, *The History Men*, London, 1983, pp. 214-22.

[4] Richardson, *Debate*, pp. 77-80, 114-18; C. Hill, *The Century of Revolution*, Edinburgh, 1961, part 1; *Reformation to Industrial Revolution*, London, 1967, parts 1-3; and *The World Turned Upside Down*, London, 1972, chap. 1; B. Manning, *The English People and the English Revolution 1640-1649*, London, 1976, *passim*.

[5] C. Hill, *Economic Problems of the Church*, Oxford, 1956; *Society and Puritanism in Pre-Rev-*

olutionary England, London, 1964; and *The World Turned Upside Down*, chaps. 8-11; cf. B. Manning, 'Religion and Politics: the Godly People', in *idem* (ed.), *Politics, Religion and the English Civil War*, London, 1973, pp. 82-123.

⁶ J.S. Morrill, 'Introduction', in *idem* (ed.), *Reactions to the English Civil War*, London, 1982, pp. 2-14; J.C.D. Clark, *Revolution and Rebellion: State and Society in England*, Cambridge, 1986, chap. 3. The American J.H. Hexter has been one of Hill's severest critics, e.g. in *On Historians*, London, 1979, chap. 5.

⁷ C. Russell, 'Parliamentary History in Perspective 1604-1629', *History*, 61 (1976), pp. 1-27; *idem*, *Parliaments and English Politics 1621-1629*, Oxford, 1979; K. Sharpe, 'Introduction' and '"Revisionism" Revisited', in *idem* (ed.), *Faction and Parliament: Essays on Early Stuart History*, 2nd edn., London, 1985, pp. ix-xvii, 1-42.

⁸ C. Russell, 'Introduction', in *idem* (ed.), *The Origins of the English Civil War*, London, 1973, pp. 12-17, 27-31; and *idem*, 'The British Problem and the English Civil War', *History*, 72 (1987), pp. 395-415.

⁹ N. Tyacke, 'Puritanism, Arminianism and Counter-Revolution', in Russell (ed.), *Origins*, pp. 119-43 (cf. pp. 17-27); and *idem*, *Anti-Calvinists: The Rise of English Arminianism*, Oxford, 1987.

¹⁰ L. Stone, 'Second Thoughts in 1985', in *The Causes of the English Revolution*, London, 1986, pp. 165-81; R. Cust and A. Hughes (eds.), *Conflict in Early Stuart England*, London, 1989.

¹¹ P. White, 'The Rise of Arminianism Reconsidered', *Past and Present*, 101 (1983), pp. 34-54, but see also nos. 114 and 115 (1987); K. Sharpe, 'Archbishop Laud and the University of Oxford', in H. Lloyd-Jones, V. Pearl and B. Worden (eds.), *History and Imagination*, London, 1981, pp. 146-64; and 'Archbishop Laud', *History Today*, 36 (August 1986), pp. 26-30.

¹² B. Hall, 'Calvin against the Calvinists', in G.E. Duffield (ed.), *John Calvin*, Abingdon, 1966, pp. 26-36; R.T. Kendall, *Calvin and English Calvinism*, Oxford, 1979; P.F. Jensen, 'The Life of Faith in the Teaching of Elizabethan Protestants', unpublished Oxford D. Phil. thesis, 1979; P. Lake, *Moderate Puritans and the Elizabethan Church*, Cambridge, 1982, and 'Calvinism and the English Church 1570-1635', *Past and Present*, 114 (1987), pp. 32-76; Tyacke, *Anti-Calvinists*, pp. 94-100. See also P. Collinson, 'England and International Calvinism, 1558-1640', in M. Prestwich (ed.), *International Calvinism 1541-1715*, Oxford, 1985, pp. 197-223.

¹³ As last note, and I.M. Green, 'Career Prospects and Clerical Conformity in the Early Stuart Church', *Past and Present*, 90 (1981), pp. 109-10.

¹⁴ These comments will be developed in my *Religious Instruction in Early Modern England*, Oxford, forthcoming.

¹⁵ W.P. Haugaard, *Elizabeth and the English Reformation*, Cambridge, 1970, chaps. 3, 6; Lake, *Moderate Puritans*, chap. 9; Collinson, 'England', pp. 213-17.

¹⁶ Thomas Cartwright's short catechism, published at the end of later editions of Dod and Cleaver's *Plaine ... Exposition of the Ten Commandments* and Perkins' popular exposition *Golden Chaine* both contain predestinarian teaching; on Whitgift and James, Lake, 'Calvinism', p. 46 (and cf. p. 34, n. 17), and J.P. Kenyon, *The Stuart Constitution*, 2nd edn., Cambridge, 1986, p. 129. On sermons see my *Religious Instruction*.

¹⁷ *Ibid.*, and my '"For Children in Yeeres and Children in Understanding": the Emergence of the English Catechism under Elizabeth and the Early Stuarts', *Journal of Ecclesiastical History*, 37 (1986), pp. 397-425.

¹⁸ H.C. Porter, *Reformation and Reaction in Tudor Cambridge*, Cambridge, 1958, pp. 376-413; H.R. Trevor-Roper, 'Laudianism and Political Power', in *Catholics, Anglicans and Puritans*, London, 1987, pp. 41-47; T.M. Parker, 'Arminianism and Laudianism in Seventeenth-Century England', in C.W. Dugmore and C. Duggan (eds.), *Studies in Church History*, 1 (1964), pp. 29-30; White, 'Rise of Arminianism', pp. 44-46.

¹⁹ Parker, 'Arminianism', pp. 21-25, 29; Trevor-Roper, 'Laudianism', pp. 51-57; J. den Tex, *Oldenbarnevelt*, Cambridge, 1973, chaps. 10, 12; Provost Potter's remark is cited by Tyacke, *Anti-Calvinists*, p. 80.

²⁰ Trevor-Roper, 'Laudianism', pp. 68-69; Kenyon, *Stuart Constitution*, pp. 26-28.

[21] Tyacke, 'Puritanism', pp. 129-31; P. Lake, *Anglicans and Puritans?*, London, 1988, pp. 173-82; this is a complex subject which requires fuller treatment than it can be given here.

[22] Green, 'Career Prospects', pp. 112-14; Parker, 'Arminianism', pp. 30-31. But now see also A. Foster, 'The Church Policies of the 1630s', in Cust and Hughes (eds.), *Conflict in Early Stuart England*, pp. 193-223.

[23] There was, however, no doctrine of resistance in Arminianism.

[24] J.P. Sommerville, *Politics and Ideology in England 1603-1640*, London, 1986, chaps. 1, 4, 6.

[25] Kenyon, *Stuart Constitution*, p. 134; Trevor-Roper, 'Laudianism', pp. 97-98; White, 'Rise of Arminianism', pp. 53-54

[26] Tyacke, *Anti-Calvinists*, p. 212; H.R. Trevor-Roper, *Archbishop Laud*, London, 1940, pp. 52-62, 179-84, 325-32.

[27] See my 'Career Prospects' and *Religious Instruction*, and the forthcoming study of the Jacobean episcopate by Kenneth Fincham; also M.J. Ingram, *Church Courts, Sex and Marriage in England*, Cambridge, 1987.

[28] The best accounts of the 1640s and early 1650s are still those of D. Underdown, *Pride's Purge: Politics in the English Revolution*, Oxford, 1971, and B. Worden, *The Rump Parliament*, Cambridge, 1974.

[29] A point stressed by Dr. C. Haigh in an unpublished paper on 'The Church of England and its People 1604-40'.

[30] J.S. Morrill, 'The Religious Context of the English Civil War', *Transactions of the Royal Historical Society*, 5th Series, 34 (1984), p. 178; and 'The Attack on the Church of England in the Long Parliament, 1640-42', in D. Beales and G. Best (eds.), *History, Society and the Churches*, Cambridge, 1985, p. 105.

[31] Morrill, 'Religious Context', pp. 162-78; and 'Attack', pp. 105-24.

[32] J.S. Morrill, 'The Political Context of the English Civil War', unpublished paper; A. Fletcher, *The Outbreak of the English Civil War*, London, 1981, pp. 417-18; P. Collinson, *The Birthpangs of Protestant England*, London, 1989, chap. 5, especially pp. 133-36.

[33] Morrill, 'Attack', p. 105, and note 6 above.

[34] Morrill, 'Religious Context', pp. 159-63.

[35] E.H. Kossmann, 'Popular Sovereignty at the Beginning of the Dutch Ancien Régime', *Acta Historiae Neerlandicae*, 14 (1981), p. 1.

[36] See following notes, and Collinson, *Birthpangs*, pp. 134-35.

[37] N.M. Sutherland, *Catherine de Medici and the Ancien Régime*, London, 1978, pp. 22-28; D. Parker, *The Making of French Absolutism*, London, 1983, pp. 13-30; H. Heller, *The Conquest of Poverty*, Studies in Medieval Reformation Thought, 25, Leiden, 1986; P.T. Hoffman, *Church and Community in the Diocese of Lyon*, New Haven, 1984, chaps. 1-2; N. Zemon Davis, 'The Rites of Violence', *Past and Present*, 59 (1973), pp. 51-91.

[38] A.C. Duke, 'From King and Country to King or Country?', *Transactions of the Royal Historical Society*, 5th Series, 32 (1982), pp. 113-35; *idem*, 'Salvation by Coercion', in P.N. Brooks (ed.), *Reformation Principle and Practice*, London, 1980, pp. 135-56; and *idem*, 'Building Heaven in Hell's Despite', in A. Duke and C.A. Tamse (eds.), *Britain and the Netherlands*, 7, The Hague, 1981, pp. 45-75; P. Mack Crew, *Calvinist Preaching and Iconoclasm*, Cambridge, 1978; W. Nijenhuis, 'Variants within Dutch Calvinism in the Sixteenth Century', *Acta Historiae Neerlandicae*, 12 (1979), pp. 48-64.

[39] As last, plus G. Parker, *The Dutch Revolt*, London, 1979, chaps. 2-4; I. Schöffer, 'Protestantism in Flux during the Revolt of the Netherlands', in J.S. Bromley and E.H. Kossmann (eds.), *Britain and the Netherlands*, 2, Groningen, 1962, pp. 67-83; and J.J. Woltjer, 'Dutch Privileges, Real and Imaginary', *ibid.*, 5, The Hague, 1975, pp. 19-35.

[40] As last, plus Duke, 'King and Country', pp. 131-32, and *idem*, 'The Ambivalent Face of Calvinism in the Netherlands', in Prestwich (ed.), *International Calvinism*, pp. 109-34; Parker, *Dutch Revolt*, p. 155; Schöffer, 'Protestantism', pp. 70, 80.

[41] J.V. Polisensky, *The Thirty Years War*, London, 1971; G. Parker, *The Thirty Years War*, London, 1984; R.J.W. Evans, *The Making of the Habsburg Monarchy*, Oxford, 1979.

[42] See the surveys by N. Zemon Davis, 'From "Popular Religion" to Religious Cul-

tures', in S. Ozment (ed.), *Reformation Europe: A Guide to Research*, St. Louis, 1982, pp. 321-41, and Kaspar von Greyerz, 'Introduction', in *idem* (ed.), *Religion and Society in Early Modern Europe*, London, 1984, pp. 1-14.

[43] For example, P.S. Seaver, *Wallington's World: A Puritan Artisan in Seventeenth-Century London*, London, 1985; Sommerville, *Politics and Ideology*; G.E. Veith, *Reformation Spirituality: The Religion of George Herbert*, London, 1985; C.C. Christensen, *Art and the Reformation in Germany*, Detroit, 1979.

[44] John Bossy, 'Holiness and Society', *Past and Present*, 75 (1977), pp. 119-37; 'Some Elementary Forms of Durkheim', *ibid.*, 95 (1982), pp. 3-18; and *Christianity in the West 1400-1700*, Oxford, 1985, pp. 167-71.

[45] C. Ginzburg, *The Cheese and the Worms*, London, 1980; D. Sabean, *Power in the Blood*, Cambridge, 1982, chap. 2.

[46] e.g. L.F. Solt, 'The Fifth Monarchy Men: Politics and the Millennium', *Church History*, 30 (1961), pp. 314-24; W. Lamont, *Godly Rule*, London, 1969, *passim*; Collinson, *Birthpangs*, pp. 127-32.

[47] For a comparison of English and German experiences, see B. Donagan, 'Codes and Conduct in the English Civil War', *Past and Present*, 118 (1988), pp. 65-95.

[48] K. Wrightson, *English Society 1580-1680*, London, 1982, chaps. 2, 6; A. Fletcher and J. Stevenson (eds.), *Order and Disorder in Early Modern England*, Cambridge, 1987, pp. 23-25, 41-57.

[49] Morrill, 'Religious Context', p. 164.

[50] G.E. Aylmer, 'Collective Mentalities in Mid Seventeenth-Century England. I. The Puritan Outlook', *Transactions of the Royal Historical Society*, 5th series, 36 (1986), pp. 6-7; and 'II. Royalist Attitudes', *ibid.*, 37 (1987), pp. 7-11, 14-15; and cf. Morrill, 'Attack', pp. 108-10, 120-24.

[51] C. Hill, *Antichrist in Seventeenth-Century England*, London, 1971; P. Christianson, *Reformers and Babylon*, Toronto, 1978; P. Heath, *The English Parish Clergy*, London, 1969, pp. 10, 106-07, 133-34, 152-53; R. O'Day, *The English Clergy*, Leicester, 1979, chaps. 14-15.

[52] W.A. Shaw, *A History of the Church during the Civil Wars and under the Commonwealth*, London, 1900, I, pp. 1-122, and II, pp. 175-85.

[53] Seaver, *Wallington's World*, pp. 164-72.

[54] Contrast Cromwell's attitude with that of the Earl of Manchester and John Hutchinson: C. Hill, *God's Englishman: Oliver Cromwell and the English Revolution*, London, 1970, chap. 3; J. Malcolm, *Caesar's Due: Loyalty and King Charles 1642-1646*, London, 1983, pp. 163-64.

[55] See above, note 50, plus Malcolm, *Caesar's Due*, chaps. 5-6.

[56] R. Ram, *The Souldiers Catechisme: Composed for the Parliaments Army*, London, 1644, pp. 1-2, 23-24; T. Swadlin, *The Souldiers Catechisme Composed for the Kings Armie*, Oxford, 1645, pp. 1-3, 9-11.

[57] Aylmer, 'Royalist Attitudes', pp. 3-7.

[58] I.M. Green, 'The Persecution of "Scandalous" and "Malignant" Parish Clergy', *English Historical Review*, 94 (1979), p. 513; J.S. Morrill, *The Revolt of the Provinces*, London, 1976, pp. 36-42, 89-111.

[59] I. Roots, 'Interest – Public, Private and Communal', in R.H. Parry (ed.), *The English Civil War and After*, London, 1970, pp. 111-23.

[60] G. Yule, *Puritans in Politics*, Sutton Courtenay, 1981; R.S. Paul, *The Assembly of the Lord*, Edinburgh, 1985; J.F. McGregor and B. Reay, *Radical Religion in the English Revolution*, Oxford, 1985.

[61] See above, note 28, plus Hill, *God's Englishman*, chaps. 6-7.

[62] R.S. Paul, *The Lord Protector*, London, 1955; R.P. Stearns, *The Strenuous Puritan*, Urbana, 1954; on Pym, see Fletcher, *Outbreak*.

[63] Compare C.M. Hibbard, *Charles I and the Popish Plot*, North Carolina, 1983, *passim*, and the work of R. Clifton, 'Fear of Popery', in Russell (ed.), *Origins*, pp. 144-67, and 'The Popular Fear of Catholics during the English Revolution', *Past and Present*, 52 (1971), pp. 23-55.

[64] Hill, *God's Englishman*, chap. 9; B. Worden, 'Providence and Politics in Cromwellian England', *Past and Present*, 109 (1985), pp. 55-99. For the careers of Thomas Morton and James Ussher, see L. Stephen and S. Lee (eds.), *Dictionary of National Biography*, London, 1908-09.

[65] K.R. Firth, *The Apocalyptic Tradition in Reformation Britain*, Oxford, 1979; Lamont, *Godly Rule*, chaps. 5-7; Hill, *Antichrist*, chaps. 2-4.

[66] See the works cited in notes 28, 60, and G.E. Aylmer, 'Collective Mentalities ... III. Varieties of Radicalism', *Transactions of the Royal Historical Society*, 5th series, 38 (1988), pp. 10-15; for the 1650s, see B. Worden, 'Toleration and the Cromwellian Protectorate', in W.J. Sheils (ed.), *Studies in Church History*, 21 (1984), pp. 199-233.

[67] Finlayson, *Historians*, chap. 4; and see the works on Wallington, Cromwell and Peter cited above, notes 43, 53, 62; and C. Hill, 'The Religion of Gerrard Winstanley', in *Religion and Politics in 17th Century England*, Brighton, 1986, pp. 185-252.

[68] The best guides through the maze currently available are those of Sommerville, *Politics and Ideology*, and Fletcher, *Outbreak, passim*.

[69] Kossmann, 'Popular Sovereignty', p. 1.

WILLIAM III AND HIS FELLOW CALVINISTS IN THE LOW COUNTRIES

Hans Bots

When on 15 January 1651 Prince William III was presented for baptism in the Grote Kerk of The Hague, the Rev. Tobias Tegneus delivered a sermon which seemed to have scant relevance to the bitter reality of that moment. Like other Orangist ministers, Tegneus had not yet realized that the role of the House of Orange was finished for many years to come and that for the time being the country had little to expect of this new scion.[1] Still, in themselves, the high expectations of this minister were not so strange; from of old the members of the House of Orange had been regarded by their fellow Calvinists, and certainly by most of the clergy of the Dutch Reformed Church, as the defenders of orthodoxy and the true religion.

The student of the relations between William III and the Dutch Reformed Church, however, should also approach the matter from a different angle. That the official church has always shown a great respect for the House of Orange is undisputed; it is therefore more important to examine the question of what position William III took in matters of religion, and to what extent he allowed his actions to be regulated by the Church. The answer to these questions unfortunately was not so simple, because the sources studied often yielded few direct clues. The tentative findings to be presented here frequently had to be developed by indirect means.

We know that the young Prince had a solidly Calvinist upbringing under the guidance of the orthodox—Voetian—court chaplain Cornelis Trigland whose instruction from William's sixth year must have taught the boy that God's almighty hand was not to be defied and that the world was God-governed. The Prince was certainly not insensible to Trigland's instruction and we have many testimonies to the fact that he was a religious, pious man with a rock-solid confidence in God's providence, even if he never became the Christian prince after the ideal of David, as described by Trigland in 1666 in his *Idea sive imago principis Christiani*.[2]

Shortly after William III had been made Stadholder in 1672 he received a moving letter from his former instructor in religion in which

Trigland once again bade his ex-pupil to be firm in the Christian-reformed religion; in addition, he called upon him to follow the example of his forefathers and not to appoint other persons to public office than 'such as are known to be orthodox and sincerely reformed, for how can any that are loose in their religion, like all sects, be faithful to God and the country?'[3] Trigland, who was to die a few weeks afterwards, had realized that now the moment had come when William III could put his religious principles into practice. From 1672 onwards, therefore, it is interesting to examine to what extent the interests of the House of Orange coincided with those of the church, the church leaders and the clergy.

It was soon to become apparent that William III, his stern orthodox upbringing notwithstanding, was not the unbending Calvinist that some God-fearing Orangists had hoped for. Of course the Stadholder, as a member of the Dutch Reformed Church, never explicitly confronted the orthodox doctrine and always in essence submitted to the decisions of the classis or the synod, but that did not mean that he lost sight of political interests or that he did not occasionally let these prevail over ecclesiastical ones. Indeed, political developments abroad served to bring the Prince and his Dutch fellow Protestants closer to one another. At the same time the Prince had a sufficient instinct for political opportunity to be aware that his foreign policy could only be successful if there was no undue tension in the domestic situation. This required a conciliatory, not overly partisan or polarizing attitude.[4]

As a true son of the Orange dynasty, William III had not remained deaf to the plea for greater toleration that had been heard constantly in the Low Countries since the second half of the 16th century. The Stadholder-King's contemporaries repeatedly lauded his tolerance. Thus the Utrecht professor J.G. Graevius emphasizes that William III was admittedly orthodox but that he also took good care that among his fellow churchmen no dissension or dispute arose on items of secondary importance upon which 'eternal salvation did not depend'.[5] A quite impressive testimony in this regard is the following note on William's attitude by Gilbert Burnet, historian and eyewitness:

> He believed the truth of the Christian religion very firmly and he expressed a horror at atheism and blasphemy: and though there was much of both in his court, yet it was always denied to him and kept out of sight. He was most exemplarily decent and devout in the public exercises of the worship of God, only on weekdays he came too seldom to them: he was an attentive hearer of sermons, and was constant in his private prayers, and in reading the scriptures: and when he spoke of religious matters, which he did not often, it was with a becoming gravity: he was much possessed with the belief of absolute decrees: he said to me, he adhered to these, because he did

not see how the belief of providence could be maintained upon any other supposition: his indifference as to the forms of church-government and his being zealous for toleration, together with his cold behaviour towards the clergy, gave them generally very ill impressions of him.[6]

Without detracting one whit from the sincerity of the Stadholder-King's orthodox religious beliefs, the liberal Anglican bishop Burnet manages to convey, in a manner which it is impossible to misconstrue, that William III refused to submit entirely to the Church leaders because his zeal for toleration would not let him. The same claim can be made retrospectively for the Prince's immediate ancestors of the Orange dynasty. His father had met his death at too early an age to make much of an impression *in religiosis*, but of his grandfather Frederick Henry it is sufficiently known that, even before he was invested with the dignity of Stadholder, he had some sympathy for individuals and groups who neither could nor would subscribe to the Dordrecht dogmas. High principle figured even more largely in the manner in which toleration had found expression, a few decades previous to that, in the person of William the Silent, who as a true Erasmian defended that variety of truth which constituted a bond between people. Inspired by a Christian humanism, William the Silent sought to promote a universal and unalloyed Christian faith under the primacy of charity.

But, like William the Silent, his greatgrandson William III was forced to make quite a few concessions to this desire for toleration. He, too, had to compromise in dealing with the various interests and factions. Thus, in a conflict between Voetians and Coccejans in 1676, he had no option but to join the orthodox side. For when in that year in Middelburg the Coccejan Willem Momma—against the wishes of the classis and through the agency of the liberal minister Johannes van der Waeyen— had been appointed and inducted as a minister, William III, in response to an appeal made to him, was compelled to intervene to uphold authority and to remove both ministers, even though he was in sympathy with the two victims.[7]

But let us return for one moment more to Burnet's testimony. The Englishman considered the Stadholder-King a religious, devout person, with a great confidence in Providence. Undoubtedly it was this confidence that in 1688 gave William the courage and the energy to launch and bring to a successful conclusion his expedition to England. In the preceding years he had been confronted with the victims of religious persecution in France, and he was increasingly persuaded that it was his duty to come to the assistance of his fellow Protestants. Also, he realized more and more that it was his mission to preserve the balance of power in Europe; against this background, a Catholic tyranny under Louis

XIV or his father-in-law James II in England was to be prevented at all costs.

The Dutch church leaders saw William III's expedition to England and the subsequent Glorious Revolution above all as a God-willed and God-blessed work, as is apparent from the messages of congratulation from the North and South Holland synods delivered to the Stadholder-King upon his first return to the Republic in 1691: ruin and disaster which had threatened God's churches in England, Scotland and Ireland, but also in the Netherlands itself, indeed in all of Europe, they said, had been happily averted by William III, who, like another Joshua, was destined to redeem his people and lead them into peace and safety.[8]

As I had occasion to observe above, the available source materials provide little relevant information on William III's direct contacts and concerns with the Dutch Reformed Church; the Prince's occasional intercessions on behalf of this or that minister which are on record, or his good word with the church authorities for a loyal servant do not, after all, add to our knowledge of William's religious opinions. Nor do they reveal the extent of his tolerance regarding subjects who were somewhat negligent in their respect for orthodox doctrine, and regarding such as subscribed to other Christian creeds or such as were entirely outside of the Christian tradition.

It is well known that William III applied to the Catholics in the Republic the policy of appeasement already adopted by his grandfather Frederick Henry. Although the Stadholder-King viewed the Catholic Louis XIV as his archenemy and although after 1678 he constantly sought to ensure that the balance of power in Europe was not disturbed at the expense of the 'true religion', he was concerned not totally to alienate from him the relatively large Catholic segment of the population. This is all the more remarkable when it is realized that, for some time after the French invasion in 1672, anti-Catholic sentiments flared up, as in numerous towns and villages Protestant churches were confiscated for the Catholic worship. Nevertheless the situation of the Catholics in the Republic was in some districts even better at the end of the seventeenth century than it had been in the first half; we know, for example, that in the Breda Barony and in the Bergen op Zoom Marquisate more Roman Catholic priests were employed at the end of the century than at the beginning.[9] Even in William's immediate entourage there were several Catholic servants; it is clear that the Stadholder-King was not a fierce anti-papist, and it has been said that the harsh repression of the Catholics in Ireland never had his personal approval.[10] Fanaticism was alien to him and he did not assume that his Roman

Catholic subjects must be potential traitors because they also recognized the authority of the Pope, who, as Locke had still argued in his *Epistola de tolerantia*, was also a secular prince. William III approached those who in his judgment had to be characterized as 'heterodox' in a balanced, realistic fashion without ever being unfaithful to his own convictions. This attitude is well demonstrated by a letter he wrote to G.F. Prince von Waldeck on 4 January 1689, shortly after the successful invasion of England. Regretting the violent anti-Papistic reactions in England, he declared to use every effort to moderate the prevailing emotions.[11]

A similarly tolerant attitude the Prince adopted vis-a-vis other religious groups in the Republic. In 1672 he had, for instance, shown considerable sympathy for the pacifism of the Anabaptists who, in compensation for the conscription enforced in times of a national emergency, had raised large sums of money. In his letter to the States of Holland of 15 May 1673, the Stadholder without hesitation officially released the Anabaptists from their duty to bear arms.[12] Similarly, Quakers who in the fifties of the 17th century had fled to the Republic from England and who had at first met with very hostile treatment on the part of the official—especially ecclesiastical—authorities, were almost everywhere in the country left in peace in the last quarter of the seventeenth century. In 1677, William Penn, one of the great leaders of the Quaker community, was not only free to attend a large national meeting in the Republic, he was also given the opportunity of an interview with Stadholder William III.[13]

Atheists and Socinians met with much less consideration, even sharp hostility, in the last half of the seventeenth century. Yet in this case, too, the Prince was unwilling to join in the fanatical hunts for heretics of some ministers. Did he realize that some forms of liberalism were too hastily being equated with Socinian sympathies? Quite possibly so; at any event William III refused to take action against Foecke Floris, a stubborn Anabaptist teacher accused first by the Frisian synod and then, in 1688, by the North Holland synod, of Socinian views and who, when forbidden to preach, defied the authorities by continuing to deliver his sermons.[14] The heterodox minister must have sensed that William III could save him from the precarious position in which he found himself; he therefore went so far as to apply to the Prince and to invoke his protection. His timing was excellent: at Hellevoetsluis the Stadholder was making preparations for the crossing to England. The Anabaptist minister had no doubt been told that William III was sailing to England under the motto *Pro religione et libertate*, and like Benjamin Furly who interceded for him with the Prince he probably took the second element of this motto as literally as the first.[15] In the view of Foecke Floris and Furly, the Prince stood to gain in credibility, if, before he brought freedom to England, he had ensured the freedom of heterodox groups in his own provinces. William III probably saw the truth of this. But like the good strategist he was, he did not wish to commit himself to either side in the conflict and before giving judgment in the matter, he desired to be more fully informed. This decision meant that in the meantime the proceedings against the minister had to be suspended. Consequently the affair was long delayed, because after his departure to England the Prince had no leisure to deal with the issue. In the event, William III never gave his final verdict: he managed so often to postpone the matter that it simply ceased to exist. If the case of Foecke Floris fizzled out like a damp squib, it nevertheless demonstrates that the Prince never unquestioningly obeyed the behests of the church authorities, let alone those of fanatical orthodox ministers.

Although indubitably a religious man and at home in the Dutch Reformed Church, the Stadholder and later King particularly sought to bring about a conciliatory, tolerant attitude towards other religious groups. Even among the people immediately surrounding him he tolerated, besides Catholics and Jews, persons to whom orthodox zealots could have all sorts of objections, such as a Romeyn de Hooghe, who had been denied Communion because he had published pornographic prints.[16] A quite remarkable expression of William III's conciliatoriness and tolerance was the Dutch resolution for peace in the Church ('tot rust in de Kerk') of 18 December 1694, adopted in consultation with the Stadholder-King. It made a forceful appeal for mutual forbearance: ministers of the church were urged to show moderation and requested not to attack fellow ministers on points of secondary importance; professors of theology were to avoid pronouncements in their lectures and writings that could give rise to confusion or fresh debate; the members of the Church were finally requested only to appoint persons of an irenic disposition to the office of minister.[17]

As we have seen, William's desire for peace and conciliation in the Low Countries was for a significant part inspired by political considerations, in particular by political developments abroad. On occasion such considerations could even prevail over William's pacific instincts; thus we know that the Stadholder was firmly opposed to a plan developed by Adriaan Paets for the reunification of Remonstrants and Contra-Remonstrants into a single, evangelically reformed church, since in the Stadholder's view this would only be to the political advantage of the Regents—that is to say, the republican, pro-French side.[18] Political reality could, after all, never be disregarded, not even if the reformed religion was at stake. A letter from William III to Anthonie Heinsius of 31 October 1697 is most revealing in this regard. In this letter, the Stadholder-King confesses that it is his duty rather 'to continue the war than to make the slightest concession conducive to the weakening of the exercise of the reformed religion'.[19] But, he goes on, how could this be done in the face of Catholic supremacy now that Sweden, Denmark, the Swiss cantons and Saxony on the Protestant side had dropped out? The preservation of the European balance of power, which William regarded as his chief mission, was certainly not served by irresponsible actions, no matter how high the principles that motivated them. And indeed the Stadholder-King always opposed such actions. Against this same European background it also becomes understandable that to William III, far from indifferent to religious issues though he was, national interests—even if they were of a Church nature—could conflict with these overriding political considerations.

[1] *Predicatie, te samen ghestelt, ter occasie van de H. Doop, bedient aan de eerst-geborene sone van ... Prins Wilhelm*, The Hague, 1651 (Knuttel Pamfletten no. 7042).

[2] Cf. several funeral orations and pamphlets published at William's death in 1702, e.g. *De doot van Josua op het afsterven van Wilhelm III*, by A. Moonen (Knuttel Pamfletten no. 14714). See also Knuttel Pamfletten nos. 14699, 14700, 14703 and 14712. Cf. N. Japikse, *Prins Willem III, de Stadhouder-Koning*, 2 vols., Amsterdam, 1930, I, pp. 60-61.

[3] '... bekende orthodoxe en opregte gereformeerde, want die los sijn in de religie gelijck alle secten, hoe kunnen die Godt en het Landt getrou sijn.' This letter was published by G.D.J. Schotel, 'Cornelis Trigland, leermeester van Willem III', *Godgeleerde bijdragen*, 49 (1865), pp. 185-89.

[4] See *inter alia* M.Th. uit den Bogaard, *De gereformeerden en Oranje tijdens het eerste stadhouderloze tijdperk*, Groningen, 1955, p. 252.

[5] '... de eeuwige saligheid niet afhangt'; J.G. Graevius, *Lijkrede over de dood van den doorluchtigsten en grootmagtigsten Wilhelm den III*, Utrecht, 1702 (Knuttel Pamfletten no. 14708).

[6] G. Burnet, *History of His Own Time*, ed. M.J. Routh, London, 1833 (Rpt. Hildesheim, 1969), IV, p. 564.

[7] For the Middelburg conflict, see C.L. Thijssen-Schoute, *Nederlands cartesianisme*, Amsterdam, 1954, pp. 577-78.

[8] W.P.C. Knuttel (ed.), *Acta der particuliere synoden van Zuid-Holland*, IV, 's-Gravenhage, 1916, pp. 171-76 (Rijks geschiedkundige publicatiën, kleine serie, vol. 16).

[9] L. Rogier, *Geschiedenis van het Katholicisme in Noord-Nederland in de 16e en 17e Eeuw*, 2 vols., Amsterdam, 1947, II, pp. 617-22; H.A. Enno van Gelder, *Getemperde vrijheid*, Groningen, 1972, pp. 144-46.

[10] Cf. D.J. Roorda, 'De Joodse entourage van de Koning-Stadhouder', in *Rond prins en patriciaat. Verspreide opstellen*, Weesp, 1984, p. 150.

[11] '... j'ay bien du chagrin que l'on est icy si violent contre les Catoliques, je faits tout ce que je puis pour moderer les choses à leur eguardt ...'; in P.L. Müller, *Wilhelm III von Oranien und G.F. v. Waldeck. Ein Beitrag der Europäische Gleichgewicht*, 's-Gravenhage, 1880, vol. II, p. 126.

[12] H.A. Enno van Gelder, *o.c.*, pp. 102-03.

[13] Cf. W.I. Hull, *The Rise of Quakerism in Amsterdam, 1655-1665*, Swarthmore, 1938; and,

by the same author, *Benjamin Furly and Quakerism in Rotterdam*, Amsterdam, 1941; H.A. Enno van Gelder, *o.c.*, pp. 72-74.

[14] See on this issue, S.D. van Veen, 'Foecke Floris', *Historische studiën en schetsen*, Groningen, 1905, pp. 411-44, and H.A. Enno van Gelder, *o.c.*, pp. 178-79.

[15] Cf. John Locke's letter to Philippus van Limborch of 25 November 1688, in E.S. de Beer (ed.), *The Correspondence of John Locke*, III, Oxford, 1978, pp. 524-25; Maurice Cranston, *John Locke. A Biography*, Oxford, 1985, p. 305.

[16] Cf. D.J. Roorda, *l.c.*, pp. 149-50.

[17] H.A. Enno van Gelder, *o.c.*, p. 235.

[18] Cf. F.R.J. Knetsch, *Pierre Jurieu, theoloog en politicus der Refuge*, Kampen, 1967, pp. 139-40.

[19] '... continueren als yets toe te geven tot vermindering van de exercitie van de gereformeerde religie.' This letter was published in F.J.L. Kramer (ed.), *Archives ou correspondance inédite de la Maison d'Orange-Nassau*, Troisième série, tome II, Leiden, 1908, p. 2.

GLORIOUS REVOLUTION AND MILLENNIUM:
THE 'APOCALYPTICAL THOUGHTS' OF DRUE CRESSENER

J. van den Berg

On 22 November 1687, Drue Cressener, vicar of Soham in the diocese of Ely, wrote to his friend Henry Plumptre:

> I have been almost buried in my Apocalyptical Thoughts for these several months ... I do now acquaint you, that I am in a condition to write Prognostications of the Affairs of almost all Kingdoms for these Hundred Years next following.

How much the subject fascinated him and how deeply he was convinced of the issue of his prognostications also appears from another letter to Plumptre, written on 21 February 1688 (O.S. 1687):

> I am more and more confident, as Apocalyptical Men use to be, of the strength of my Conclusions; And from thence send you the News of a continual increase of the flourishing State of the Church very shortly to begin, and to continue to the end of the World; And therefore desire you to take special Care of your Health, and to desire all good People to do so, that they may be so happy as to live to see a full confirmation of this Prediction ....

Cressener supposed the next year (1689) would be 'a year of Wonders for the Recovery of the Church'. He was thrilled at the prospect: 'My Pen runs before I am aware of it; For my Head is full, and I think I have got one to ease my self upon, and so I desire you to bear it patiently ....'[1]

While he followed the great events of his own time with deep intensity, Cressener himself had a very uneventful life.[2] Born in 1642 in Bury St. Edmunds, in his sixteenth year he went up to Cambridge, where he studied first at Christ's College, later at Pembroke Hall, of which he became a fellow in 1669. In Christ's he no doubt was taught by Henry More, who in the period after the Restoration would become the most prominent Anglican millenarian.[3] Cressener was ordained in London in 1677; in the same year he became vicar of Waresley, in 1678 also proctor of the University of Cambridge. In 1679 he moved to Soham, where he stayed as vicar till his death in 1718. From 1700 he was also prebendary of Ely; perhaps he owed his appointment to the influence of the Bishop of Ely, Simon Patrick, with whom he was acquainted since the turbulent years which preceded the Glorious Revolution.

It was in those years that he started writing his first book, *The Judgments of God upon the Roman-Catholick Church. From its First Rigid Laws for Universal Conformity to it, unto its Last End*. What follows on the title-page is in fact a summary of its contents; we are informed that the book gives

> A Prospect of these near approaching Revolutions, Viz. the Revival of the *Protestant* Confession in an Eminent Kingdom, where it was totally suppressed. The last end of all *Turkish* Hostilities. The general Mortification of the Power of the *Roman Church* in all Parts of its Dominions. In Explication of the *Trumpets* and *Vials* of the *Apocalypse*, upon Principles generally acknowledged by *Protestant* Interpreters.

The book contained testimonies from a number of people, among them Simon Patrick, Thomas Burnet and Henry Plumptre, which should make it clear that the main part was written before the events of the Glorious Revolution.[4]

Patrick was a leading figure in the circle of London ministers who strongly opposed the growing influence of Rome in the reign of James II and who welcomed the Glorious Revolution; as a theologian, he was a typical representative of the Latitudinarian tendency in the Church of England.[5] It is not clear whether he himself was a millenarian. Cressener wrote that Patrick's encouragement 'was the great Motive to me to enter into the more obscure and uncertain parts of the Prophecy'[6], which at least seems to indicate that Patrick was in sympathy with millenarian studies, though his support for Cressener may have been caused as much by Cressener's uncompromising anti-Catholic stand. Thomas Burnet, master of the Charterhouse, was also a prominent Latitudinarian. He was deeply interested in scientific subjects, especially in the theories about the origin and development of the earth. In 1681 he published the first part of his *Telluris theoria sacra*; it appeared in 1684 in an English version: *Theory*—from the fourth edition (1719) onward *The Sacred Theory*—*of the Earth*. When Cressener had almost finished his book, probably in May 1688 (he had come as far as the nineteenth chapter) he received a manuscript copy of the second part of Burnet's *Theoria*, which apparently circulated among his London friends.[7] Cressener was highly pleased with the 'Learned and Ingenuous Discoveries' of his 'Honoured Friend', whom no doubt he knew since their common time at Christ's College[8]:

> I do wholly subscribe to his opinion about the necessity of the literal Acceptation of the first part of the 21st Chapter of the *Apocalypse*, concerning the Resurrection of the Saints: And from thence to acknowledge the unquestionable grounds we have for a Blessed *Millennium* here upon Earth.[9]

Their thoughts on the Millennium ran parallel, though as we shall see the centre of gravity of Cressener's work differed from that of Burnet.

Henry Plumptre probably was the Plumptre of Nottingham who was involved in a conflict, caused by James II's proceedings against the charter of Nottingham corporation.[10] If so, he certainly shared the political views of the London circle of Latitudinarian clergy; no doubt he was a close friend, as Cressener entrusted him with his private 'Apocalyptical Thoughts'.

Furthermore, William Lloyd, Bishop of St. Asaph's, was interested in Cressener's work.[11] He asked for the manuscript, which he received before June 1688, when together with six other bishops he was sent to the Tower.[12] He was a convinced millenarian; John Evelyn, who on more than one occasion discussed with Lloyd the subject of biblical prophecy, called him 'this prophetick bishop'[13]—perhaps not without a tinge of irony.[14] He propagated his millenarian views till the end of his life; there is an amusing story about a meeting between Queen Anne and Lloyd in 1712, at which the old bishop tried to convince the Queen that within four years the Church of Rome would be utterly destroyed and the Millennium would begin.[15]

The millenarianism of men such as Thomas Burnet, Lloyd and Cressener was indeed marked by a strong, sometimes even vehement anti-Catholic bias, which especially in the period between the Popish Plot and the Glorious Revolution fell in with the mood of many Anglicans who saw the Anglican establishment threatened. The combination between apocalyptical expectations and anti-Catholic fervour was combustible material, which could become dangerous when used by the opponents of James II. Though, as Margaret Jacob points out, Burnet's work as such did not justify active resistance, there were difficulties with regard to the obtaining of a publishing licence.[16] The second part of the *Theoria* was published after the Revolution, in 1689.[17] We may assume that because of similar difficulties the licensing of Cressener's *Judgments* was held up. It was not published until after the Revolution, in 1689, the same year in which the second part of Burnet's book appeared, and it contained a long dedication to the new King, in which Cressener remarked that to those who would believe his interpretation of prophecy they would be like 'a Voice from Heaven, not only for present comfort to themselves, but to call for their best assistance to Your Conduct'. William received a special place in the series of apocalyptical events: 'We have seen you at the Head of almost all the several kinds of *Peoples*, and *Nations*, and *Tongues*, that would not suffer the *dead Bodies* of *the Witnesses* to be buried. We our selves were thereupon in a manner made the First-fruits from the Dead upon their approaching *Resurrection*.'[18]

One year later, in 1690, appeared his second and last book, *A Demonstration of the First Principles of the Protestant Applications of the Apocalypse*;

like his first work published in London, though this time not printed for Richard Chiswell, as his *Judgments* had been, but (for reasons which we shall discuss below) for another London bookseller, Thomas Cockerill. The second work is an attempt to corroborate the main points of the first book by means of reasonable argumentation; almost inevitably it does not contain much new material. The contents of the book are summarized in a number of 'rules' or 'propositions', not only printed in the text but also on folding pages. In June 1691, a few months before the decease of the venerable Puritan theologian Richard Baxter, Cressener sent him a letter on the subject and the system of the book:

> Sir, this I did offer to the censure of some learned criticks before I printed it; And their encouragement as well as mine owne greater scepticalnesse in the whole processe of my endeavour under it, does make me very desirous to have your cautious examination of it.

But in fact Cressener wanted to convert Baxter, whom he knew to be more fundamentally 'scepticall' with regard to millenarian speculations, to his own views regarding the identification of Rome with Antichrist:

> I should think it is a very happy advantage to the Reformation if after your former opposition of it you should now impartially owne, that its Great Adversary is so pompously set forth to the world in this Prophecy, as the Great Antichrist.

Cressener also gave practical advice: 'To save ye trouble of turning to the quoted Rules ... bee pleased to let the Tables of ye Propositions lye open before you, As is usuall in Mathematicall proof.'[19]

The use of the latter term is indicative of Cressener's method. Joseph Mede had tried to interpret prophecy according to 'the law of synchronistical necessity', and Henry More had claimed that his method of interpretation gave as much certainty as the translation of a Latin or Greek author in accordance with 'the rules of grammar and the known interpretations of Dictionaries'.[20] For Cressener, however, this was not sufficient: 'there is still wanting a clearer Evidence.' Especially in regard of 'the Friends of the Grotian way' it was necessary to show that Cressener's interpretation (which fundamentally was in line with that of Mede and More) was 'much more certain' than that of Grotius, whom Baxter seconded.[21] Still, Cressener realized that even his method, built like that of Mede and More on the idea of a 'synchronistical' relationship between the prophecies in Daniel and the Apocalypse which made it possible to chart with more or less precision the course of history, did not guarantee 'a Mathematical Evidence about such matters'. But he tried to come as near to such evidence as was possible: the only way to make the Apocalypse appear as 'the Word of God to *us*' (i.e. as a prophecy, delivered for the instruction and comfort of the Church of his own days) was 'to prove and not to guess at the meaning of it'.[22]

This time, too, Cressener had some difficulty in having his book published, though now for different reasons. In the dedication—now to Queen Mary—he attributed the unwillingness of the publishers to a general lack of interest in millenarian studies: 'The Enquiry into these matters is so out of fashion, and lies under so general a prejudice, that I found the Press every-where affrighted from undertaking the Charge of this Publication.' Ultimately, thanks to Simon Patrick's warm recommendations he had been able to find a publisher.[23] Perhaps the publishers were also deterred by Cressener's way of writing; he himself feared 'that the dry strictness of the Reasonings in it, will turn away more from perusing it, than the strength and cautiousness of it will please'.[24]

Cressener attributed a high value to his predictions. In the Dedication he wrote: 'If they prove to be satisfactorily clear, Religion and Empire being the Subject-matter of them, they seem to be the most proper Object of the Meditation of Christian Princes.' He hoped that Her Majesty's favourable regard of his performance would procure 'the Royal Stamp' upon it and thus make it 'the Currant Study of the Age again'.[25] But this hope was not fulfilled: in the coming years, interest in millenarian speculations would be at a low ebb, and apparently Cressener did not feel stimulated to write more on the subject. With regard to millenarian publications, his pen, which had once 'run before him', was at rest for the remaining part of his life. Still, in later years, too, the study of the subject occupied him, as appears from a letter to Simon Patrick on the prophecies of Daniel, which ends on a charming note of self-knowledge: 'But when I am upon this subject, I am apt to bee too tedious for wch I beg your pardon for.'[26]

Cressener had not always been an opponent of 'the Grotian way'. In his younger years he was much impressed by Grotius' irenicism, which in the view of English millenarians was closely bound up with his non-millenarian interpretation of the Apocalypse:

> I was once very much taken with the mollifying pleas of *Grotius*, and others of the Reconciling way; and apprehended it possible for the chief Heads of the *Roman* Communion to condescend to an expedient for a general Reconciliation. But when I came to be acquainted with Mr. *Mede*'s Demonstrations, and had compared them with the monstrous evasions, and absurd strains of wit, that *Grotius* and others were fain to flye to, to turn off the force of them, I gave over all thoughts of the comprehending way.[27]

One may wonder whether the political and religious developments in England made him turn from the irenical Grotius to the militantly anti-

Catholic Mede. The personal influence of his teacher More, who was a pupil and admirer of Mede, may also have played a part. However this may be, it is clear that Mede, who had succinctly formulated his millenarian views in his *Clavis apocalyptica* (1627), became his great authority. But just as other followers of Mede did, he tried to vindicate his independent judgment by criticizing the great master on details. 'Apocalyptical thoughts' leave ample scope for a range of minor variations.

While the framework of Cressener's millenarian concept is essentially that of Mede, he was indebted to the Huguenot theologian Pierre Jurieu for the application of his scheme within the context of contemporary political developments. Jurieu, too, was a millenarian in the spirit of Mede.[28] One year after the revocation of the Edict of Nantes, in 1686 (he was then in exile in the Netherlands) he published his main exposition of the subject, *L'Accomplissement des prophéties*; it appeared in English translation in 1687.[29] When Cressener read this work, either in the French edition or in the English translation of 1687, but at any rate before he wrote his *Judgments*, he was deeply struck by Jurieu's interpretation of the two witnesses of Rev. 11. Understandably, in millenarian circles there was much speculation about the identity of the witnesses and the place and time of their death and resurrection. Mede, who identified the witnesses with the churches of the Reformation, saw their death and resurrection as a future event, 'adhuc implendum'.[30] In 1629 he wrote: 'I conceive not this *Clades [Testium]* to be such as should extinguish the persons or whole materials (as I may so speak) of the Reformed Churches, but the publick Fabrick of the Reformation ....' He was uncertain, however, with regard to the exact nature of the event: 'It would make somewhat perhaps for understanding the degree of this *Clades*, if we could certainly tell what were that πλατεία τῆς πόλεως, wherein the *Witnesses* should lie for dead; and whether those of the *nations, tongues* and *people*, which should hinder the putting of them into graves, were *friends* or *foes*. They may seem to be *friends* ....'[31]

For Jurieu, the death of the witnesses was not an object of speculation, but grim reality.[32] In France, the antichristian powers had silenced the voice of the faithful witnesses. But there was hope for the future: according to the prophecy of Rev. 11 the witnesses would rise again and stand upon their feet. Jurieu expected that the resurrection of the true church in France would take place by means of a conflict between the French king and the Pope which would shatter the power of Antichrist as embodied in Rome. In a publication of 1687, *Apologie pour l'accomplissement des prophéties*, which was not translated into English and which perhaps escaped Cressener's attention, Jurieu declared that his predictions with regard to the dates of the great events were his private opinion. This does not detract, however, from the fact that he expected a speedy revival of the true church. After some time, this would be followed by the fall of the papal power. Patience was needed: 'Il faut assigner un temps de quelque longueur pour la dernière chute du Papisme'[33], but it would certainly not be an interminable time; in this context, Professer Knetsch speaks of the 'short-windedness' of Jurieu's apocalyptical concept.[34] According to Jurieu, the destruction of Antichrist would take place in the beginning of the next century and be followed by the reign of Jesus Christ on earth.[35]

In the dedication of his *Judgments* to William III Cressener described Jurieu's interpretation of the prophecy of the two witnesses as a 'discovery', and in the preface he wrote: 'Monsieur *Jurieu* must indeed be allowed to have given the World the first Alarme of the death of the Witnesses at this present time.' At the same time, however, he noticed that in England the grounds which Jurieu gave 'had the ill fortune ... to be received but as his Conjectures'. The apparently lukewarm reception of Jurieu's work made Cressener decide 'to clear up the foundation, that he depended upon, and to add a new proof of mine'. When his *Judgments* was published (as we saw, after the Glorious Revolution) Cressener was afraid that his work would be seen as a *vaticinium ex eventu*, 'a politick conjecture from the present State of Affairs'; therefore he was at pains to procure testimonies which made it clear that his work was written at a time when there was 'the thickest cloud' over the Reformed Churches in almost all parts of Europe.[36]

The 'thickest cloud' was, of course, the actual or threatening persecution by Rome. Jurieu, a Huguenot exile in the Netherlands, wrote from the background of the dispersed Reformed church of France, whose witness in the mother country had almost totally been silenced. He was also deeply impressed by the fate of the Waldensians, driven from their valleys in Savoy; in 1686, he was asked to become their intercessor with the Dutch States General.[37] Cressener wrote from the vantage-point of the English church, still by law established, but (as many thought) threatened in its existence by the Romanizing politics of James II. It is difficult to assess to what extent these fears were realistic. On the one hand, the events of 1679 and the year after, when all England was in the grip of the threat of a 'Popish Plot', had shown how easily unfounded rumours and accusations could lead to an anti-Catholic hysteria which was out of touch with reality. On the other hand, the letters, written by James's Catholic secretary Edward Coleman in the years before 1679 were, indeed, incriminatory.[38] After his accession to the throne in 1685, it was clear to all observers that James looked forward to the triumph of

Catholicism in England, which, he hoped, would come about by means of infiltration and conversions, and after 1686 his attitude towards the Anglican church became definitely hostile; as one historian writes: 'He blundered on with the blind optimism of a man whose mind was determinedly closed to any thought of failure.'[39] The fate of the Huguenots strengthened the anti-Catholic mood in England, and the support James officially gave them was not quite unambiguous.[40] To us, it seems incredible that in the 1680s a religious landslide could have taken place in England, but we should not forget that less than half a century before, in the period of the Commonwealth, the Church of England had almost been wiped away by a landslide to the other side. Also in later seventeenth-century England the religious and political equilibrium was precarious, though perhaps less than some feared and others hoped.

The events of 1685 gave new fuel to the anti-Catholic mood, and led to a renewed emphasis on the traditional identification of the Catholic church (or the papacy) with Antichrist. On this point, Cressener was not less explicit than Jurieu, but he wanted to strengthen the equation of Rome with Antichrist by means of a coherent and consistent exegetical argumentation. In this context, the identification of the Beast, mentioned in the Book of Revelation, with the fourth Beast of Daniel 7 is pivotal. Therefore, Cressener strongly criticized Grotius's historical interpretation of the term 'the Beast'[41], which made its application to the present-day Roman church impossible. According to Cressener, 'the Beast, and the false Prophet are the chief Ruling Power of the present Church of Rome', and '*Babylon* signifies the City of *Rome* in a state of Ecclesiastical Domination'.[42] In the Dedication of his *Demonstration* to Queen Mary, he complained about the 'General Unconcern' with regard to this point, which he saw as 'the effect of the Popish Marriages in the Three Last Reigns'.

> Nothing was more the Doctrine of our Church to the end of the Reign of King *James* the First, than the Charge of *Babylon*, and Antichrist, upon the *Roman* Church; but it seemed something too rude a Charge, both to Church and Court, when the Queen came to be concerned in it ....[43]

In his defence of the antiquity of his doctrine over against the modern interpretation, given by Grotius and his followers, he appealed to Archbishop James Ussher, who had given a long list of authorities in support of his thesis that Babylon signified Rome under the Pope and that the Papacy may be said to be 'the *Beast* that *was*, and *is not*, and yet *is*'.[44] And by means of rather tortuous reasoning he even tried to show that the fifteen arguments, used by Bellarmine to prove that the Church of Rome was the true church in fact proved that is was Babylon.[45]

When Cressener wrote his *Judgments*, the 'Witnesses' were still in sack-cloth, the 'Beast' still triumphant. According to Cressener, one of the main sins of the Roman church was 'the forcing Men against their Consciences to reverence the Roman Authority in Points of Faith and Worship for the only Rule and Standard of Christian Truth'. The sin of the heathen emperors was their tyranny against the church; the Christian emperors became spiritual dictators to the consciences of men; now the degenerate church wants to enforce all to 'an Uniformity in the Roman Worship'. This is the great provocation, which calls for God's judgments.[46] These judgments will begin within a short time. The witnesses are dead, but thanks to their friends they are not buried; no doubt, Cressener thinks here of the reception the exiled Huguenots had found in other Protestant countries. The time of their resurrection is near: 'the Recovery of the True Church' will take place in 1689, or ultimately in 1690.[47]

Cressener acknowledged that he derived his interpretation of the prophecy of the two witnesses from Jurieu:

> however different I am from *Monsieur Jurieu* in almost every thing else, yet I was extreamly surprised with the light that he has given to the Prophecy about the Death of the Two Witnesses from the present face of the Protestant Churches all over *Europe*.[48]

Even the probable dates he gives for their resurrection are the same as those we find in Jurieu's works.[49] Just as it is the case with Jurieu, his expectations, seemingly based on nothing but his interpretation of biblical prophecy, are in fact to a large degree determined by the political situation. In 1687, change was already in the air. When, only one year later, the Glorious Revolution took place, Cressener saw the events in England as a sign that the Protestant cause would also prevail in those countries where the witness of the Reformed Church had recently been silenced. The passage in the Dedication on the death and the resurrection of the witnesses[50] of course refers primarily to France, where only recently the witnesses had been killed.

Initially, he identified the killing of the witnesses with the Revocation. Contrary to Jurieu, whose interpretation of ἐπὶ τῆς πλατείας he rejected, Cressener asserted that the resurrection of the witnesses could take place outside France. But that was only a theoretical difference: '...it is very difficult to imagine, where this can happen, but in the Kingdom of *France*.' For various reasons, other countries did not qualify for the great event, but 'the Gallican Church, in the present state of it, seems to be already on the fair way to a thorough Reformation'.[51] Possibly Cressener had in mind the *Four Gallican Articles* of 1682, which had denied the dominion of the Pope over things temporal.[52] In Huguenot circles, there was some sympathy for the Gallican theory—Jurieu saw the Huguenots as consistent Gallicans—, but it was mixed with deep disappointment at the fact that it was the Gallican church itself which persecuted the Huguenots.[53] For Anglicans it was still more easy to see a parallel between their own church and the Gallican church; only some decades later the broadminded Archbishop Wake suggested that a new reformation might ensue from a union between the Anglican and the Gallican church.[54] Cressener was very sanguine. Now was the time when the fourth vial (Rev. 16.8, 9) was to be poured out over the sun, which in its turn would scorch men with heat. In Cressener's scheme, the sun stood for the Sun-King, Louis XIV, whose quarrels and wars would vex and humiliate 'the Papal and Imperial Interest'.[55] Here, knowledge of contemporary political events and ignorance with regard to their background are mixed in a curious way: at that time, Protestantism had more to fear from a fanatical King than from a moderate Pope. But even if he had known this, it probably would not have changed his views. In the apocalyptic times in which he lived anything was possible; to Plumptre he wrote: 'Upon this occasion I cannot but mention to you, that the King of *France* either has not long to live, or must be really made *The Most Christian King* within these few Years.'[56]

The pouring out of the last vials would mean the utter destruction of the Beast and thus usher in a new era, the time of the Millennium. Just when he started the nineteenth chapter of his work, which would deal with the Millennium, he received, as we saw, a manuscript copy of the second part of Thomas Burnet's *Theoria*. The works of Cressener and Burnet had a different scope: while Cressener was mainly interested in the relation between prophecy and history, Burnet was primarily interested in the relation between prophecy and geology. His interest in the future fate of the earth coloured Burnet's millenarian views, which, in their turn, influenced those of Cressener, in particular with regard to the theory of a conflagration which would change the face of the earth. We find the connection between conflagration and Millennium already with Mede, who based it on 2 Peter 3: 'Christ our Lord shall come, when the *Beatum Millennium* is to begin ... in flaming fire; by the Divine and miraculous efficacy whereof the *World* that now is shall be refined, and delivered from the bondage of corruption ....'[57] More saw the idea of a conflagration confirmed by 'the Opinion ... of ancient Heathens and Jews'.[58] Burnet's point of departure in his description of the conflagration was 'the doctrine of the Stoicks'; Scripture (especially, of course, 2 Peter 3) was for him 'a second witness'.[59] Cressener wrestled with the subject. With Burnet, he believed that the great judgments of God upon the world are ordinarily executed by the concurrence of the natural disposition of things.[60] Now, the consummation of God's judgments on the Church of Rome would be brought about by the pouring out of the last three vials and the sounding of the last trumpet, which would inaugurate 'the Last Ruine of *Babylon* and the Beast'[61], or—in terms of the doctrine of a conflagration—'the burning of the Seat of Antichrist'. The progress of the conflagration would be gradual and slow; so much so that there would be room for a pure state of the Christian Church 'betwixt the ruine of the Beast and the last end of the Conflagration'. The Christian Church would not only continue but increase after the conflagration of the Roman territories. The partial conflagration of the world (which might lead to a change for the better of the climate in other parts of the world) would be the means for the conversion of Jews and heathen in all parts of the world, 'the Conversions [*sic*] of the Kingdoms of this present World, into the Universal Kingdom of the Lord and of his Christ. And from that time may Christ be said to begin to Reign with his Father for ever, tho the *Millennium* will be his more peculiar share of that Reign'. The last sentence is unclear: it reflects an uncertainty in Cressener's thinking with regard to the place of the Millennium in the context of the apocalyptical scheme—either within the time of the conflagration, 'in those parts of the world which were yet untouched and entire', or after the conflagration, when the New Jerusalem would descend form heaven.[62]

Cressener's expectations seemed to find a partial fulfilment through and after the Glorious Revolution. A greater revolution in the state of affairs of the world was still to come, but—as Cressener wrote in his dedication to William—'that which makes the fairest promise of the near approach of this time, is Your Majesty's unexpected success in these Nations, which has given a perfect new turn to all the affairs of Europe .... It is manifest, That in all appearence the next causes are now in Action.' For the adversaries—Cressener thought here first of all of the persecutors of the Huguenots in France—no other way would be open but to grant freedom of religion; this would lead to a conversion of the whole Kingdom of France without any violent methods, and to a general mortification of the Roman church in all parts of its dominion, 'as would make it sink by degrees into nothing'.[63] But for the Reformed churches a new future would dawn; they are 'but scattered Altars, and particular Synagogues, till they come all to be united into one Universal Temple at the end of the Consecration of the Christian Church, that is, at the end of the Vials and of all the Enemies of Christ'.[64]

Cressener wrote all this before or in March 1689. In the summer of the same year, not the conversion of France, but the 'glorieuse rentrée' of the Waldensians into the valleys of Piedmont took place; an event which created a deep impression in England. John Evelyn mentions a conversation between a number of leading clergymen in the London residence of Bishop Lloyd. All of them were 'not a little surpriz'd at what had happened in *Savoy*'; even, it seems, Lloyd himself, though he had already for a long time affirmed that the Waldensians were 'the 2 Witnesses spoken of in the Revelation who should be Kild, and brought to life againe'.[65] Cressener tried to fit the 'glorieuse rentrée' into his chronology of the death and resurrection of the witnesses. If their death did not take place at the time of the Revocation itself, but just a bit later, at the time of 'the last Considerable Abjurations of the new Converts', then the resurrection of the witnesses three days [= years] after their death 'must fall just about the time that the *Vaudois* did Revive'. He added—we find it in the dedication of his second book, *Demonstration*, to Queen Anne—:

> The *Proper* Kingdom of *France* did indeed seem from the present Posture of Affairs, to be the most likely to be the first Scene of this Revival. But it has been shewn, that there is nothing in the Prophecy that does fix the first beginning of it there; And that the Persecution in *France*, and *Savoy*, being executed by the same Instruments, may very well pass for one and the same thing.

The fact that the Turkish power—the second woe of the Apocalypse—seemed to come to an end strengthened his conviction. All evidence pointed the same way.[66] Of course, like so many millenarian schemes, his scheme, too, was adaptable to circumstances. But his belief in the essential value of his 'apocalyptical thoughts' remained unshaken: 'The Foundation of a Building may be setled upon a Rock, though some parts of the Superstructure should fall for want of immediate and close coherence of it.'[67]

Does Cressener's further silence on the subject mean that he was a disappointed man? In his lifetime, William and Mary both died. The tide did not turn in France, and though in England the future of Protestantism was now safe, in large parts of Europe the power of Rome was as strong as ever. And while he was not in all respects a man of the past—I think here in particular of his sympathy for the theories of Thomas Burnet, which with regard to the dramatic aspects of the apocalyptical events contained a demythologizing element—in general his approach was, as he knew himself, indeed out of fashion. But in his aversion from Rome and his hope for a revival of Protestantism he reflects something of the fears and hopes of at least a number of contemporary Anglicans in the time of the Glorious Revolution. Perhaps this event, through which he believed his predictions would be confirmed and his expectations would be fulfilled, was also his glorious moment, his finest hour.

[1] Cf. his letter to Plumptre of 28 February 1688 (O.S. 1687), in which he wrote that he agreed with Jurieu that a resurrection of the 'Reformed Religion' in France in 1689 was highly probable. The letters of Plumptre are printed in D. Cressener, *The Judgments of God upon the Roman-Catholick Church*, London, 1689, sigs. Tt1-3.

[2] Dru[e] Cressener, son of Thomas, was baptized on 13 January 1641/2; see Bury St. Edmunds, St. James Church Parish Registers, Baptisms 1558-1800 (with thanks to Suffolk Record Office, Bury St. Edmunds). The list of incumbents in Soham Parish Church mentions him as Drugo Cressner. For his life, see *DNB* s.v. (gives a wrong birthdate); J. Venn and J.A. Venn, *Alumni Cantabrigienses*, vol. I, Cambridge, 1922, s.v.

[3] For More's millenarianism, see J. van den Berg, 'Continuity within a Changing Context: Henry More's Millenarianism, Seen against the Background of the Millenarian Concepts of Joseph Mede', *Pietismus und Neuzeit*, 14 (1988), pp. 185-202.

[4] Patrick, Burnet and Plumptre declared in March 1689 (N.S.) that they had read the chapters 1-19 'near a year ago'. Thomas Paget and Samuel Freeman wrote that these chapters were in their hands 'when the Bishops were sent to the *Tower* [June, 1688], and then offered [apparently for approbation] to Lambeth': *Judgments*, sigs. A4r-v.

[5] For his theological position, see J. van den Berg, 'Between Platonism and Enlightenment: Simon Patrick (1625-1707) and his Place in the Latitudinarian Movement', *Nederlands archief voor kerkgeschiedenis*, 68 (1988), pp. 164-79.

[6] Cressener to Plumptre, 22 November 1687, *Judgments*, sig. Tt2v.

[7] See M.C. Jacob and W.A. Lockwood, 'Political Millenarianism and Burnet's *Sacred Theory*', *Science Studies*, 2 (1972), p. 270.

[8] Referring to this early relationship Margaret C. Jacob even suggests that Cressener may have been one of the Anglican sources of Burnet's millenarianism: *The Newtonians and the English Revolution 1689-1720*, Ithaca (N.Y.), 1976, p. 108. Anyhow, both Burnet and Cressener were pupils of Henry More. As appears from his testimony, Burnet had read Cressener's manuscript in the early spring of 1688; by then his *Theoria sacra* had already appeared. Neither there, nor in the millenarian expositions in his *De statu mortuorum et resurgentium tractatus* (London, 1727), does Burnet directly refer to contemporary authors; besides, his expositions have not, as those of Cressener have, an explicit historical scope. In the aftermath of the Glorious Revolution, however, his eschatological views were influenced by the great events of those days: while in 1727 he wrote that the resurrection of the witnesses had not yet taken place, in 1691 he wrote in a letter to John Patrick: '... the resurrection of yᵉ Witnesses goes on very well in Savoy and Dauphiné'; Burnet to J. Patrick, prebendary of Peterborough, Bodleian Library, Oxford, MS Tanner 26, f. 44. The letter can be dated from a P.S. in which the surrender of Dublin to the Duke of Ormonde is mentioned.

[9] *Judgments*, p. 288.

[10] *DNB*, s.v. Henry Plumptre (the son), president of the Royal College of Physicians.

[11] For Lloyd, see A. Tindal Hart, *William Lloyd 1627-1717*, London, 1952.

[12] *Judgments*, sig. [b4v].

[13] E.S. de Beer (ed.), *The Diary of John Evelyn*, vol. V, Oxford, 1955, p. 25.

[14] Cf. Evelyn, *Diary*, vol. V, p. 20, on Lloyd's 'long since opinions concerning great Revolutions to be at hand for the good of the Christian orthodox Church', or p. 322, on Lloyd's 'old discourse' concerning the destruction of Antichrist etc.

[15] Note of Lord Dartmouth (who was present at the meeting) to Gilbert Burnet's *History of my Own Time*, 2nd ed., I, Oxford, 1723, pp. 327f.; cf. Tindal Hart, *William Lloyd*, pp. 177f.; Jacob, *Newtonians*, p. 127.

[16] Jacob, *Newtonians*, pp. 118f., 112.

[17] Or perhaps already in December 1688: Jacob and Lockwood, 'Political Millenarianism', p. 270, note 11.

[18] *Judgments*, sig. A[2r-v].

[19] Cressener to Baxter, 2 June 1691, Dr. Williams's Library, London, Baxter Correspondence III, f. 15 (= item 135). For Baxter and Cressener, see also W.M. Lamont, *Richard Baxter and the Millennium*, London, 1979, pp. 59-62, and for Baxter's 'former opposition', Van den Berg, 'Continuity', pp. 199f.

[20] Van den Berg, 'Continuity', pp. 189, 193.

[21] *Demonstration*, pp. xxiiif.

[22] *Judgments*, sig. b2r-v.

[23] *Demonstration*, sig. a1r.

[24] *Demonstration*, p. i.

[25] *Demonstration*, sig. a1v

[26] Cressener to Bishop Patrick, 15 September 1694, Bodleian Library, MS Tanner 25, f. 216.

[27] *Demonstration*, p. xiii.

[28] For Mede's influence on Jurieu, see F.R.J. Knetsch, *Pierre Jurieu, theoloog en politicus der refuge*, Kampen, 1967, p. 206.

[29] *The Accomplishment of the Scripture Prophecies ... Faithfully Englished from the New French Edition ... Enlarged with the Applications of Daniel, and the Revelation*, London, 1687.

[30] 'De occisione testium', *The Works of ... Joseph Mede*, London, 1677, p. [924].

[31] Mede to William Twisse, 11 November 1629, *Works*, p. 761.

[32] For this and what follows, see Knetsch, *Jurieu*, chap. 14, and 'Pierre Jurieu (1637-1713) and his Comment on the Glorious Revolution' in this volume.

[33] *L'Accomplissement des prophéties ou la délivrance prochaine de l'Église*, Rotterdam, 1686, p. 149 (*in margine*).

[34] Knetsch, *Jurieu*, p. 209.

[35] Cf. the sub-title of *L'Accomplissement*: 'Ouvrage dans lequel il est prouvé, que le Papisme est l'Empire Antichrétien; que cet Empire n'est pas éloigné de sa ruïne; que la persecution presente peut finir dans trois ans et demi. Après quoi commencera la destruction de l'Antichrist, laquelle s'achevera dans le commencement du Siecle prochain: Et enfin le regne de Jesus-Christ viendra sur la terre.'

[36] *Judgments*, Dedication and Preface, sigs. A[1]v, b4r-4.

[37] J.F. Martinet, *Kerkelyke geschiedenis der Waldenzen*, 2nd ed., Amsterdam, 1775, p. 108.

[38] J. Kenyon, *The Popish Plot*, London, 1972, *index*; R.W. Jones, *The Revolution of 1688 in England*, London, 1984, p. 78; J. Miller, *Popery and Politics in England 1660-1688*, Cambridge, 1973, pp. 137ff.

[39] Miller, *Popery*, p. 202.

[40] Jones, *Revolution*, pp. 112f.

[41] Grotius saw 'Bestia quarta terribilis atque mirabilis' of Dan. 7.7 as the Macedonian dynasties which ruled over Syria and Egypt; *Annotata ad Vetus Testamentum*, II, Lutetiae Parisiorum, 1644, p. 436; cf. p. 414 (on Dan. 2.40).

[42] *Judgments*, 'Suppositions for the Second Part', nos. 1 and 5 (on folding page, unpaginated).

[43] *Demonstration*, sig. a1v.

[44] *Demonstration*, p. iv; 'The Consent of the Ancients Concerning the Fourth Beast in the Revelations', London, 1690 (printed as an appendix to *Dem.*), p. 35. See N. Bernard (ed.), *The Judgments of the Late Arch-Bishop of Armagh, and Primate of Ireland, of Babylon (Rev. 18.4) Being the Present See of Rome*, London, 1659, esp. pp. 126f.

[45] *Demonstration*, p. 8; see R. Bellarminus, *Disputationes de controversiis Christianae fidei adversus huius temporis haereticos*, ed. 3a, I, Ingolstadii, 1590, Lib. IV 'De notis ecclesiae', cap. 3-18 (c. 1299-1363).

[46] *Judgments*, pp. 55-65.

[47] *Judgments*, pp. 96-98.

[48] *Judgments*, p. 82.

[49] Knetsch, *Jurieu*, esp. p. 207f.

[50] See above, p. 136.

[51] *Judgments*, p. 140.

[52] For 'la Déclaration' or 'les Quatres Articles de 1682', see *Dictionnaire de théologie catholique*, IV, Paris, 1924, pp. 185-205.

[53] Knetsch, *Jurieu*, p. 104.

[54] N. Sykes, *William Wake, Archbishop of Canterbury 1657-1737*, I, Cambridge, 1957, p. 260.

[55] The attitude of Innocent XI with regard to the Glorious Revolution was initially passive, though it seems that at a later stage he regretted not having come to the assistance of James II; J. Orcibal, *Louis XIV contre Innocent XI*, Paris, 1949, p. 75, n. 350; for James II and the Pope, see Miller, *Popery*, pp. 229-38.

[56] Cressener to Henry Plumptre, 28 February 1687/8, *Judgments*, sig. [Tt4r].

[57] Mede, *Works*, p. 618.

[58] H. More, *Theological Works*, London, 1708, p. 28.

[59] Thomas Burnet, *The Theory of the Earth*, Book II (1691), new. ed. under the title *The Sacred Theory of the Earth*, London/Fontwell, 1965, p. 251.

[60] *Judgments*, p. 292.

[61] *Judgments*, p. 215.

[62] *Judgments*, pp. 290-95.

[63] *Judgments*, sigs. [A1v, A3r].

[64] *Judgments*, p. 187.

[65] Evelyn, *Diary*, V, p. 25 (18 June 1690).

[66] *Judgments*, pp. 110ff.

[67] *Demonstration*, sigs. A3v, 4r.

PIERRE JURIEU AND THE GLORIOUS REVOLUTION ACCORDING TO HIS 'LETTRES PASTORALES'

F.R.J. Knetsch

Introduction

When trying to understand the period of the Glorious Revolution and the persons who played roles in it or who attempted to explain it to their contemporaries, the title of Paul Hazard's famous study *La Crise de la conscience européenne*, which was published more than fifty years ago, inevitably comes into our minds. Things were changing rather quickly in those days, but to the protagonists it was not quite clear in which direction. Authors were constantly commenting on the events of their time and the new ideas which were propagated and they did so in small books and pamphlets. 'Our time doesn't like big books', Pierre Jurieu himself stated at the beginning of a rather voluminous one;[1] generally he was a skilled pamphleteer who could also handle a rather new kind of publication, the periodical. Booksellers called his *Lettres pastorales* 'la Gazette ecclésiastique'; later on they were nicknamed by his opponents 'la Gazette prophétique'.[2] These examples make us aware of the critical tensions to which that period was subjected. A constantly flowing stream of publications reflected the differences in outlook which prevailed among the opinion makers of that time.

A rather important antithesis was that between rationalism and fideism. The question was what to take as the starting-point of thinking (in the widest sense of explaining the world): in the intellect, which has to postulate a supreme intellect governing the universe by eternal and unchangeable laws, or in the will, which postulates a supreme will ruling the world according to its inscrutable decisions, of which we find some traces, some 'vestigia' in revelation and history. It may be clear that the intellectualist line of thinking is much more eager to reduce the number of miracles than is the voluntarist one, although at the time nobody totally denied the possibility of miracles. They might occur and if so, then you had to interpret and to believe them. My point is that Pierre Jurieu, trained in the French Calvinist 'Académies', had started his career as an intellectualist of the scholastic type and had only gradually and partially developed a voluntaristic view. This evolution is one of the main sources of the opposition he was confronted with, especially from his former friend Pierre Bayle.

The third remark I want to make is that the opposition between Bayle and Jurieu was clearly aggravated by the division between 'Prinsgezinden' and 'Staatsgezinden'—'Orangists' and 'Republicans'— which dominated the political climate in the Dutch Republic. The attitude of both parties was based on the issue whether the sovereignty of the Dutch Republic was vested in the States of the separate provinces ('*Staatsgezind*') or in the 'the Prince', the Stadholder. Stadholder originally meant deputy of the monarch, but since the Revolt the unity of the Low Countries, established by the Burgundian-Habsburg aspirations but by then reduced to the territory of the northern provinces, was embodied in him. So the 'Stadholder' was not simply the highest officer in the service of the States, as the Republicans wanted to interpret his position, his function had a fuller meaning, something extra which, moreover, appealed to the politically unemancipated common people. At the time Bayle and Jurieu were nominated in Rotterdam as professors of the recently established 'Illustre School', a rather small local College, the city fathers were 'Staatsgezind'. Bayle soon became a close friend of Adriaan Paets, the most prominent of them, whereas Jurieu kept a certain distance. From the time of his grand-uncle André Rivet and of his aunt Marie du Moulin onward Jurieu's family had had connections with the court of the stadholders, and he himself continued this line.[3]

This brings me to my fourth and last preliminary remark. During periods of strong tensions, people in the seventeenth century still used to stick to family ties more than to any other loyalty. The political parties or factions were to a certain degree knit together by family relations and Pierre Jurieu's family was no exception to this rule. On the contrary, the subsequent versions of Jurieu's will show how strongly he was attached to the Du Moulin 'clan' to the end of his life. It is time now for a glance at some of its most important data.

Life of Pierre Jurieu

Pierre Jurieu was born in 1637 as the last of five children of Daniel Jurieu, reformed minister of Mer (now Department Loir-et-Cher), and his wife Esther du Moulin, a daughter of the famous French theologian Pierre du Moulin. She died eleven months afterwards in the house of her brother Cyrus du Moulin. Thirty years later, Jurieu married the elder daughter of this uncle, Hélène; her sister Suzanne married Jacques Basnage, Bayle's friend, and their only brother Pierre became an officer in the army of the Republic and possibly a secretary to the Stadholder. According to a letter of Bayle[4] he died in Holland after being appointed governor of Surinam. We should keep these facts in mind in order to understand Jurieu's outlook and behaviour: as a member of a family to which belonged a number of important persons.

At the time Jurieu was a student, his grandfather, a professor of theology in Sedan, was still alive. Having started his career in England, he afterwards became a professor at Leiden[5] and later a reformed minister at Charenton/Paris. If Louis XIII had not prevented the French delegation from attending the Synod of Dordrecht (1618-19), Pierre du Moulin would have been a member of the synod. He later became one of the most ardent propagandists of the 'canons' of this synod in France. He finished his career as a professor at Sedan and as a tenacious opponent of Moïse Amyraut of Saumur.[6]

Two of Pierre du Moulin's sons emigrated to England; his namesake became a canon of Canterbury, Louis on the contrary a non-conformist; it is significant that Jurieu was to defend the honour of the family against the latter, whereas he highly exalted the learning and character of the former.[7] He knew them both very well, because he finished his studies by travelling to England. This must have taken place during the Restoration; the notice that he had been ordained by an English bishop has to be taken very seriously, although it has not yet been verified.[8] Returning from his British tour he joined his father in the ministry of Mer to which he was ordained according to the French reformed, i.e. Presbyterian rules. During his stay at Mer he received a call from the Rotterdam Walloon community, to become its pastor. After a long time he declined the invitation, without any explanation. It is, however, not very difficult to find the reasons for his refusal. His parish was in danger of becoming one of the victims of an anti-Huguenot action as it was forced to demonstrate the 'right of ancient possession' of its church. Not being able to do so, the reformed inhabitants of Mer were ordered to demolish the building and to rebuild it outside the city centre.[9] This must have been a very frustrating experience. During the judicial actions which preceded these unhappy events Pierre Jurieu married his cousin and with her, together with her father, mother and sister he went to live in the vicarage of Mer in 1667. As a result Jurieu was not able to leave his parish until 1672. That year he went to Vitry-le-François and two years later he was nominated as a professor of the Protestant Academy of Sedan.

Here he deployed a remarkable skill in writing books on the Catholic-Protestant controversy, defending the Reformed Church against its opponents. It is also noteworthy that he was the most ardent and in the end successful supporter of the nomination of Pierre Bayle, at that time still a young man, as professor of philosophy. The lengthy letters written by the latter to his family provide us with many details about this period, during which Jurieu acted as the elder friend and patron of Bayle.[10] In 1681 the French government closed down the Academy, whereupon Bayle departed to look for a new job. Jurieu stayed, as he was also a minister of the local Reformed church. But being warned that the police suspected him of having written the small but very well composed booklet *La Politique du clergé de France*[11], he took refuge in the Netherlands and settled in The Hague. It was there that he was informed by a deputation from Rotterdam about his nomination as a professor and his call as second minister of the Walloon church. He accepted both nominations and moved to the Hoogstraat in Rotterdam where he stayed for the rest of his life. Many indications show that his life in Rotterdam was a continuation of what had started in Sedan. He now published the books he had written there and added others on the same topics, and he acted as the head of the family as he had done in Sedan. But there were two striking differences: the authorities were not hostile as the French had been, and Bayle did not visit him as frequently as he had done in Sedan. This does not mean that they were enemies yet; they just drifted away from each other. On the other hand they had the same concern, because they both knew for sure that the revocation of the Edict of Nantes was imminent and therefore they did their utmost to avert what seemed inevitable.[12] In the end their different reactions to the revocation were the cause of their final rupture. From 1685 onwards Bayle followed the line of advocating submisson to the authorities and at the same time preaching mutual tolerance, whereas Jurieu found comfort in scriptural prophecies and in developing a theory of popular sovereignty combined with the right of resistance. These activities are the main subject of this article, but before turning to them we must finish this outline of his life.

The Glorious Revolution was seen as a blessing by Jurieu but as a disaster by Bayle. Anonymously Bayle wrote against it, undetected by Jurieu until 1690. Unceasing and open hostility then broke out between the two men until the death of Bayle in 1706. In the meantime Jurieu increasingly identified himself with the English cause. Together with the wine merchant Etienne Caillaud, he even organized an intelligence service which transmitted information from French harbours to the English Secretary of State. His own activities in this field virtually ended with the conclusion of the Peace of Rijswijk (1697); later, during the War of the Spanish Succession he left this task to younger people.[13] During the War of the League of Augsburg—which by its mere duration was a threat to his expectations—Jurieu could not always bear the tensions. He got involved in a series of useless doctrinal polemics, especially with

the Utrecht minister Elie Saurin.[14] After the war and in spite of its un-
favourable conclusion for him and the other Huguenots—of which he
published a rather detailed *Relation*[15]—he became a new man. Besides
the aforementioned *Relation* he wrote a second *Relation*, this time on the
cruelty used against the Protestants on the French galleys,[16] and also
two books in connection with the Quietist controversy, a corrected version of thirty of the old Genevan metrical psalms and an edition of his
lectures on the Old Testament and history of religion. On 20 November
1703 he wrote a letter to the Grand Pensionary Heinsius and in 1705 a
pamphlet, both in favour of the Camisards, the revolting Calvinists of
the Cevennes. His last publication, in 1706, was an incisive, almost brilliant book against his worst enemy, 'le philosophe de Rotterdam'.[17]
Seven years later he died, commemorated by the Walloon synod of the
Netherlands with the highest praise.

Ideas

In his earlier works, Jurieu maintains the orthodox Reformed doctrine against such Catholic opponents as Antoine Arnauld, Jacques-Bé-
nigne Bossuet, Louis Maimbourg and David-Augustin Brueys. The only
notable difference from the publications of the majority of his colleges
is, apart from the vivacity of his style, his defence of private baptism. In
his writings dating from after the revocation there are more differences
to be noted. His explication of the Revelation of St. John is of course not
unique, but Dutch theologians in particular did not like its application
to contemporary events. In my opinion it was this kind of explanation
which brought about another change in his theological views: he turned
away from the usual intellectualism of seventeenth-century reformed
scholasticism to a more voluntaristic view of God and man. He developed a more vivid and flexible concept of God than the Infinitely Perfect Being who was at the basis of the reasonings he had employed in his
Sedanese lectures. A God whose hand can be seen in the events of the
time is more 'actus purus' than was usually admitted. On the other
hand, man who is chosen by this God to be his instrument, is not a
thinking but an active being, who is able to say 'je croy parce que je
veux', I believe because I will, and not I think, because the Holy Ghost
has inspired in me correct ideas about the Eternal Being. Unfortunately
Jurieu did not succeed very well in elaborating this view. He simply did
not have enough time and rest to do so. And so his remarkable attempts
to find another concept of God and the world had no result and did not
influence his students or others. In his later struggle with Bayle he even
returned to his earlier opinions.

In his ecclesiology Jurieu also developed ideas which differed from those commonly held by the reformed. In his refutation of the congregationalist views of Louis du Moulin he had already opted for a federalist concept of Christianity, which in his opinion was built up from the basic congregations to larger territorial entities. Thus national churches could assemble in councils but never be governed by one priest, because no single priest could know a 'national' flock. As the pope is an impertinent usurper, kings as first members of their churches are obliged to defend them against the unjust pretentions of Rome. Here we see the Erastian vein in his thought; he strongly advocates the Establishment against Catholicism and Independentism alike. That he could do so as a Frenchman was for two reasons. Firstly, the Edict of Nantes could be interpreted as the official recognition of the Reformed Church of France, that is to say as a secondary established church. But secondly, there was a deeper and more hidden reason for his defence of the Establishment. He most ardently wished that the Gallican Church would shake off popish tyranny and become the French counterpart of the English Church. His line of defence against the attacks of Bossuet was to ask constantly why this bishop, who minimized the differences between Catholicism and Protestantism, nevertheless refused to take a single step in the Protestant direction by drawing the consequences from his own Gallican conviction. We, the French Reformed, are the only true and consistent Gallicans, Jurieu repeatedly stated.[18]

But the French Reformed had (and still have) a presbyterian church-government, which has never been adopted by any adherent of the idea of a Gallican church. How to overcome this difference? Here we meet with one of the most important questions in connection with our subject, Jurieu's defence of the Glorious Revolution. I have mentioned that Jurieu builds up the organisation of the church from its base, the separate congregations. It is here that people meet publicly, and it is to this basis that God has given sovereignty. 'The movement of power is circular', he says.[19] Sovereignty does not descend from God to the pope, from him to the emperor and so right down to the lowest level; on the contrary: it descends from God to the people, who are fully entitled to bestow it on whom they please, stipulating the conditions and restrictions they want. So the people have the right to delegate the power of the keys to a body of venerable men, the consistory (Reformed church-council), or to one pious person, the (Anglican) bishop. Aristocracy and monarchy are both recognized forms of government according to the generally accepted theory of Aristotle, so why not apply it to the church?

Perhaps it would be better to say: to the churches, because Jurieu also tries to explain the pluriformity of the church. The consistories or bishops are fully entitled to meet in provincial, national, international or even world councils in order to settle doctrinal differences. But in case of irrevocable dissent, as for instance between Calvinists and rigid Lutherans (mark the use of the adjective!), both parties can go their own way and have their separate religious meetings. In this sinful world, it is inevitable to have churches of a higher and a lower grade of purity, but how can simple laymen know which one is best? The only responsible persons are the leaders of schisms. At the Last Judgement they will have to answer for having jeopardized the unity of the Church, but simple followers then will be considered as being innocent.

After the revocation of the Edict of Nantes Jurieu extended these theories as widely as possible—even Socinianism and Islam he considered as (dead) branches of the Church—in order to brand persecution as totally unjust and even anti-Christian. He explains that the Roman Catholic church is a real member of the whole church because it sticks to the fundamental truths of Christianity. Unfortunately it is virtually impossible to find the way to salvation in that church because it has 'polluted' the truth by dangerous additions such as transsubstantiation and the adoration of saints. Perhaps only young children who have died soon after baptism, or totally ignorant heathens recently converted by misionaries and unable to read the Scriptures, will be saved. But those who are better instructed, among them especially former Protestants, will find out that the additions are mortally poisonous. This very interesting 'True System of the Church'[20] has to be kept in mind as the background of the *Lettres pastorales*.

Yet there is another idea which he gradually worked out: that of popular sovereignty and its corrolary, the right of resistance. During his discussions with Catholic opponents, especially the former Jesuit Louis Maimbourg, he was forced to defend the conduct of the Huguenots during the sixteenth century, and also their theories, notably that of the Monarchomachs, among them George Buchanan. Whereas he condemned the authors, he accepted the nucleus of their thought, and in this way he ended up as an adherent to the doctrine of the original governmental contract and of the right of resistance against violations of the contract by the authorities. 'Salus populi suprema lex esto' had become one of the fundamental principles of his political theory before the revocation. I want to stress this point because some scholars tend to underline Jurieu's opportunism and versatility particularly in his political doctrines.[21] Having shown what his difficulties were I hope to have made it clear that he did overcome them without sacrificing the consistency of his theoretical basis.

Revocation

The Edict of Fontainebleau of 22 October 1685, which was the formal revocation of the Edict of Nantes, did not find Jurieu unprepared. Nevertheless the uncompromising harshness of the revocation shocked him. The arrival of so many refugees in the Netherlands, telling their stories, was a harrowing experience, especially to those who had arrived earlier under much better conditions, as Jurieu himself who had been able to save his fortune.[22] His immediate reaction was threefold: he assisted as many refugees as possible, especially in finding jobs, he wrote accounts of and protests against the cruelties to which his fellow-members of the Reformed church had been exposed and he studied the biblical prophecies in order to find indications pointing towards a better future. His guide was Joseph Mede's *Clavis apocalyptica*. In March 1686 his own version, *L'Accomplissement des prophéties*, was published, and soon it was more widely distributed than the almanacs of the year, as he himself reported a few years later in his *Lettres pastorales*.[23] As he also summarized his views in this periodical, we can restrict the account of the book here to one point on which Joseph Mede had not decided: the death and resurrection of the two witnesses in Revelation 11:1-13.

In order to understand why Jurieu concentrated on this detail, we have to realize that the most disheartening of the anti-Huguenot actions in France had been what Jurieu called 'the dragoons' mission', the conversion of Protestants by means of billeting on their houses, which had proved to be very effective. After the employment of this kind of missionary activities, virtually no sign of Protestant life was left. The witnesses had been killed. But they had not yet been buried. They were still visible as—partly very uneasy—'Nouveaux Convertis' or 'Nouvelles Catholiques' (N.C.). And now the prophetic indication that the two witnesses (two because of their relatively small number) would be resurrected after three and a half days, was the clue to Jurieu's explanation and to his subsequent action.

In his opinion, as in Joseph Mede's, prophetic days are the equivalent of normal years. The witnesses represented the protest against the kingdom of Antichrist, the pope, as it had been proclaimed by medieval sects, most numerous in France, and afterwards by the Reformation. This protest had never been silenced, and one could only guess the exact time this suffocation had taken place, at the start of the 'dragonnades', at the revocation as a legislative act or at the expulsion of the Waldensians from their valleys by the Duke of Savoy. Anyway, the margin left by this uncertainty was no more than half a year, so within a very near future the 'resurrection of the two witnesses' could be expected. In Jurieu's opinion this resurrection would be some kind of restoration of

Protestantism in France. It has to be noted here that the whole picture is extremely Francocentric. France is the oldest daughter of the church, and so it is the country where all important events will happen. What also has to be noted is the fact that at that time on the one hand many people were not uncritical as to such explanations and that Calvinism had a strong anti-apocalyptical tradition, but that on the other side there certainly was a tendency to give such prophecies at least the benefit of the doubt. It is on this basis that Jurieu went on and became active during the second half of 1686.

What had to be done was to prevent the two witnesses from being buried, i.e. to keep alive the feeling of the N.C. that they were not real Catholics. On this point Jurieu's old opponent Bossuet showed him the path he had to take. At Easter 1686 Bossuet addressed a 'Lettre pastorale' to the new sheep of his flock, in order to congratulate them on their conversion to the church of their ancestors. He denied that there had been any dragoons in his diocese and so he stressed the voluntariness of their step. This point is vital because all agreed on the moral worthlessness of forced conversions. How to make this clear to the N.C. became Jurieu's most urgent concern. He found a brilliant solution by sending *Lettres pastorales* of his own hand to the former Protestants in France in order to keep active their old convictions which would preclude their inward apostasy or, in other words, prevent the dead bodies of the two witnesses from being buried. On 1 September 1686 the first issue appeared, to be followed twice a month by the subsequent issues.

Its formula was as simple as it could be: every issue had a size of eight quarto pages printed quite compactly in two columns. In each of them Jurieu treated three main topics: an exposition of reformed doctrinal 'commonplaces', an outline of the history of the church and its dogma and, very important, pieces of news from France, especially pertaining to what happened to the last handful of unbending Huguenots and the actions of the N.C., who fled their country or gathered in underground meetings. The last two topics are very interesting so far as they show a changing attitude in Jurieu. He had started to tell the Huguenots, as all his colleagues did, that they had to flee from Babylon, meaning they had to leave France in order to find 'repos ailleurs', their (spiritual) rest elsewhere. But soon the incitement 'flee from Babylon' got a different meaning: leave the Catholic Church and organize services in hidden places to read and explain the Word of God, as in the South of France some already did.

It needs hardly to be mentioned that the doctrinal and historical expositions had a strictly polemical shape: Jurieu refuted what Catholic controversialists, Bossuet, Nicole and Pellisson in the first place, had advanced against Protestantism. But the pieces of news also had a polemical undertone, e.g.: Bossuet tells you that there has been no violence in his diocese, but what about the panic roused by the violence they exerted elsewhere? And somewhat later on he published a letter testifying that there really had been dragoons in Meaux and that its bishop must have been fully aware of the fact. Conclusion: if these 'convertisseurs', these proselyting priests, are lying in cases which quite easily can be checked, how can you trust them as they deal with historical or doctrinal evidence?[24]

We can quite safely assume that it was a tense moment for Jurieu as he started the third volume of his periodical, on 1 September 1688. This year would be decisive. The start, however, was disappointing. He was discussing the doctrine of the infallibility of the Church, so much emphasized by Pellisson, which meant that the 'notae ecclesiae', the characteristics of the true church, were at stake. Both parties agreed that the holiness of the church consisted in the holy conduct of its members, culminating in martyrdom. Some pieces of news published by Jurieu quite clearly had the scope to show that the Reformed Church of his time did not lack martyrs. But in the second Letter of the third year Jurieu told his readers that somewhere in the South there had been a raid on a house full of N.C. However, it turned out to be a 'debauch' and not a holy meeting at all! What a shame to be able to demonstrate in court that you did not serve God because you were serving your pleasure!, he exclaims.

Fortunately there were indications of more satisfying conduct. A document was circulating with 600 signatures cancelling the previous 'reunion' with the Catholic church. But the most inspiring news from France was published by Jurieu in the third Letter: the story of the shepherdess from Crest in the Dauphiné, Isabeau Vincent, who, though illiterate, in a kind of 'lethargy' said 'excellent and divine' things. Jurieu did his utmost to maintain the facts against other reformed who denied them and also to demonstrate that it was a divine miracle. This is an interesting point because it shows that many reformed believed that the time of miracles was over and that similar phenomena had to be explained by natural causes. Jurieu did not hold this opinion. God still gives supernatural signs of his goodness. And of course, during the time of the completion of his Kingdom, God will work as many wonders as He did at the beginning. They even have been announced: the conversion of the Jews (a reason for Jurieu to advocate tolerance!) and of the remaining pagans and of course the fall of Babylon. An additional motive for this defence of the possibility of contemporary miracles was for Jurieu the idea he too shared with the Catholics that the occurrence of true miracles was a mark of the true church. Consequently he was very happy to be able to show some in the débris of his church.

The Glorious Revolution

After having said all this on the 15th of October 1688, Jurieu was ready to give his 'advice on the circumstances of this time', and so he did after a month. It is clear that he considered the enterprise of Prince William III as one long chain of miracles and would describe it as such. Nevertheless he started very carefully, for, however large in other parts of Europe the number of his readers may have been, the only audience he was really publishing for were the N.C. in France. He opens his Letter of 15 November with an assault on Bossuet's 'Book of Variations' before he turns to the situation in France. As a consequence of the moves of the Dutch fleet the authorities of Normandy had taken the precaution of disarming the N.C., which suddenly shed a glaring light on their ambiguous position as unreliable subjects. Jurieu of course makes the most of it by inciting them to see the consequences of this treatment by returning to Protestantism. The fact that they do not possess arms any more is a guarantee to the authorities that their secret meetings can only have a peaceful goal. However, in case the persecutions are further increased, they should try to leave the country. This country, France, is surrounded by enemies which it has provoked by its impudent attitude. But the attitude of the French government with regard to its own people is no better, we are told on 15 December. Its clerical advisers are very stupid, advocating persecution instead of leaving people in peace. But remain steadfast, after the Diocletians God always sends Constantines, and, moreover, the present-day confusion is the apocalyptic earthquake which will cast down the walls of Babylon.

And then, in the first Letter of the year 1689 (III, 9), Jurieu for the first time touches on English affairs. He counters the French point of view in the following words: 'That great and sudden revolution ... is the abomination of the bigots.' The N.C. should be on their guard against false interpretations of 'an affair which is not only the most innocent but also the most glorious and great one since several centuries'. And they should also keep in mind that 'being King of England and a Catholic at the same time is as incompatible as being the pope and a Lutheran'. The laws of the kingdom not only prohibit this, but they outlaw Roman-Catholicism as such. In eight points Jurieu explains this situation in a way which is almost specific, combining the validity of positive law with the absoluteness of natural law. In his opinion positive laws have the virtue of contracts which cannot be violated without committing a serious crime. Because James II did not possess the qualities required for a king of Great Britain, there should have been a regency or the succession should have devolved on the next heir. But the English Church and the English people had the magnanimity not to exclude James II from the crown, so he had 'religiously to observe the oaths made at his coronation to conserve the religion and the laws' as they were at that time. But he did not; on the contrary, mass was celebrated publicly, the bishops were constrained to violate their conscience and on top of all this a Jesuit was made a member of the Royal Council, i.e. master of the kingdom and master of the established church.

It was against these abuses of power by James II that the English called in the aid of his son-in-law and nephew, Prince William III of Orange. Rendering this, the noble Stadholder became the target of all the fury in France as if he had violated the laws of nature instead of following a real vocation. Jurieu rejects this opinion as being unrealistic because if William had refused to assist the English, they would have acted without him, but at the expense of a civil war, resulting perhaps in a new Charles I and, who knows, a new and even worse Cromwell. So the action of William III was not only to the benefit of James's daughters Mary and Anne, who were first in line to the succession of the throne, and the State, but even of James II himself! And his success is a sign that God has used him as his instrument to carry on his grand design. Doing so, the Prince did not touch one hair on the head of his uncle and father-in-law. It was the king himself who suddenly descended from the throne and deserted. That is why he lost his crown. And you should acknowledge and adore in all this God's profound judgements. According to the prophecies of the New Testament, this is the first blow of the ruin of Antichrist's empire. This surprising revolution will be followed by other revolutions of the same kind.

After his justification of the attitude of the English nation and of the acts of the great Prince of Orange, Jurieu in his next letter justified the United Provinces. In his opinion they were fully entitled to lend their fleet and army to the Stadholder for his enterprise which consisted in the liberation of a people who had asked for it. There is nothing wrong in it, especially not because 'Nous sommes dans un païs où le bon sens demeure degagé de ces ridicules et pernicieuses maximes qui font les peuples pour les Roys. Nous faisons les Roys pour les peuples', that is, we are in a country where the common sense remains free from those ridiculous and pernicious maxims which make nations for the king's sake. We make kings for the nation's sake! This sentence is a clear reminder of the 'Acte van Verlatinge', the abjuration of the Spanish king by the free Dutch provinces in 1581. And then Jurieu asks: why do the French blame the Dutch zeal for their religion after their own assistance to the Duke of Savoy in massacring his Protestant subjects? And finally he points out that the Dutch were perfectly aware of the fact that James II always had been their personal enemy. Well then, the teachings of Jesus Christ do not prevent us from anticipating an enemy.

The Letter of February 1st, 1689, again focuses attention upon the French scene: the revocation of the Edict of Nantes is branded as stupid, because it neither expelled the Protestants as Austria did, nor degraded them to second class subjects as the Turks did to Christians, but instead tried to keep the Huguenots in France, while at the same time extirpating their religion. After three years this proved to be a failure because the massive flight of the Huguenots, the steadfastness of a large number of confessors and the secret religious meetings still being held in France. These facts only are a fraction of the miracles of this time, Jurieu says, but before looking at the next letter where he gives an account of the expedition of the Stadholder, we should look back to the previous one, just to note that Jurieu in his refutation of Bossuet's *Histoire des variations* reached the point where the mighty prelate starts his polemics against the ideas of a simple parson, i.e. of Jurieu himself. As a result of this hardly accidental coincidence Jurieu had the opportunity to defend his explanation of the scriptural prophecies in the same context in which he gave an account of their beginning 'accomplishment' (to use his word). An extra advantage of this procedure was the possibility of showing the connection between the affairs of England and France.

In the next Letter, dated 15 February 1689 (III, 12), more than 50 points are enumerated, showing why Jurieu was convinced that 'le Pape est l'Antechrist et le Papisme est l'Antichristianisme'. Trying to summarize the most important arguments we find that Antichrist is an apostate sitting in God's temple, elevated over kings and emperors, whose capital is built on seven hills and whose empire will last for 1260 years. This means that the end is near, yea, that it has started already at the invasion of the Turks in Europe, but in the meantime persecution has been so severe that the true believers had to be compared to the two witnesses. Here we find a very interesting point because Jurieu, after the last series of comparisons in his account of the history of those days, returns to the two witnesses and posits point blank:

> Nous vous disions que ces deux témoins morts sur la place de la grande cité, c'est l'Eglise Reformée abbatuë en France. Et nous ajoutions que ceux qui empêcheront leur sepulture et leur totale extinction. Ce sont les tribus, peuples, langues et nations, c'est à-dire divers peuples circonvoisins, etc. Il y a apparence, disions-nous, que toute l'Europe contribuera à empêcher que la France ne vienne à bout de son dessein, d'extirper la verité.

This has come true litterally, he adds, for even the House of Austria and the pope himself have joined the adversaries of France, and France's most faithful slave, the Duke of Savoy, is going to break away.

To these miracles Jurieu adds the willingness of the United Provinces, generally not very keen on having troops on their soil without an explicit purpose, to consent to the recruitment and finally to the expedition against James. This unanimity was a marvel in a state where one city could block any decision, and how risky a decision this was! The expedition itself is also described by Jurieu as one long chain of miracles in which God's hand could be seen very clearly. After the 29th of October the fleet was heading for the North but a storm dispersed the ships at night. Twelve days later a fresh start was made and with James II and his army in the North, the course now was West, where God turned the wind at the right time. There was no armed resistance at the dangerous moment of the landing, neither was there any assistance. In Exeter only 'le petit peuple' were cheering the Prince, but the bishop had gone and the mayor and other notables were in hiding. They realized too well the fate of Monmouth and his supporters three years before. After a fortnight's stay in Devon there had been no increase in troops, but on the other hand in this county full of rocks and hedges where 500 troops would have been able to stop the march, nobody appeared. Finally the armies met near Salisbury but there—marvel of marvels—the king's soldiers refused to fight.

In the next Letter, that of 1 March (III, 13), Jurieu defends the explanation of Joseph Mede (Leo I the first real pope; starting of the kingdom of the Antichrist) against Bossuet, and then he continues his account of the marvels of the time by comparing James II and Louis XIV to the kings of Psalm 2, whose schemes were confounded by the Almighty. 'God has saved his Church by the mistakes of those who aimed at its destruction', Jurieu says, treating the most stupid mistakes of James II in the next Letter (15 March, III, 14). One mistake was his failing to have unchallengeable witnesses of the birth of his son, the other his sudden flight. In this letter Jurieu also announces the publication of an exact relation of the miracle of Dauphiné and Vivarets: the 200 or 300 little prophets, children who in their sleep 'annoncent les choses merveilleuses de Dieu', pray, exhort, menace, promise, 'chantent les Pseaumes de David' and even predict future things, but after their awakening return to their usual simplicity.

That the situation in France is Jurieu's principal concern also appears from the 15th Letter of the volume, undated but clearly from 1 April 1689. He discusses 'libelles qui viennent de France', which in fact consist in one only, Bayle's *Réponse d'un N.C. à la lettre d'un réfugié*, ascribed by Jurieu not to a N.C., but (very justly so) to an old pupil of the Jesuits.

Over against the latter's imputation that Protestantism is in favour of the persecution of heretics, Jurieu says, wait and see whether we shall force the consciences of the people in occupied territories. And on the other hand he gives an account of the furious persecution raging at the time in Southern France: 'c'est la piété catholique.' But Protestants do not murder kings, as Catholics did and still want to do. This point is given in the testimony of a monk, quite recently arrested in Rotterdam because of his offer to kill Louis XIV. In a holy contrast to this, Jurieu establishes that the N.C. return from their error and show a spirit of true martyrdom.

Political Theory
    Writing his next Letter on 15 April 1689 (III, 16) Jurieu shows he is aware of two things: firstly that his readers are more interested in his 'reflexions sur les affaires du temps' than in doctrinal discussions, and secondly that he should give a summary of his political theory in order to counter immoderate claims as to the total submission of subjects to the government. At the same time this would be the best defence of the British! Total submission had been advocated in a virulent libel against the stadholder from France called *Le Vray portrait de Guillaume Henri de Nassau, nouvel Abçalom, nouvel Hérode, nouveau Cromwell, nouveau Néron*, as well as in a pamphlet of Elie Merlat, a refugee minister in Lausanne, entitled *Le Pouvoir absolu des souverains*. With the remark that tyrants do not need lessons in absolutism and good kings do not follow these, Jurieu introduces his ideas which he outlines in nineteen short sections spread over three Letters.
1. The first sentence goes straight to the point: 'We are convinced that all humans are naturally free and independent from each other.' It is sin which made domination and subordination inevitable, so domination is not 'de droit divin naturel'. It is neither 'de droit divin positif', because there is not an express commandment of God establishing the power of masters over slaves or of sovereigns over subjects. Original sin only makes it safer to live together under a government. 2. The form of this government can be freely chosen: Monarchy—absolute or mitigated—, aristocracy or democracy are all possible and none of them is 'de droit divin' in itself. But once the choice is made, obedience is an obligation 'de droit divin', because, 3. any voluntary and free transfer of real or abstract goods, e.g. delegation of power, establishes a lawful title and this is why kings are called God's lieutenants and even his living images. Nevertheless, 4. this origin of human power teaches us its limits: *a*) in a way, the nation is more than the king as in the Gallican tradition the church is more than the pope. *b*) The people can not transfer rights it

does not possess, c) e.g. the people cannot legitimatize tyranny over consciences or freedom to commit crimes. d) As the nation has taken a king for the sake of its own conservation, the latter does not have the right to destroy it, for 'le salut du peuple est la souveraine loy'—welfare (and salvation!?) of the people is the supreme law. This is why no obedience is due to a king who violates the fundamental laws of the state and who ruins society. Just as all political (and even all human) relations, government is based on a 'mutual pact' which implies, at least tacitly, that governmental power is always restricted. 6. The restrictions, however, are very different, and can vary from an elective to an absolute kingdom. 7. The latter is not contrary to nature, because the entire sovereignty can be transferred. 8. Absolute power, however, is not unlimited. This would conflict with all God's institutions since God himself does not want absolute power but has tempered it by his covenants with men.

In the following Letter of 1 May 1689 (III, 17) Jurieu, after observing that the eight points would suffice to justify the English, goes on in order to produce all possible evidence. He continues his eighth point in showing that even Grotius, who virtually denies the Christians a right of resistance, admits that alienation of the State and dissolution of society are to be countered by the people. Then in his ninth point Jurieu draws a tentative conclusion:

> Le peuple est la source de l'authorité des Souverains, le peuple est le premier sujet où reside la Souveraineté, le peuple rentre en possession de la souveraineté aussi-tost que les personnes ou les familles à qui il l'avoit donnée viennent à manquer; le peuple enfin est celuy qui fait les Rois.

These are the principles he wants to corroborate. He does so in quoting again Grotius in his tenth section. Grotius also has the theory of the original contract, and Jurieu adds: the only point in litigation is to what extent a people can surrender ('se livrer') to a sovereign. 11. Experience and (biblical) history show that the people can make legitimate kings, all others are usurpers. Even in French history the crown has been transferred from the first to the second 'race' and then even to the third, which proves that there is no unlimited power. The welfare and conservation of the people constitute its limits. In case of violation of these limits obedience can be renounced. 12. Those who deny this and appeal to Christian patience are inconsistent if they do not demand it from wives who suffer from domestic tyrants; on the other hand, if they extend the appeal to patience even to those abominable situations, they subject those wives to the most horrible excesses. 13. And the maxim, 'princeps legibus solutus est', is limited by this one, 'salus populi suprema lex esto', which is superior. Moreover Jurieu notes that 'princeps' means 'sovereign', i.e. the institution which makes the laws. In

England this is done conjointly by king and parliament. These sovereigns are only above those laws they can change, not above the laws of God, nature or 'those depending from the right of nations' ('qui sont du droit des gens').

The authority which is decisive in these matters is the Word of God but, he says, you can hardly believe your eyes when reading the examples produced in favour of unlimited power: Saul who kills the priests at Nob or David who kills Uriah and takes Bathsheba. Jurieu grimly adds: and on the next page we expect to find the sentence that gangsters have the right to kill and to rob because they have the power. The strongest argument against the right of resistance (and by implication in favour of unlimited power) is of course David's refusal to kill Saul, but Jurieu replies: this only shows the rejection of regicide, not more. Otherwise, what would be the use of commanding 400 armed men if David was holding the opinion that he did not have the right to resist the unlimited power as used by Saul? And then Jurieu adds: in *our* opinion, David was not authorized to resist Saul because he was only a private person. It should be noted that during the revolt of the Camisards Jurieu dropped this scruple and permitted private individuals to unite in order to resist abuse of power.[25] The rest of this Letter, nearly two pages, is consecrated to the defence of the little prophets who had caused much confusion in Southern France by preaching in trance as reformed ministers. Jurieu denies that the whole thing could have been forged. There must have been something supernatural behind it. And by this piece of news he was able to draw attention to France right in the middle of a discussion of British affairs.

This discussion he rounds off in the Letter of 15 May 1689 (III, 18). 14. The correlate of unlimited power is unlimited, passive obedience, defended by scholars who want to avoid any trace of defence of regicide. Jurieu dryly replies, 15. that even the most strict theories don't have any impact on forsworn mutineers like Cromwell and his companions, and that his own views don't justify regicide. The question is, which kind of government is the best, an absolutist régime or a limited one. In his opinion Britain is much better off than France, because there have been many more troubles in France than in the British Isles. And if one wants to see the effect of power without any limits, look at the Turks, who have reduced all captured places to a most lamentable state without being able to prevent sedition and revolt. Jurieu ventures upon the thesis that the prosperity of a country is in proportion to the limits of its government. He admits, however, that armed resistance has its severe drawbacks, and that it is only allowed under strict conditions: no armed protection of private interests nor of minor general material interests is admissible, and in serious cases it only is allowed after more gentle remedies have been used.   After this exposition, Jurieu considers the defence of William's intervention a simple matter. He uses Grotius who was an opponent of armed resistance but for a few exceptions: if non-absolutist kings aspire to absolutism, if a king has abdicated and his rights consequently have become equal to those of any private individual, if a king tries to usurp the whole sovereignty which he constitutionally shares with a 'Senate' or if he does things to which according to the constitution ('dans le transport qu'on a fait de la Souveraineté' ...!) resistance is allowed. These principles are virtually identical with ours, Jurieu says, and so he can not agree with Merlat's demand for unconditional submission of the people. 17. He adds one important point: even a hereditary crown is not the private possession of a certain family, because sovereignty originates from the people, who have transferred it in behalf of their conservation. 18. So the British were fully entitled to do what they did *a*) because a nation can transfer the sovereignty to whom they want, certainly to another member of the royal family, *b*) in case the ruling member violates stipulations of the mutual pact, *c*) e.g. those concerning religion. *d*) Moreover, the ruling member, James II, had abdicated, *e*) after having tried to usurp the whole sovereignty and *f*) consequently to diminish the liberty of the people. *g*) To this end he even had raised troops. So William was right in doing what he did and the Anglicans were wrong with their too restricted ideas concerning the right of resistance. 19. The last difficulty Jurieu deals with is the fact that no written article of the English constitution expressly excludes a Roman Catholic from the throne. He answers that as far as he knows no article of the Spanish constitution excludes a Lutheran, but whereas the qualification 'Catholic' is incompatible with Lutheranism so the function of head of the Church of England is incompatible with Catholicism. James II simply had misused the indulgence of the nation on this point. As an extra, Jurieu defends the legitimacy of the Convention, invoked during the Revolution, stating that the English Parliament has the right to assemble on its own authority and that in this case it has done nothing contrary to natural right or to the right of the nations—'and that's what we have proved rather extensively in this short tract on the power of kings. But it is time to stop now.'

On the last page of this Pastoral Letter Jurieu mentions the religious meetings which continue to assemble in Southern France, in spite of the heavy persecution and he resumes his defence of the activities of the young prophets. One of them now living in Geneva, does not prophesy anymore, but his manners resemble those 'de nos Trembleurs'—of our

Quakers! The calumny to which they have been exposed is due to the ignorance of the true character of inspiration and prophetism. That is why they have been taken for fanatics, and Jurieu promises to discuss this in his next letter—which he did not do. Instead he published an account of the persecution he had received from Castres. Anyway, he concentrated on the events in France and in the Letter of 15 June 1689 (III, 20) he gave an extensive treatise on prophets and prophetism. From the great number of prophets combined with the cruelty of persecution he deduced that the last days before the millenium had come. He tried to compare the modern prophets with the inspired of biblical times, stressing that not only saints are true prophets (Balaam!), and that not every word they speak has been inspired by the Holy Spirit. So, while we should never uncritically accept what they say, we should not reject all their words. The whole phenomenon is a sign of God, to which we have to pay attention.

On 1 July 1689 Jurieu writes the last Letter (III, 21) of the volume; of its thirteen pages, nine are consecrated to 'Reflexions on chapter 11 of the Revelation of St. John with regard to the present events'—a very interesting piece of work because Jurieu says: 'the events are the true and nearly the only interpretation of the Prophecies.' They decide whether the predictions are true or false, and therefore Jurieu tries to interpret the interpretations, and of course to show the right meaning of his work *L'Accomplissement des prophéties*. He pursues two lines in doing so. Along the first line he shows that the death of the 'two witnesses' cannot be confined to one day: it was the dragoons' action during a great deal of 1685 which has to be taken as the killing of the two witnesses and consequently their resurrection also will consist in a series of events. These events in his opinion are to be found in the increasing number of 'assemblées' in the South, where the same people who apostatized in 1685 even before the dragoons had reached their city or village, now take much more serious risks to hear the preaching of God's Word. The other line of interpretation is the English one. On 16 February 1685, Charles II died and was succeeded by James II. The coronation took place on 25 May of the same year. That coincided with the start of the dragoons' mission in Béarn. Nearly three and a half years after this event William III arrived in England, and just at that time the zeal of the N.C., as well as the number of the victims among them, rose considerably. The coronation of William and Mary took place on 21 April, exactly three and a half years after the revocation of the Edict of Nantes. Since that time the courage of the N.C. has been incredible and so has the panic of their persecutors. A fire in a shed at the coast was sufficient to make whole villages spring to arms calling 'the Prince of Orange is coming.'

And Jurieu finishes his account by saying, I have given William III a much greater part in the execution of God's design than I have ever done before. This is not because I am his prophet, I am no prophet at all. The only thing I am doing is to explain and apply the prophecies and 'mes conjectures n'ont gueres manqué'. 'The king of England is my witness that the last time I had the honour to speak to him, I took the liberty to tell him that if my conjectures were right he would be master of England before the end of the year 1688.' This proved to be quite accurate: the Prince entered London on 28 December of that year! And so I sincerely hope that we will soon see the happy days predicted by the prophet in which 'justice and peace will kiss each other'. That is how Jurieu managed to knit together his expectations of a new future for the Reformed Church of France and of the Glorious Revolution in Britain.

Conclusion

To conclude, again the fact has to be emphasized that the audience to which Jurieu addressed his account and his defence of the Glorious Revolution were the 'Nouveaux Convertis' in France. Their courage had to be strengthened, not to plan revolutionary actions, but to obey God rather than men, i.e. to leave the Roman Church and return to the Reformed faith and practice. Doing so they would see miracles worked by God in their favour. But this exhortation did not remain uncontradicted. During the same year 1689 in which the coronation of William and Mary took place, which, according to Jurieu was a miracle, another miracle occurred: the Waldensians returned to their valleys. Nevertheless, the first phrase of Bayle's anonymous *Avis important aux refugiez sur leur prochain retour en France* ran: 'Now the famous year 1689 expired without anything very memorable having taken place.' In Bayle's opinion the glorious return of the Waldensians was nothing more than a seditious enterprise of a handful of peasants.

As the descendants of those peasants planned an extensive commemoration of this event in 1989, I was greatly honoured to be asked to contribute to it with a study of the fierce controversy which arose between Jurieu and Bayle on this point, for Jurieu defended the Waldensians strongly. But most strikingly, he was not able to justify them as he had justified the Glorious Revolution. As we have seen before, Jurieu had demonstrated that the Glorious Revolution had been so glorious because it was in accordance with the Laws of God, of nature and of nations. But now he had to face the fact that the return of the Waldensians had taken place in flat contradiction to their sovereign's edict. And so Jurieu had to admit that they were wrong according to human laws and even to the revealed Laws of God, but that they were right according to

Gods hidden plans, just as biblical saints had been, who did forbidden things under divine inspiration.

By taking this line of defence, Jurieu tacitly conceded that the old-fashioned theological explanations of the scholastic type failed to justify political actions. Nevertheless he merits the title theologian of the Revolution because his ideas, however erroneous in part, have shown a remarkable fertility, and this not in spite of, but rather thanks to the apocalytic perspective in which he had propagated them.

[1] [Pierre Jurieu], *Histoire du Calvinisme & celle du Papisme mises en parallele*, vol. I, Rotterdam 1683, Preface, first line: 'Dans le siècle où nous sommes on n'aime pas les gros livres, ni les longues Prefaces.

[2] Erich Haase, *Einführung in die Literatur des Refuge*, Berlin, 1959, p. 116; cf. Elie Saurin, *Remonstrance aux églises*, 1695, p. 37 (1st col.): '... une Gazette prophétique des operations et du succez de la Campagne prochaine et des suivantes ....'

[3] F.R.J. Knetsch, 'Pierre Jurieu, réfugié unique et caractéristique', *Bulletin de la Société de l'Histoire du Protestantisme Français*, 115 (1969), pp. 450-52.

[4] Elisabeth Labrousse, *Pierre Bayle*, I, The Hague, 1963, p. 175 (letter to his brother Jacob, 26 November 1678).

[5] J. van der Meij, 'Pierre du Moulin in Leiden', *Lias*, 14 (1987), pp. 15-40.

[6] F.P. van Stam, *The Controversy over the Theology of Saumur, 1635-1650* (Doct. thesis, Amsterdam Free University), Amsterdam/Maarsen, 1988, treats this controversy at length.

[7] Pierre Jurieu, *Traité de la puissance de l'église*, Quevilly/Rouen, 1677, Dedication, p. 2.

[8] J.-G. de Chaufepié, *Nouveau dictionnaire historique et critique*, III, La Haye, 1750-56, s.v. Jurieu, remarque A.

[9] Paul de Félice, *Mer—son église réformée*, Paris, 1885, pp. 53-58.

[10] Labrousse, *Bayle*, I, pp. 131-67.

[11] Jacques Solé, 'La Diplomatie de Louis XIV et les protestants français réfugiés aux Provinces-Unies, 1678-1688', *Bulletin de la Société de l'Histoire du Protestantisme Français*, 115 (1969), p. 628.

[12] F.R.J. Knetsch, 'Pierre Jurieu, 1637-1713, face à la Révocation', in J.A.H. Bots and G.H.M. Posthumus Meyjes (eds.), *The Revocation of the Edict of Nantes and the Dutch Republic, 1685*, Amsterdam/Maarssen, 1986, pp. 107-09.

[13] The monograph on this subject by Joseph Dedieu, *Le Rôle politique des protestants français, 1685-1715*, Paris, 1920, which contains all relevant documents in an Appendix, pp. 281-331, is inadmissably biassed against Protestantism, as I showed in my *Pierre Jurieu theoloog en politikus der Refuge*, (Doct. thesis Leiden University), Kampen, 1967, pp. 346-50.

[14] E. Kappler, 'Bibliographie chronologique des oeuvres de Pierre Jurieu, 1637-1713', *Bulletin de la Société de l'Histoire du Protestantisme Français*, 84 (1935), pp. 429-30, nos. 91-92. See also my supplement, 'Un contributo alla bibliografia di Pierre Jurieu, 1637-1713', *Rivista di storia e letteratura religiosa*, 9 (1973), pp. 471-72, nos. 66, 70-76, 79-81.

[15] [Pierre Jurieu], *Relation de tout ce que s'est fait dans les affaires de la religion reformée, et pour ses interêts, depuis le commencement des négociations de la Paix de Reswik*, Rotterdam, 1698; a short serial publication.

[16] [Pierre Jurieu], *Relation de la cruauté qu'on exerce au'jourdhuy envers nos freres de France sur les galeres*, Amsterdam, 1700 (14 pp.), republished in Knetsch, *Pierre Jurieu*, pp. 438-45; in its meeting of 14 November 1700, the Rotterdam Walloon church council had asked Jurieu to publish this pamphlet. It is not listed in Kappler, 'Bibliographie'.

[17] See for these topics, Kappler, 'Bibliographie', pp. 430-35, nos. 103-05, 107, 110; cf.

Knetsch, 'Contributo', pp. 473-74, nos. 85-88, 91-94; p. 476, nos. 27, 29-30.

[18] This idea is at the base of Jurieu's *Abbrégé de l'histoire du Concile de Trente* [du Fra Paolo Sarpi], 2 vols., Geneva, 1682 (2nd ed. Amsterdam, 1683), and clearly expressed in his 'Avis aux protestants de l'Europe', published in *Préjugez légitimes contre le papisme*, 2 vols., Amsterdam, 1685.

[19] *Traité de la puissance*, p. 91: 'les synodes ... ont ce pouvoir dérivé du Peuple, il ne leur a pas été donné de Dieu immediatement ... c'est une autorité qui monte et dont le mouvement est circulaire.'

[20] Pierre Jurieu, *Le Vray systeme de l'église et la véritable analyse de la foy*, Dordrecht, 1686.

[21] Guy Howard Dodge, *The Political Theory of the Huguenots of the Dispersion, with Special Reference to the Thought and Influence of Pierre Jurieu*, New York, 1947, a book to which I am greatly indebted, has a slight tendency to this direction. On the same line we find the remarkable study by Robin J. Howells, *Pierre Jurieu: Antinomian Radical*, Durham, 1983; see pp. 58-60 for an interesting interpretation of Jurieu's account of the Glorious Revolution, quite different from mine. In full opposition to the results of Dodge and me is Hartmut Kretzer, *Calvinismus und französische Monarchie im 17. Jahrhundert. Die politische Lehre der Akademien Sedan und Saumur, mit besonderer Berücksichtigung von Pierre Du Moulin, Moyse Amyraut und Pierre Jurieu*, Berlin, 1975. The latter's *Calvinismus versus Demokratie respektive 'Geist des Kapitalismus'?*, Oldenburg, 1988, partly in French, does not add much to the debate.

[22] Knetsch, 'Pierre Jurieu réfugié', p. 450.

[23] [Pierre Jurieu], *Lettres pastorales addressées aux fideles de France qui gemissent sous la captivité de Babylon*, 3rd year, no. 21, p. 166 of the quarto edition.

[24] *Lettres pastorales*, I, no. 1, p. 7 (2nd col.); also I, no. 8, pp. 61-62.

[25] [Pierre Jurieu], *Avis à tous les alliez, protestans et catholiques romains, princes et peuples, souverains et sujets, sur le secours qu'on doit donner aux soûlevez des Cevennes*, n. pl., 1705.

RELIGIOUS AND THEOLOGICAL BOOKS IN THE ANGLO-DUTCH BOOK TRADE AT THE TIME OF THE GLORIOUS REVOLUTION

P.G. Hoftijzer

On 8 February 1689 (New Style), some two months after the successful invasion of England by William of Orange, Johan Lucas Wetstein, a member of a leading Amsterdam bookselling family, wrote to his London correspondent Samuel Smith—in French, for his control of the English language was slight: 'Je crains que depuis mon départ de Londres le négoce n'aura pas valu de delà beaucoup plus qu'icy; au part toutes ces troubles chaqu'un craint & ne se souci[e] pas d'estudier ou lire des livres.'[1] Indeed, there can be little doubt that the exciting events of 1688-89, for the moment at least, will have distracted people's attention both in Britain and the Netherlands from such lofty pursuits as the reading of books. Still, much more damaging to the book trade was the disruption of the flow of books between the British Isles and the European mainland during the aftermath of the Revolution, the two wars fought between the Anglo-Dutch alliance and France for almost twenty-five consecutive years.

During this long period traffic both at land and at sea was frequently interrupted by the protracted hostilities. The English, moreover, in contrast to the Dutch closed their borders to all French goods. 'C'est un malheur général à présent le misérable état de la librairie, laquelle ne désire que la paix ... On imprime fort peu à présent dans nos pais comme aussi partout', another Amsterdam bookseller, Johannes Janssonius van Waesbergen, lamented in a letter to the same Samuel Smith at the end of 1689.[2] The disastrous effects of the war on the international book trade were equally felt at the international bookfairs of Frankfurt and Leipzig. Referring to his inability to provide all the books Smith had ordered, the Frankfurt bookseller Johann David Zunner wrote to him:

> ... quelques uns en restent encore, que je n'ay pas pu trouver à la foire, puisque les imprimeurs n'estoient pas icy en personne et les autres craignoient le payement des voitures à cause des destours et de la guerre, principalement pour ce qui est des livres qui sont imprimés à Genève, à Basle et autres lieux de cette contrée.[3]

Yet, despite these serious problems the book trade between England and
the Dutch Republic in the years following the Glorious Revolution remained a substantial affair. As book exports to Britain from booksellers
in France were virtually cut off after 1688, the Dutch readily moved in
to take their place and increase their already strong hold on the English
market for imported books. Statistics based on English customs records
show a marked preponderance of book imports from the United Provinces over all other countries from the early 1690s until deep into the
eighteenth century.[4] In this contribution we will try to look more closely
into the Anglo-Dutch book trade during the last decades of the seventeenth century, especially with regard to the commerce in books of a religious or theological nature, which formed such a considerable part of
the total number of books exchanged.

The European book trade was, obviously enough, only one of several
vehicles for the distribution of knowledge and ideas in early modern
Europe. Within the international *respublica litteraria* various other means
of communication were available. 'Academic travel'—then perhaps
even more than now—was almost a professional necessity for anyone
who wished to keep abreast of the latest developments in scholarship,
learning and science. Equally important was the exchange of letters with
like-minded people all over Europe, an exchange, moreover, which was
gradually being supplemented by the emergence of a truly international
learned periodical press. Yet book trade records, such as the archives
and correspondence of individual booksellers, book catalogues, order
lists etc., do constitute a valuable source for our knowledge of the early
modern history of ideas, not least because they are more detached from
the predilections of the individual reader. These records often can provide a good picture of communication through the printed word during
the *ancien régime*.

One of the most important documents for our knowledge of the
Anglo-Dutch book trade at the end of the seventeenth century is the letter-book, now in the Bodleian Library at Oxford, of the London bookseller Samuel Smith, from which the quotations at the beginning of this
paper have been taken.[5] Samuel Smith (d. 1708), a former apprentice of
the notorious London bookseller Moses Pitt, appears to have set up his
business in 1682, in the shadow of St. Paul's Cathedral which at that
time was still being rebuilt after its destruction in the Great Fire of
1666.[6] In 1693 Samuel Smith would move his premises to the shop of
John Martyn, the former publisher of the Royal Society, 'at the sign of
the Bell' in St. Paul's Churchyard, a shop which, according to the
chronicler of the London book trade of this period, John Dunton, was

'very beautiful and well furnished'.[7] Until his death in 1708 Smith was a respected member of the trade, working closely together with his partner and brother-in-law Benjamin Walford.

Not long after his establishment as an independent stationer Smith was appointed bookseller to the Royal Society as well as publisher of its *Philosophical Transactions*, an important position which brought him the custom of many of the Society's Fellows. He also began publishing books by some of the greatest English scientists of his day, men such as Robert Boyle, John Ray, Thomas Sydenham and Martin Lister, while he had a major share in the distribution of Isaac Newton's *Principia mathematica*.[8] Another regular customer of Smith's was Robert Hooke, the versatile Curator of Experiments to the Royal Society and an ardent book-lover, who noted his frequent visits to Smith in his diary.[9]

Samuel Smith belonged to a small group of English booksellers who specialised in the so-called 'Latin trade', the import of scholarly, mostly Latin books in all fields of learning from the continent. The emphasis of this Latin trade at the end of the seventeenth century was clearly on scientific books: works on medicine, physics, botany and the like. Thanks to the growing interest in the natural sciences these books were being published in increasing numbers on the continent as well as in Britain.[10] But Smith also dealt in a multitude of other books, editions of the classics, books on law, philosophy and history, which he sold either to his London clientele or distributed among booksellers in Oxford and Cambridge and the rest of the country. Works on religion, theology and ecclesiastical history were also abundantly available from his stock; his 1687 catalogue of recently imported books included no less than twelve pages of theological works.[11]

Most of his foreign stock Samuel Smith obtained through booksellers on the continent. This is extensively documented by his letter-book, which contains the incoming correspondence from a great many booksellers in the German States, France, the Southern Netherlands and the Dutch Republic over the years 1683-1692. His most important source of supply without question were the Dutch, who at a time when the United Provinces were regarded as the intellectual store-house of Europe,[12] dominated the international book trade. Partly through personal visits to the Netherlands Smith had established good relations with the most prominent representatives of the Dutch book trade, booksellers and publishers such as Johannes Jansonius van Waesberge and Hendrik Wetstein in Amsterdam, Reinier Leers in Rotterdam and Pieter van der Aa in Leiden. It is in their letters and order lists that detailed information can be found on many aspects of the Anglo-Dutch book trade of this period.

What works on theology, religion and related subjects are to be found in this Anglo-Dutch book trade? In the case of one exceptional correspondent of Samuel Smith the answer is quite easy to give. From 1685 to 1691 he exchanged letters with Johannes Leusden (1624-1699), professor of Hebrew at the University of Utrecht, who was the editor of important new editions of the Hebrew Bible and Book of Psalms and the prolific author of numerous biblical compendia, as well as of various dictionaries, grammars and manuals of the oriental languages.[13] As an author Leusden was exceptional in that he was personally involved in the printing and selling of his books, an uncommon practice which must have earned him a considerable additional income. As Samuel Smith was willing to buy large quantities, Leusden in some cases accomodated his English customer by providing the books with a London imprint on the title page. Thus in 1690 he sent 600 copies of his recently published *Compendium Graecum Novi Testamenti* to Smith with the occasional imprint 'Londoni, Sumptibus Samuelis Smith, ad Insigne Principis in Cemiterio D. Pauli, 1688'. Interestingly, Smith one year earlier had acted also as Leusden's middleman in the dispatch of 50 copies of his edition of the Hebrew Book of Psalms across the Atlantic. The books were intended for the use of American students at Harvard College in New England, being a gift to Increase Mather, the well-known Boston minister and rector of Harvard, with whom Leusden kept up friendly relations.[14]

As regards Smith's correspondence with his Dutch colleagues it is more difficult to come up with a satisfactory answer concerning the nature of religious or theological books shipped across the North Sea, mainly because of the great mass of titles listed in the letters and order lists. Moreover, for the most part the books are described only in a short and condensed way, which often makes their identification problematic. This is not so much the case with the books sent by Smith to the Low Countries. The sale of English books on the continent was a very modest affair during the seventeenth and eighteenth centuries, mainly due to the comparatively high prices of books produced in England and because of the poor knowledge of the English language among continental readers. In the years before the Revolution small numbers of English religious books and pamphlets, mostly of a Puritan or anti-Stuart nature, had been exported to the Netherlands, where many British religious and political exiles had fled. That Smith had had some part in this illicit trade can be gathered from his correspondence with Abigail May, the widow of the Amsterdam bookseller Steven Swart. Abigail May was herself descended from a family of English Brownists which had fled to Amsterdam at the beginning of the century. Being closely watched by English spies in Amsterdam she was reported to be supplying her

British exile clientele in Amsterdam with the latest from England. In her letters to Smith she frequently asked him to send anything newly printed, especially on the subject of the 'popish controversy' in England.[15] Predictably this demand decreased after 1688, when most of the exiles returned to Britain.

Yet there was also an increasing demand in the Low Countries for serious theological literature from England. In the letters which Smith received from his Dutch correspondents there are frequent requests for such ponderous theological books as the *Works* of Isaac Barrow (4 vols., London, 1683-87) and John Lightfoot (2 vols., London, 1684), or Matthew Poole's *Annotations upon the Holy Bible* (2 vols., London, 1683-85). Writing to Smith in October 1685, the widow Swart urged him finally to send her the books she had ordered, adding somewhat irritatedly: 'If you have no conveenjens to send when I writt for them, you ou[gh]t nott to delay with me. I mi[gh]tt have sould Pools Annotations twise or 3 tymes before now.'[16] Reinier Leers of Rotterdam, whose business with Smith was mainly in cheap Dutch editions of the classical authors, ordered substantial numbers of religious works, such as Archbishop James Ussher's *Historia dogmatica* (London, 1689), Henry Dodwell's *Dissertationes in Irenaeum* (Oxford, 1689) and William Cave's *Historia literaria scriptorum ecclesiasticorum* (London, 1688).[17] Some of these books may have been intended for members of the thriving and well-educated British merchant community in Rotterdam,[18] but among the consumers of the English books ordered by Leers also were Pierre Bayle, 'le philosophe de Rotterdam', and his friend Henri Basnage de Beauval, editor of the *Histoire des ouvrages des savans* (1687-1709), a scholarly journal published by Leers in which many English works were reviewed and discussed.[19]

The bulk of the commerce between Samuel Smith and his Dutch colleagues, however, was in books shipped from or through the Low Countries to England. Among these books were works published in the Dutch Republic, often by Smith's correspondents themselves, as well as books purchased on Smith's behalf at the bookfairs of Frankfurt and Leipzig. A third category consisted of 'bound', i.e. antiquarian books bought on Smith's specific orders at Dutch book auctions. Many of these books can be traced in the various printed catalogues of Samuel Smith's foreign stock which have survived, but whereas these catalogues only list titles of books, the letter-book provides interesting additional information, for instance about the prices he had to pay for them, and about the numbers of books he ordered. Thus it is possible to deduce, up to a point, the extent of his theological imports and the demand for specific titles. A few examples may illustrate this.

A large number of the books listed in the correspondence consist of editions of the Bible or the separate Old and New Testament in various languages, particularly Hebrew, Greek, Latin and French. Partly these bibles must have been intended for bible study and exegesis, such as the 30 copies of the Greek New Testament which Smith received from the Amsterdam bookseller Johannes Jansonius van Waesberge in September 1688 at a total cost of 30 guilders (approximately £3).[20] Partly too the bibles may have served more practical needs: a regular item in the order lists are copies of the so-called *Testamentum Mons*, the popular French Protestant edition of the Old and New Testament, which most probably were retailed among the growing population of French Huguenot refugees in London.[21] Editions of the Latin Vulgate are listed quite frequently in the letters written to Smith before the Revolution, no doubt because of the toleration of Roman Catholic worship during the reign of James II. In this respect it is worth noting that until November 1688 Smith had excellent commercial relations with various booksellers in the Southern Netherlands, such as Jean Baptiste Verdussen (father and son) at Antwerp and the Serstevens family in Brussels, who supplied him with a large variety of Catholic books, including missals, breviaries and diurnals.[22]

Another important category of theological books in the letters of Samuel Smith's Dutch correspondents consists of works on ecclesiastical history. The diversity here is quite remarkable, covering studies on the history of practically any conviction within the Christian church from the earliest times to the present, and written by authors of all religious denominations. One of the most frequently listed works in this category is the *Summa historiae ecclesiasticae*, a handbook written by the Leiden professor of theology Fridericus Spanheim jr. which was published in 1689 with a dedication to King William as the 'maintainer of the reformed religion and liberator of oppressed Europe'. Within a few years Smith purchased well over a hundred copies of this work at a price of slightly more than two guilders per copy. Very popular also appear to have been accounts and histories of the numerous Catholic church councils, from the meetings of the early Church to the Council of Trent. Smith regularly obtained copies of the *Historia conciliorum generalium* (Cologne, 1683) by the Gallican theologian Edmond Richer, of Pietro Pallavicino's *Istoria del Concilio di Trento* (Rome, 1656-57, 2 vols.), and especially of the *Summa conciliorum* (Lyon, 1683), composed by the sixteenth-century Bishop of Toledo Bartholomeo Carranza; of this last work Smith in one shipment alone received some 50 copies in September 1687 from the Leiden bookseller Pieter van der Aa. It is well possible that the vehement controversy between Anglican and Roman Catholic theologians, which had flared up once again during the reign of James II, accounts for this particular interest, as both parties tried to find support for their arguments in the writings of the Church Fathers and the proceedings of the early church.

The majority of the works on church history in the correspondence, however, are listed only by an occasional one or two copies. Examples out of a multitude of titles would be the *Historia Pelagiana* (editions Padua, 1673 or Leipzig, 1677) by the Italian theologian Enrico Noris, the Bollandist *Acta Sanctorum*, a serial publication published at Antwerp from 1643 onwards, the *Annales Anabaptistici* (Basel, 1672) by the Swiss theologian Johannes Henricus Ottius, or the *Historia ecclesiastica et politica* (Leiden, 1671) by the Leiden professor Georgius Hornius.

A significant proportion of the religious works purchased of Samuel Smith consists of works of a humanist, moderate and rational theological nature. Perhaps this may be explained by the circumstance that many of the members of the Royal Society, who constituted such a notable part of Smith's clientele, adhered to the latitudinarian form of Anglicanism, a liberal and tolerant Christianity that has been associated with the success of the Newtonian revolution in science.[23] Erasmus, the prince of humanists, is well represented, but even more so are the liberal Dutch theologians who claimed to be his heirs, Arminians such as Hugo Grotius, who perhaps was the most widely-read Dutch author in England, and Philippus van Limborch, professor at the Remonstrant Seminary in Amsterdam. Significantly the latest edition of Grotius's *Opera omnia theologica* had appeared in 1679 in a combined Anglo-Dutch publishing venture, but, judging from the continuous requests by Smith for new copies, this work had become rare by 1688.[24] Of the first edition of Van Limborch's major work, the *Theologia Christiana*, published in Amsterdam by Hendrik Wetstein in 1686, altogether some hundred copies are listed in the correspondence until 1692, when it had sold out completely.[25]

Smith also had some part in the distribution in England of private copies of another book by Van Limborch, the *De veritate religionis*, published at Gouda by Joost van der Hoeve in 1687. In September of that year he had been asked by his Amsterdam correspondent Johannes Janssonius van Waesberge, on behalf of Van Limborch, to act as intermediary in the dispatch of nine copies of this book to friends and relations of the author.[26] Proof of a further connection between Van der Hoeve, Van Waesberge and Van Limborch can be found in another of Van Waesberge's letters to his London colleague. In August 1689 he informed Smith that he had shipped one hundred copies of a 'curious treatise on tolerance', which he supposed would sell well in England.[27]

Indeed it did, for the treatise was John Locke's *Epistola de tolerantia*, written originally as a personal letter to his friend Van Limborch in 1687 and published anonymously in 1689 by the same Joost van der Hoeve at Gouda. But although Van Waesberge in subsequent letters to Smith wrote that he was willing to send additional copies if wanted, his expectations of excellent sales on the British market were soon thwarted by the rapid publication in London of various English editions and translations.

Of course this brief survey of the contents of the trade in religious and theological books between Britain and the Netherlands at the end of the seventeenth century cannot but show the tip of the proverbial iceberg. Moreover, much research on the correspondence still remains to be done, particularly on the identification of many of the titles listed, some of which have rather intriguing titles, such as a frequently mentioned work briefly entitled *Revelator arcanorum*, or the 25 copies which Johannes Janssonius van Waesberge in June 1688 sent to London, bearing the enigmatic title *Philadelphia secta christiana*. And what is one to make of the following French, presumably mystical or pietist tracts, entitled *Clef de l'apocalypse*, *Nouveau ciel et terre* or *Théologie du coeur*? Some books, too, are conspicuously absent from the order lists in the correspondence, especially those works of a more controversial theological nature. For instance, there are hardly any references, direct or indirect, to the writings of Spinoza, whose heretical theological works were certainly read in Britain. Was it because the book trade of Samuel Smith was too much exposed to inspection by the authorities, and is therefore the conclusion justified that works of this nature were exchanged through other channels? On the other hand, on 7 September 1691 Johannes Janssonius van Waesberge openly informed Smith that a ninth volume of the Socinian *Bibliotheca fratrum Polonorum* was about to appear in Amsterdam, and that he could supply him with any number wanted, which indeed he did a few months later.[28] Evidently at the end of the seventeenth century Holland was still 'the gateway for Socininanism into England', as H.J. MacLachlan has put it.[29] Also the fact that Smith hardly ordered any copies of another highly controversial book of the period, Richard Simon's *Histoire critique du Vieux Testament* (Paris, 1678; after its prohibition in France reprinted at Amsterdam in 1685), can not be attributed to any concerns about seizures by the government: an English translation had appeared in 1682, which must have saturated the market.

All in all it can be concluded that, where so few records of a similar nature have survived, the letter-book of Samuel Smith is a highly important source for our knowledge of the Anglo-Dutch book trade as well as of the exchange of knowledge and ideas, theological or otherwise, between Britain and the European continent. To be sure, it is a source with limitations, the most conspicuous one being that the letter-book represents only one half of the correspondence, as Smith's outgoing letters unfortunately have not survived. Also it must be stressed that the 'Latin trade' of Samuel Smith and some of his colleagues in London supplied an exclusively well-educated and reasonably well-off clientele, whose interests should not be taken as representative of those of the average English reading public. Yet it is hoped that the publication and further study of the letter-book can yield a rich harvest to historians from various disciplines.

In the same letter of 8 February 1689 which was mentioned in the beginning of this article, Smith's Amsterdam correspondent Johan Lucas Wetstein, after having enquired whether Mrs. Smith would prefer to have 'a Westfaly hamm or a peece of smoak'd beef' to be sent to her as a token of his friendship, added in a post script, written in English in stead of his usual French:

> I have not forgot yet the Bibel for M[ada]m Smith. She may be shure to have it in the next bale that is to be sent to you. I shall hide it that this sully Hills shal never find it, if the rogue is not turned out allready. I hope you will bee borgemaster in his place.[30]

'Sully Hills' was Henry Hills the Elder, a notorious printer and bookseller, who as Master of the London Stationers' Company was in charge of searching ships coming into port for illicit books, and, to make things worse, had turned Catholic in the last year of James II's reign. By the beginning of 1689, however, Wetstein's anxiety had become superfluous, for in December 1688 the large printing works of Hills at Blackfriars, where many publications defending the policies of the king had been printed, had been plundered and destroyed by an anti-Catholic mob, and like James II Hills had been forced to flee to France where he was to die shortly after.[31] Samuel Smith would never attain the position of Master of the Stationers' Company, but, it must be said, the Glorious Revolution of 1688-89 did not do him any harm either.

[1] Bodleian Library, Oxford, Rawlinson MSS, Letters 114, letter-book of Samuel Smith (henceforth Smith Correspondence), f. 33.

[2] Letter dated Amsterdam, 16 December 1689 (Smith Correspondence, f. 188).

[3] Smith Correspondence, f. 338. Unfortunately the date of this letter has been torn but it can be dated after the autumn fair of 1689.

[4] G. Barber, 'Aspects of the Booktrade between England and the Low Countries in the Eighteenth Century', *Documentatieblad Werkgroep 18e Eeuw*, 34-35 (1977), pp. 47-63, and *idem*, 'Book Imports and Exports in the Eighteenth Century', in R. Myers and M. Harris, *Sale and Distribution of Books from 1700*, Oxford, 1982, pp. 77-106.

[5] See note 1. A full and annotated edition of this correspondence is in preparation by the present author and will be published in a forthcoming volume of the Publications of the Sir Thomas Browne Institute. For an excellent introduction to the letter-book, see N. Hodgson and C. Blagden, *The Notebook of Thomas Bennet and Henry Clements (1686-1719). With Some Aspects of Booktrade Practice*, Oxford, 1956, pp. 9-27.

[6] 'A l'enseigne de[s trois] plumage[s] dans le Coémitière de St. Paul' is the address usually given on the covers of letters received by Smith during these years from his continental correspondents.

[7] John Dunton, *Life and Errors*, ed. J. Nichols, London, 1818, p. 207.

[8] Cf. A.N.L. Munby, 'The Distribution of the First Edition of Newton's *Principia*', in *Essays and Papers. Edited, with an Introduction, by Nicolas Barker*, London, 1978, pp. 43-54. Occasional copies of Newton's book are listed in the letters of the Leiden bookseller Pieter van der Aa (see e.g. Smith Correspondence, f. 275v).

[9] For Hooke's later diary see R.T. Gunther (ed.), 'The Life and Work of Robert Hooke. Part IV: Diary, 1688 to 1693', in *idem, Early Science in Oxford*, vol. X, Oxford, 1935, *passim*.

[10] On the Latin trade see A. Ehrmann and G. Pollard, *The Distribution of Books by Catalogue from the Invention of Printing to A.D. 1800, Based on Material in the Broxbourne Library*, Cambridge, 1965, chap. 4.

[11] *Catalogus librorum rariorum, tam veterum quam recentiorum, ex regionibus Transmarinis in Angliam, nuperimè advectorum, per Sam. Smith bibliopolam. Et apud eum venales extantium, ad insignia principis in coemiterio D. Pauli*, Londini, 1687 (an incomplete copy is preserved in the British Library, s.c. 251 [2]).

[12] Cf. G.C. Gibbs, 'The Role of the Dutch Republic as the Intellectual Entrepôt of Europe in the Seventeenth and Eighteenth Centuries', *Bijdragen en mededelingen betreffende de geschiedenis der Nederlanden*, 86 (1971), pp. 323-49.

[13] On Leusden see L. Hirschel, 'Johannes Leusden als hebraïst (with notes and additions by A.K. Offenberg)', *Studia Rosenthaliana*, 1 (1967), pp. 23-50.

[14] See more extensively P.G. Hoftijzer, 'The Utrecht Hebraist Johannes Leusden and his Relations with the English Booktrade', in C.W. Schoneveld (ed.), *Miscellanea Anglo-Belgica. Papers of the Annual Symposium of the Sir Thomas Browne Institute, Held on 21 November 1986*, Leiden, 1987, pp. 18-26.

[15] In a letter, dated Amsterdam, 31 May 1686, she wrote to Smith: 'I pray if theare is anything worth sending niewly printed which is worth sending, pray send it me in this bundell, and also that of Popery Represented and Misrepresented ... or anything of that nature wich is printed, or any popish boockes'; Smith Correspondence, f. 232v, printed in P.G. Hoftijzer, *Engelse boekverkopers bij de Beurs. De geschiedenis van de Amsterdamse boekhandels Bruyning en Swart, 1637-1724*, Amsterdam/Maarssen, 1987, p. 336.

[16] Smith Correspondence, f. 218, printed in Hoftijzer, *Engelse boekverkopers*, pp. 325-26. Although the widow Swart was a member of the large English community living in Amsterdam, her control of English in writing had clearly deteriorated.

[17] Cf. Smith Correspondence, f. 88, Reinier Leers to Samuel Smith, Rotterdam, 11 February 1690 (Old Style), printed in O.S. Lankhorst, *Reinier Leers (1654-1714). Uitgever & boekverkoper te Rotterdam. Een Europees 'libraire' en zijn fonds*, Amsterdam/Maarssen, 1983, p. 231.

[18] No doubt the most well-read English merchant in Rotterdam at this time was Benjamin Furly, a quaker who possessed an enormous library. John Locke stayed with him during the last two years of his exile. Cf. J.A. van Reijn, 'Benjamin Furly. Engels koopman (en meer!) te Rotterdam, 1636-1714', *Rotterdams jaarboekje*, 9e reeks, 3 (1985), pp. 219-48.

[19] In a letter to Smith, dated 23 November 1687, Leers wrote: 'Je vous prie aussi d'y ajouter pour mon usage un ex[emplaire] des *Sermons* de Tillotson, 8° complet, et s'il y a quelque chose de nouveau, en Latin ou en Anglois, que vous croyes propre pour mon journal, je vous prie aussi de m'en envoyer un'; Smith Correspondence, f. 87, printed in Lankhorst, *Reinier Leers*, p. 229. On Basnage and his journal see H. Bots (ed.), *Henri Basnage de Beauval en de 'Histoire des ouvrages des savans', 1687-1709*, 2 vols., Amsterdam/

Maarssen, 1976. Surely Samuel Smith was not the only channel through which English books arrived in Rotterdam; cf. John Feather, 'English Books on Sale in Rotterdam in 1693', *Quaerendo*, 6 (1976), pp. 365-73.

[20] Smith Correspondence, f. 181 (28 September 1688). The Testaments cost 12 Dutch *stuivers*.

[21] In the same shipment of September 1688 Johannes Janssonius van Waesberge sent 28 copies of this French Testament which had been recently been reprinted. They cost 36 *stuivers*, i.e. 1 guilder 16 *stuivers*, per copy (*ibid.*, f. 182).

[22] For a list of missals etc. to the value of some 300 guilders, which Smith in 1687 or 1688 received from an anonymous bookseller in the Southern Netherlands, see Smith Correspondence, f. 363 (possibly the list is an annex to a letter from Jean Baptiste Verdussen sr, dated 5 May 1688). The Amsterdam booksellers, however, were no less able to supply these books, as can be concluded from the following 'catalogue de les livres catholiques que nous avons', with prices in guilders and *stuivers*, which Johannes Janssonius van Waesberge in December 1687 sent to Smith (Smith Correspondence, f. 173):

Breviarium Romanum 8°	5.4
---------- Carmelitar. discalceatorum 8°	5.4
---------- ---------- idem 12° 4 voll.	9.–
---------- Romanum 12° 4 voll.	6.8
---------- ------- 18° 4 voll.	4.16
Diurnale Romanum 24°	–.18
-------- ------- 32°	–.14
Litaniae variae 24°	–.10
Missale Romanum fol.	7.12
Officium B.M. Virginis 24°	–.14
-------- 32°	–.13
------- hebdomadae sanctae	–.12

Tout argent contant sans rabais.

[23] For this association with its strong political implications see Margaret C. Jacob, *The Cultural Meaning of the Scientific Revolution*, New York, 1988, chap. 4: 'Crisis and Resolution: The Newtonian Enlightenment', pp. 105-35.

[24] The publishers of this edition had been Joan Blaeu of Amsterdam and Moses Pitt, the London bookseller to whom Smith had been apprenticed around 1680. As early as 1686 Johan Lucas Wetstein informed Smith that in his opinion Grotius' *Opera* would soon become difficult to obtain, 'ne restant que fort peu d'exemplaires'; Smith Correspondence, f. 24, letter dated 24 May 1686.

[25] On 23 May 1692 (N.S.) Johannes Janssonius van Waesberge wrote to Smith: 'Les Limborch Theologia ... on ne trouve plus'; Smith Correspondence, f. 203. A second edition of this work was published by Wetstein in 1695; rare issues of the third edition of 1700, published by the Amsterdam bookseller S. Petzold, have a combined Amsterdam/ London imprint, naming Smith and Walford as vendors (Wing L 2305 lists only one copy in the Law Society Library, London).

[26] Van Waesberge wrote on 30 September: 'Dans la balle que nous envoyons par Godfrey [a skipper] nous avons envoyé 9 exemplaires de Limborg de Veritate religionis pour l'auteur, qu'il vous plaira envoyer à son addresse suivant les 7 lettres que vous trouverez dans un tome de la Bibliothèque Universelle tome 6'; Smith Correspondence, f. 168. Apparently Smith did not comply with this request, for two (!) years later, on 7 October 1689 Van Waesberge wrote: 'L'année passé [*sic*] nous avons addressé à vous quelques exemplaires du livre de Monsr. Limborg pour envoyer à quelques évèques et autres de ses amis; vous nous obligeres de nous avertir avec occasion s'ils n'en sont tout rendu à ses addresses, de quoy nous ne doutons, mais comme l'auteur a reçu nouvelles d'un doyen de Salisbury qu'il n'auroit reçu son exemplaire, l'auteur nous a prié de nous informer là dessus chez vous, et si la lettre n'en soit rendu avec l'exemplaire, vous nous obligeres de nous informer afin de satisfaire à Monsr. Limborg'; Smith Correspondence, f. 187.

[27] Johannes Janssonius van Waesberge to Smith, 25 August 1689: 'Dans la balle nous avons envoyé deux traités curieux de Tolerantia et Pace ecclesiastica, qui se débiteront bien aisément chez vous' (Smith Correspondence, f. 185). The treatise 'De pace ecclesiastica' was written by the German theologian Samuel Strimesius, who was of Dutch-English descent and had studied both at Cambridge and Oxford. The title probably refers to one of his earlier irenic works (the *De pace ecclesiastica* appears not to have been published before 1697).

[28] 'Il paroitra dans peu de jours icy un livre in folio à la même forme que les Bibliothèques Sociniennes [de] Crellio, Slichting etc., et presque de la même matière et qui pourroit servir pour une tome neuvième. Le titre ne m'est pas encore connu, mais si vous auriez loisir d'en prendre un nombre et de les avoir premier et tout [ensemble?] je crois que nous aurions l'occasion de vous les faire avoir à un prix raisonnable. Il sera environ 240 feuilles, mais il faudroit se déclarer bientôt, car il y [a] des autres qui le désirent. Le prix nous ne pouvons marquer ...'; Smith Correspondence, ff. 199-97v (leaves bound incorrectly). Apparently this 'ninth volume' of the *Bibliotheca fratrum Polonorum* was Samuel Przipcovius's *Cogitationes sacrae* (Eleutheropolis, 1692), of which Van Waesberge in April 1692 sent 50 copies to Smith (at 8 guilders per copy); on 12 April he wrote: 'Le 9e tome de Fratrum Polonorum étant achevé nous n'avons voulu manquer de vous l'envoyer par la première occasion comme nous avons fait aujourd'huy par Rotterdam ...'; Smith Correspondence, f. 202.

[29] H.J. McLachlan, *Socinianism in Seventeenth-Century England*, Oxford, 1951, chap. 3.

[30] Smith Correspondence, f. 34.

[31] See R. Beddard, 'Anti-Popery and the London Mob, 1688', *History Today*, 38 (1988), p. 39.

WILLIAM III AND THE CHURCH IN UTRECHT
AFTER THE FRENCH OCCUPATION
(1672-1673)

F.G.M. Broeyer

In 1664 William III Prince of Orange, who was then 13 years old, received a number of beautifully bound manuscripts with his initials in golden letters on the back.[1] The young Prince was presented with the books by Lodewijk van Renesse, minister at Breda, a learned man who was an honorary doctor of Oxford. In the United Netherlands Van Renesse had won distinction by his work as a reviser of the authorized version of the Dutch Bible, published in 1637. The synod of Utrecht had appointed him to this task when he was a minister in the province of Utrecht. In his preface to the manuscripts Van Renesse spoke about the prayers of many people, who hoped that the Prince would be saved for the good of the Dutch Republic and the church. He reminded William of the example of two very young kings of the past, namely Josiah, King of Judah, and Edward VI, King of England.[2]

What were those manuscripts that the Prince had received? They were minutes and regulations for the government of church life, drawn up by synods of the Dutch Reformed Church. Van Renesse's gift thus shows in a striking way the ambivalent character of the affection of the Dutch Orangist ministers. They expected a Prince of Orange to protect the rights of the church and oppose infringements of them. Their Orangism was nourished above all by the hope that the actions of a Prince of Orange would benefit the church. Whereas the Grand Pensionary John de Witt and his adherents tried to exclude William III from the offices that had long been held by his ancestors, a majority of the ministers hoped for a change-over which would win him the Stadholdership. They cherished this hope because they felt that the partisans of De Witt oppressed the church.[3]

Gisbertus Voetius

In Utrecht the situation was similar. For five decades the church of Utrecht had had its great man in Gisbertus Voetius. Having come to Utrecht in 1634 to the professorate of theology, he in 1637 had also become a minister of the Reformed church there and by the influence originating from these two important offices he had made Utrecht a stronghold of orthodoxy.[4] Voetius was a man who detected the dangers of heresy everywhere and immediately took up the pen in defence of the true doctrine. He was extremely worried about the philosophy of Descartes, with whom he disputed in such a fierce manner that he even exceeded the bounds of decency.[5] Later on he polemized against Johannes Coccejus, his colleague in Leiden, because of the latter's doctrine of the covenant, which appeared dangerous to Voetius on account of its implications for the observance of the Sabbath and the doctrine of Redemption.[6] In the church of Utrecht Voetius had succeeded in surrounding himself with a circle of kindred spirits who supported him in this endeavour. In the rest of the country he was held in such respect, that the party of Voetians was named after him.[7]

It is largely owing to Voetius that Utrecht had become a major spiritual centre in the United Provinces. Nevertheless he was not always successful and in 1660 he suffered an especially crushing defeat. After fighting for years against the use of the property of the five old chapters in Utrecht for other than pious ends, he was defeated disastrously. This needs some explanation. During the Middle Ages there were five chapters in Utrecht. With the Reformation the episcopal see was surpressed, but not the chapters, which were secularized. Noblemen and patricians could now obtain the chapter offices, which yielded attractive incomes. Moreover, the men who held those benefices were eligible for a number of seats in the States of Utrecht. Long before the arrival of Voetius in Utrecht this state of affairs had led to controversy. However, more than any other before him he did his utmost to put an end to this use of the rich property of the chapters for private means. After some small successes during the preceding years, from 1658 onwards Voetius and his adherents among the Utrecht ministers stepped up their pressure by trying to prevail on the prospective prebendaries to refuse chapter benefices. In the beginning this succeeded, but after a number of failures tension mounted to a high degree. In 1660 the magistrate of Utrecht took action against the inflammatory sermons of some ministers and two of them, Abraham van de Velde and Johannes Teellinck, were exiled from the city by the States of Utrecht.[8]

For Voetius and his supporters this was a great set-back. They had intended to create a situation in Utrecht which was in accord with their theocratic ideal, but their efforts to reform public life seemed to have failed. The realization of another of their aims, a re-modelling of the individual's way of life, also proved to be a more arduous task than had been anticipated, owing to the lack of cooperation on the side of the authorities. However, there was still one thing they could hope for, another government. So there is no reason to doubt the words of Cornelis Gentman, who preached the funeral sermon for Voetius in 1676, when he spoke about Voetius's high expectations with regard to William III. According to Gentman, in the time of John de Witt, Voetius had repeatedly said that the state of affairs would change for the better as soon as Prince William was given the dignities that earlier members of the House of Orange had held.[9] The leaders of the church of Utrecht were themselves devout believers so they expected the members of the government to repent in times of trouble too. Hence in 1672, when the Dutch Republic was threatened by enemies from all sides, they returned to an old project for the further reformation of public and individual life, which had been drawn up after the bad tidings about the battle against the British fleet near Lowestoft in June 1665.[10] After the French occupation, which lasted from July 1672 to November 1673, the church of Utrecht once more took up this programme, which contained recommendations for a society agreeable to the commandments of God. In the memorandum of 1665 excesses such as luxurious meals and too fashionable clothes especially had been a target for the men of the church. Measures were to be taken amongst other things against swearing, excessive drinking and card games. It also asked for a strict observance of the Sabbath and reminded the authorities that they should assist the church in achieving its aims. Twice the word 'interest', a key word of the period, was used.[11] The first reference pointed out that one of the major faults of the authorities was their lack of consideration for the advancement of religion as the highest interest of city and country; instead private interest was given priority, or at best the material welfare of the country.[12] This point was repeated at the end of the memorandum. It had to be made clear to the authorities that the honour of God ought to be the greatest interest of a government, and not prosperity, let alone private interest.[13]

But what happened at the end of the French occupation? Supporters of Voetius tried to take the helm and they had ample opportunity to do so, as the new situation was very unsettled. The province of Holland strove to punish Utrecht because, according to Holland, it had capitulated far too easily to the French. It even wanted to deprive Utrecht of its place among the United Provinces in the States General. William III on his part wished to break the power of those men in Utrecht, who had sided or seemed to have sided with De Witt.[14] A few days after the retreat of the French troops a military government was set up in the province and the city council of Utrecht and the States were suspended by order of the States General. However, a petition against the existing authorities also played a significant part. Notable was the fact that many

of the subscribers were Voetians, including former and present members
of the consistory. It was to this petition that the commander of the
troops of the States General, William Count of Horne, referred when he
announced the suspension of the governing bodies.[15]

The True Interest

In April 1674 William III had to go to Utrecht and settle matters
there. In opposition to Holland, he had seen to it that Utrecht should
regain its place in the union. He set up a new city council and also renewed the States of the province. Shortly thereafter the consistory sent
delegates to give their best wishes and especially God's blessing to the
new city council and the States. It was on that occasion that the project
of 1665 for further reformation was again warmly recommended to the
authorities of the city.[16] The timing seemed right as many men who had
held office in the consistory had been appointed to positions in the government. They were acquainted with the document of 1665. The delegates of the consistory even had reason to expect that they should re-
member something at least of what should be the true interest of everybody and especially of the magistrate.

Somehow expectations must have been running high. For another
committee, sent by the consistory a few days earlier to congratulate William III on his elevation by the new States to the hereditary Stadholdership of Utrecht, had been given a remarkable extra assignment. The
committee, of which Voetius—now in his eighties—was one of the
members, had to ask for the cancellation of the resolution of 1660
against the ministers Teellinck and Van de Velde. From the report that
the members of the committee delivered to the consistory, it appears
that they did not achieve any success at all. The military governor of
Utrecht, Horne, told them after a short interview with the Prince that
the time was not yet ripe to discuss the return of the two exiled ministers.[17]

Besides, it was ominous that William III submitted to the new States
of Utrecht a statute with elaborate provisions for the use of the prebends
of the five chapters and that of the secularized property of the former
convents. The new arrangement was very favourable to the Stadholder,
as the statute gave him a great deal of control over the bestowing of the
benefices and the spending of the money, through which he could ensure
that people became indebted to him. It had become quite impossible to
dream about the ideal of the exclusive use of the prebends for pious
ends, as Voetius, a number of his Utrecht fellow-professors and the
majority of the ministers in the city had advocated during the 1650s.
Also by other regulations the new statute for the government of the

province implied a gigantic enlargement of the Stadholder's authority. He was invested with the right to appoint and discharge so many low and high government officials, that theoretically he wielded absolute power in the province and city of Utrecht.[18]

All in all those days of congratulations and celebration of the change of government offered few reasons for real joy for the party of Voetius. But it is highly questionable whether Voetius and his men were aware of this in the euphoria of those days. The more so as the consistory had got its way in one of its points. Since 1660 the church had had to accept over and over again that proposals on its part for the calling of a minister were refused. This had been the case in 1672 and 1673 with a minister of Woerden, Henricus de Rijp. Repeated attempts to get this calling approved had failed.[19] The delegates, sent to transmit the best wishes to the city council, had been specially instructed to ask for De Rijp's calling to be approved. And in this they succeeded. The agreement of the city council could be announced as soon as the next meeting of the consistory.[20] The approbation seemed promising.

But the optimism of the Voetians was unwarranted. As early as June 1674 the consistory was confronted with the case of a man, referred to in the minutes as N.N., who had had a benefice presented to him. The problem of this benefice was that it had been expressly withdrawn from the circulation for private means, as it had been 'mortified'. By its having been handed over to N.N. this mortification had been undone.[21] From later minutes of the consistory it appears that this N.N. was a former deacon of the Utrecht reformed church, Gijsbert van Brienen.[22] Naturally the consistory which so ardently wished to see the interest of the church put before private interest and the interest of city and country, could not ignore this. At first, however, the church council was content with Van Brienen's excuse that he had not known about the change.[23]

Voetius himself may have been in a rather hopeful mood about the end of this affair, or else he was now too old to get angry. Otherwise it would be difficult to understand why he acted as witness to the marriage of his grandson Paul Voet van Winssen and a daughter of the man who had accepted the prebend, Gijsbert van Brienen in 1675.[24] However, one of the best known ministers of Utrecht in those days, Jodocus van Lodensteyn, was in very low spirits about the situation. When in 1674 several church buildings were severely damaged by a hurricane and the nave of the cathedral collapsed, he delivered a sermon in which he interpreted the hurricane as a judgment of God.[25] A few months later William III thought it necessary to use the Utrecht minister Cornelis Gentman to convey a message to his colleague Van Lodensteyn. The

Prince ordered Van Lodensteyn to be more careful about political matters in his sermons. The fact of this censure is apparent from a letter directed by Gentman to William III on 20 November 1674.[26] He wrote that he had passed down the reprimand to Van Lodensteyn and that the minister in question had promised henceforth to take the Prince's point of view into account.

Gentman appears to have thought that William III owed him a favour in return for this service. As a result of the death of the alderman Cornelis van der Voort, a former burgomaster, there happened to be an important vacancy in the government of Utrecht. Gentman made an appeal to the Stadholder to confer this office on his son Adriaen, as the post would be highly attractive for his son on account of his planned marriage. After all, with his income as a minister he was unable to give the necessary financial support. If the Prince acceded to his request, he would confess 'eternally' that His Highness had given his family social prestige.[27] On 7 December the city council was acquainted with the decision of the Stadholder to appoint Adriaen Gentman to the aldermanship.[28]

The request of Cornelis Gentman does not leave a very good impression of him, but such things were quite common in those times. In April 1674 Adriaen Gentman had been one of the Voetians brought into the new government by William III as a member of the city council.[29] Now he had taken another step up the social ladder. No doubt Cornelis Gentman soothed his conscience with the thought that the preferment of his son was to the advantage of the Voetian party. On 21 November 1674, a day after Gentman, Gisbertus Voetius and Andreas Essenius—another professor of theology in Utrecht—also wrote a letter to the Stadholder.[30] Probably the day of thanksgiving on 13 November ordered by the States to commemorate the retreat of the French army a year previously had given them this idea.[31] They congratulated the Prince on his successful military campaigns, esteemed by them as a blessing of the Almighty, and asked him to shield the reformed religion. Above all things they gave utterance to their hope that he would protect it against the dangerous novelties that were creeping into the universities and the church and were contrary to the purity of the faith and the correct exposition of the Holy Scriptures, as found in the annotations of the Dutch Bible, 'faithfully' rendered by order of the States General and by the resolution of the Synod of Dort, and 'thus expounded'.[32] In 1672, at his elevation to the Stadholdership, Cornelis Trigland, the minister who had been William III's religious mentor during his youth, had insisted in his congratulatory letter that only sincerely orthodox reformed men should be nominated to town councils.[33] Consequently Voetius and Essenius may have hailed with great satisfaction the subsequent nomination to the aldermanship of the son of their fellow minister.

However, the expectations with respect to the role of the Voetians in the government did not materialize. Adriaen Gentman was steward of the secularized property of the church for the use of pious ends. It was of no avail. The consistory did its very best to persuade Van Brienen that he ought to give up his benefice in order that it might be used again for pious ends.[34] It did the same with a similar prebend which was given to a nobleman some time later.[35] In the autumn of 1675 the consistory decided that Van Brienen had no right to shelter behind excuses any longer and it excluded him from partaking of Holy Communion.[36] Van Brienen reacted with a reference to the resolution of the States General, which, he claimed, had authorized William III in April 1674 to have all offices and prebends in Utrecht at his disposal. Thereupon he appealed to the Prince. Reacting to this request the Stadholder asked the consistory to inform him about the rights as to the benefice in question. The church council drew up a circumstantial account with data about the historical background of the dispute. It accused Van Brienen of notorious untruths in his petition. Van Brienen's complaint about his exclusion from the Holy Communion was purely a church affair. In the opinion of the members of the consistory, submitting it to the Prince was in violation of Article 31 of the book of discipline drawn up by the synod of Dort, that was in force in Utrecht.[37] During an interview with the Prince delegates of the consistory were allowed to elucidate their point of view. But they could not bring the Prince any further than the pronouncement that the case had to be settled.[38] In the mean time William III had experienced how profitable the use of the property of the chapters and the convents was for other than pious means. On 12 June 1674 the States of Utrecht had presented him with the very rich treasury of St. Marie, so that now he himself enjoyed an income from the property of the chapters.[39] The dissension between the consistory and Van Brienen was a long drawn out affair. On 23 February 1677 the church council felt obliged to admit that the demands as to the benefices had no chance of success. Van Brienen and the other person who benefitted from a mortified prebend were admitted to the Holy Communion again on the understanding that they had to judge its lawfulness in their own consciences. The consistory decided to wait for a better opportunity before trying again.[40] In January 1679 an acceptable arrangement was considered possible, but still to no avail. In their final resolution of 3 March 1679 the consistory advised utter prudence to the ministers in their public remarks concerning the question of the mortified prebends.[41]

As early as 1675 relations between the church and the government were far from friendly. On 1 November 1675 the consistory passed a resolution to complain to the classis about the infringement on the rights of the church by the civil authorities and to call in the assistance of the classis. Means were needed, as the consistory put it, to restore the power of Christ in his Kingdom on earth.[42] It was understandable that the church of Utrecht worried about the situation. A few weeks later the consistory even had to protest against the appointment of a reader by the States. The consistory thought it very wrong that the States wanted to decide who should read the lessons and direct the community singing. In the petition against the new reader it was said again, that the right of the church had to be considered as the right of Christ. Obviously the consistory found it hard to accept these developments.[43]

'The sin of their predecessors'

The most disheartening problem for the church was the development around the exile of the ministers Teellinck and Van de Velde. The consistory wrote several letters to them. All these letters show, that the church looked upon their exile as an utter injustice. The members of the church council believed that Teellinck and Van de Velde still belonged by right to the church of Utrecht, for the church of Utrecht had never agreed to their departure.[44] The ministers concerned tried in vain to bring the consistory to some realism. Teellinck wrote that there was probably not enough money in Utrecht to pay the two supernumerary ministers.[45] Van de Velde suggested that many people thought differently about the claim of Utrecht and hinted that he himself did so too.[46] All this was of no avail. Teellinck died in May 1674, but the consistory nourished high hopes, when in May of the following year William III gave permission to Van de Velde to visit Utrecht. As a result of this visit to Utrecht some petitions were presented to the consistory requesting once again his permanent return. Objections to his sojourn were expressed as well. The president of the States of Utrecht, Johan van Reede Baron of Renswoude, said in a letter to William III that the case was causing serious divisions within the city council.[47] He warned him of the dangerous effects of any seditious sermons that might be delivered by Van de Velde, and any conventicles he might organize. The government would run unacceptable risks. In his turn Van de Velde defended himself against such allegations in a detailed apology directed to the Stadholder.[48] On 19 June 1676, after a long period of preliminary contacts, the consistory decided to ask the States of Utrecht for the repeal of the resolution of 1660 against Van de Velde and Teellinck.[49] Like Van Lodensteyn, the consistory spoke about the judgments of God, which had come upon the city and the province in consequence of the expulsion of the two ministers. The recent change of government, brought about by the wonderful providence of God, now offered an opportunity to take away the cause of those judgments. The consistory voiced the supposition that the men of the new government might have received their power from God on purpose to undo the injustice suffered by the two ministers. It expressed its sincere hope that they would not be guilty of the sin of their predecessors.

The States reacted angrily to the wording used in the petition and the members of the consistory were informed immediately.[50] Three weeks later, on 6 July, a more official answer was received. The president of the States, Johan van Reede, gave the consistory to understand that the States considered the resolution of 1660 as valid with the addition that they were ill-pleased that the church council had dared to send a petition like that.[51] In February 1677, when the consistory still continued to remind them of the wickedness of the resolution of 1660, the States of Utrecht came to the decision that it should be upheld under all circumstances. In the future no petition about this case should be accepted.[52] However, for the consistory it was a matter of principle, indeed, a matter of the right of Christ. Therefore it made a new attempt after the death of Van de Velde in May 1677. The church council persuaded itself that the negative attitude of the authorities had been caused by the troublesome personality of Van de Velde, whom they did not find acceptable in Utrecht. Therefore the consistory addressed itself to the city council with the request to intercede on behalf of the church with the States of Utrecht. On 18 March 1678 the consistory's delegates for the cause of the two exiled ministers finally had to report that there was no possibility that the States would withdraw and cancel their 1660 resolution.[53]

Peace and Quiet

William III was involved both in the case of the negotiations about the property of the chapters and in that of the resolution of 1660. It is clear that if he had wished the consistory would have succeeded. William III's power was nearly unlimited in Utrecht because of the statute for the government of the province of 1674. The striking thing is, that in some conflicts elsewhere the Stadholder intervened in favour of the Voetian orthodoxy. His education had been orthodox-calvinistic and he considered himself spiritually akin to the adherents of that tendency in the Dutch Reformed Church. Why then did he not do likewise in Utrecht and choose to favour the Voetians? The reason is, that the conflicts elsewhere, in Middelburg and Leyden, were more than anything else conflicts within the church,[54] while in Utrecht the relation between church and state was at stake. The Dutch historian D.J. Roorda has described William III as 'a politically gifted pragmatist'.[55] William III thought apparently, that the interest of the church of Utrecht could not take precedence over the interest of city and country. He regarded his policy as the true interest of the country and of the Dutch church as well. All other interests had to be instrumental to that great interest.

William III was very much set on peace and quiet at home. Therefore he increasingly came to appreciate a policy of toleration. In this he was in line with the views of his close adviser Gilbert Burnet, who, though himself an Anglican—after the Revolution he became Bishop of Salisbury—was able to preach to the English presbyterian community at Utrecht without any problem.[56] During the 1680s and 1690s new theological controversies arose as a result of the growing rationalism in the Dutch Republic. William III exerted himself to bring about a resolution for peace and quiet in the province of Holland to put an end to all those quarrels.[57] This happened in 1694, and a year later Utrecht followed. The Utrecht resolution of 8 June 1695 began with a statement about its aims: 'Nothing', it says among other things, 'does please His Majesty the King of Great Britain so much as unity and mutual love in the Church.'[58] The resolution was signed by the secretary of the States of Utrecht. Naturally a secretary of the States was not in a position to refuse signing a resolution, but he held a high office which could not be associated too readily with opponents of the official policy. Who was that secretary in 1695? It was Paul Voet van Winssen, the grandson of that indefatigable fighter for an orthodox Reformed church, Gisbertus Voetius, who did not accept the slightest deviation in doctrine and life. He too wanted peace and quiet, but in quite another way.

[1] Algemeen Rijksarchief, The Hague, Archief Staten van Holland 1572-1795, 4381.

[2] *Ibid.*, Volume 'Behelsende alle de Nationale Synoden', Dedication, 22 September 1664.

[3] T. uit den Bogaard, *De gereformeerden en Oranje tijdens het eerste stadhouderloze tijdperk*, Groningen, 1955; G. Groenhuis, *De sociale positie van de gereformeerde predikanten in de Republiek der Verenigde Nederlanden voor ca 1700*, Groningen, 1977, pp. 90-91.

[4] A.C. Duker, *Gisbertus Voetius*, 4 vols., Leiden, 1897-1915 (reprint Leiden, 1989).

[5] K. van Berkel, 'Descartes in debat met Voetius. De mislukte introductie van het cartesianisme aan de Utrechtse universiteit (1639-1645)', *Tijdschrift voor de geschiedenis der geneeskunde, natuurwetenschappen, wiskunde en techniek*, 7 (1984), pp. 4-18; R. Descartes and Martin Schoock, *La Querelle d'Utrecht. Textes établis, traduits et annotés par Theo Verbeek*, Paris, 1988.

[6] W.J. van Asselt, *Amicitia Dei. Een onderzoek naar de structuur van de theologie van Johannes Coccejus (1603-1669)*, Ede, 1988.

[7] C. Gentman, *Allon bachuth, of lijck-predikatie, over de dood van den hoog-beroemden heere Gisbertus Voetius*, Utrecht, 1677, p. 19.

⁸ Rijksarchief Utrecht (RA Utrecht), Archief Staten van Utrecht, 232:29, Resolutions of 19 July 1660.

⁹ Gentman, *Allon bachuth*, p. 21.

¹⁰ Gemeentelijke Archiefdienst Utrecht (GA Utrecht), Archief Hervormde Gemeente, 8, Acta Kerkeraad, 28 June 1665.

¹¹ The idea of 'interest' had been introduced by the Florentine author Francesco Guicciardini and had come into use thanks to Henri Duke of Rohan's *De l'Interest des princes et estats de la Chrestienté*, n. pl., 1639. Cf. L.A. McKenzie, 'Natural Right and the Emergence of the Idea of Interest in Modern Political Thought: Francesco Guicciardini and Jean de Silhon', in *History of European Ideas*, 2 (1981), pp. 277-98; M. van der Bijl, 'Pieter de la Court en de politieke werkelijkheid', in *Pieter de la Court en zijn tijd (1618-1685). Aspecten van een veelzijdig publicist*, Amsterdam/Maarssen, 1986, p. 67.

¹² GA Utrecht, Hervormde Gemeente, 8, Acta Kerkeraad, 28 June 1665: 'ende sijn derhalven tot dien einde bijsonderlijk te bestraffen ... Ook dat men 't hoogste interest van ons land en stad niet en stelt de Religie en de bevorderinge des selven, maer of sijn eigen interest, ijder uit sijn eigen einde, of ten besten genomen de neringe en lichamelijke welvaert van 't land.' For the complete text of the memorandum, see F.A. van Lieburg, *De Nadere Reformatie in Utrecht ten tijde van Voetius. Sporen in de gereformeerde kerkeraadsacta*, Rotterdam, 1989, pp. 25-29.

¹³ *Ibid.*: 'Ook aen de Overigheid te recommanderen dat doch 't hoogste einde of oog-merk van 't gansche land en des selfs Regeringe mogte sijn de eer van God Almagtig en de welstant van 't Coninkrijke Jesu Christi, en niet als 't bijsonderste interest van staet de neringe en lichamelijke welvaert van 't volk, of ook niet eigen interesten, en voordeel.'

¹⁴ D.J. Roorda, 'Prins Willem III en het Utrechtse regeringsreglement. Een schets van gebeurtenissen, achtergronden en problemen', in H.L.Ph. Leeuwenberg and L. van Tongerloo (eds.), *Van standen tot Staten. 600 Jaar Staten van Utrecht, 1375-1975*, Utrecht, 1975, pp. 104-17.

¹⁵ *Ibid.*, pp. 110-11.

¹⁶ GA Utrecht, Hervormde Gemeente, 10, Acta Kerkeraad, 20 April 1674. For the version of the project for further reformation of 1665 in the petition to the city council, see *ibid.*, 8, Acta Kerkeraad, 7 July 1665 (text between 28 June and 3 July 1665), and Van Lieburg, *De Nadere Reformatie in Utrecht*, pp. 30-33 (with wrong date).

¹⁷ GA Utrecht, Hervormde Gemeente, 10, Acta Kerkeraad, 14 and 20 April 1674.

¹⁸ Roorda, 'Willem III en het Utrechtse regeringsreglement', pp. 91, 92, 119-23; cf. R. Fruin, *Geschiedenis der staatsinstellingen in Nederland tot den val der Republiek*, H.T. Colenbrander (ed.), 's-Gravenhage, 1922 (Rpt. 's-Gravenhage, 1980), pp. 288-93. For the text of the statute see RA Utrecht, Staten van Utrecht, 232:37, Resolutions of 16 April 1674. Cf. also Roorda, 'Willem III en het Utrechtse regeringsreglement', p. 128, note 3.

¹⁹ GA Utrecht, Hervormde Gemeente, 10, Acta Kerkeraad, 21 April, 15, 20 May, 8, 10 June 1672; 19, 22 May, 7, 23 July 1673.

²⁰ *Ibid.*, 20 and 23 April 1674. Cf. 23 March and 24 May 1674.

²¹ *Ibid.*, 25 June 1674.

²² *Ibid.*, 29 March 1675.

²³ *Ibid.*, 2 April 1675.

²⁴ Duker, *Gisbertus Voetius*, III, p. 325, note 4. The wedding took place on 13 June 1675.

²⁵ J.E.A.L. Struick, *Utrecht door de eeuwen heen*, Utrecht/Antwerpen, 1968, pp. 227, 238

²⁶ Letter of Cornelis Gentman to William III, 20/30 November 1674 (contrary to Holland Utrecht still used the Julian calendar), in *Correspondentie van Willem III en van Hans Willem Bentinck, eersten Graaf van Portland*, N. Japikse (ed.), I, 2nd part (Rijks Geschiedkundige Publicatiën [RGP], Kleine serie, vol. 26), 's-Gravenhage, 1932, p. 527. Cf. G.W. Kernkamp, *De Utrechtse Academie*, I (1636-1815), Utrecht, 1936, pp. 273-74; J.C. Trimp, *Jodocus van Lodensteyn. Predikant en dichter*, Kampen, 1987, pp. 156-57. Trimp shows that there may be a connection between a sermon of Van Lodensteyn delivered on 23 September 1674, in which he had severely criticized the Utrecht magistrate, and the reprimand by the Prince.

²⁷ Letter of Cornelis Gentman to William III, 20/30 November 1674 (see note 26): '... en ik eeuwelijk erkennen mag dat U Hoogᵗ. mijn huis geformeert heeft.'

²⁸ GA Utrecht, Archief stad Utrecht, 2:121, Vroedschapsresoluties, 7 December 1674.

²⁹ *Ibid.*, 2:117, Lijst van de leden van het stedelijk bestuur, 1528-1723, Extract resoluties, 17 April 1674.

³⁰ Letter of Andreas Essenius and Gisbertus Voetius to William III, 21 November/1 December 1674, in *Correspondentie van Willem III*, I, 2nd part, pp. 528-29.

³¹ RA Utrecht, Staten van Utrecht, 232:37, Resoluties, 6 October 1674. Cf. *ibid.*, 232:38, 5 November 1675. Henceforth a day of thanksgiving was held on the Thursday before 13 November.

³² Letter of Andreas Essenius and Gisbertus Voetius to William III (see note 30): 'tot stuiting en weering der gevaerlike en rust-verstoorende nieuigheden, die al vast door eenige in de hooge Scholen en Kerken worden ingevoerd; strijdig tegen de rechte eenvoudigheid en suiverheid des Geloofs, welk eenmael den Heiligen was over-geleverd; en tegen de geduerige Schrift-matige uitleggingen van Gods H. Woord, in de Randteikeningen onses Bibels, door last van de Hoog-Mog: Heeren de Staten Generael der Vereenigde Nederlanden, en volgens 't besluit van de Synode Nationael, welke tot Dordrecht gehouden is in de jaren 1618 en 19, in onse Nederlandsche tale neerstig en getrouwelik over-gesett, en soo verklaerd.'

³³ Letter of Cornelis Trigland to William III, no date (1672), in E.J.W. Posthumus Meyjes, *Kerkelijk 's-Gravenhage in vroeger eeuw*, 's-Gravenhage, 1918, pp. 22-23.

³⁴ GA Utrecht, Hervormde Gemeente, 10, Acta Kerkeraad, 29 March, 3, 17, 31 May, 7, 21, 28 June, 3, 19 July 1675.

³⁵ *Ibid.*, 1 October 1675. The nobleman in question was Johan Louis Godin, Lord of Maerssenbroeck.

³⁶ *Ibid.*, 1 October 1675. Cf. for Godin, *ibid.*, 3 April 1676.

³⁷ *Ibid.*, 8 October and 27 and 28 December 1675.

³⁸ *Ibid.*, 24 January 1676.

³⁹ Koninklijk Huisarchief, The Hague, A 16, VII 5d, Acte van overdracht van landen, tienden enz. van de thesaurie van St. Marie, 12 June 1674. Cf. RA Utrecht, Staten van Utrecht, 232:37, Resolutions, 12 June 1674.

⁴⁰ GA Utrecht, Hervormde Gemeente, 10, Acta Kerkeraad, 23 February 1677.

⁴¹ *Ibid.*, 27 January, 17 February and 3 March 1679. Cf. the text of the interesting attestation of Johan Louis Godin, *ibid.*, 21 July 1679.

⁴² *Ibid.*, 1 November 1675. Cf. RA Utrecht, Archief Hervormde Classis Utrecht, 5, Acta Classis, 2 and 3 November 1675, art. 18.

⁴³ GA Utrecht, Hervormde Gemeente, 10, Acta Kerkeraad, 29 November 1675. Cf. *ibid.*, 22 November, 6, 13, 20 December 1675, 17 January 1676. The name of the reader was Frederick van Bemmel.

⁴⁴ *Ibid.*, 10 February 1674, 16 and 23 August 1675.

⁴⁵ *Ibid.*, 5 and 13 February 1674.

⁴⁶ *Ibid.*, 16 and 23 August 1675.

⁴⁷ Letter of Johan Reede, Baron of Renswoude to William III, 6 July 1675 in *Correspondentie van Willem III*, I, 2nd part, pp. 45-46.

⁴⁸ Letter of Abraham van de Velde to William III, no date (July 1675), *ibid.*, pp. 50-52.

⁴⁹ GA Utrecht, Hervormde Gemeente, 10, Acta Kerkeraad, 19 June 1676.

⁵⁰ *Ibid.*, 26 June 1676.

⁵¹ *Ibid.*, 6 July 1676.

⁵² RA Utrecht, Staten van Utrecht, 232:39, 8 February 1677. Cf. GA Utrecht, Hervormde Gemeente, 10, Acta Kerkeraad, 11 June 1677 and also 29 December 1676 and 19 February 1677.

⁵³ *Ibid.*, 11 June, 24 December 1677 and 18 March 1678.

⁵⁴ M. van der Bijl, *Idee en interest. Voorgeschiedenis, verloop en achtergronden van de politieke twisten in Zeeland en vooral in Middelburg tussen 1702 en 1715*, Groningen, 1981, pp. 25-26,

81, 313-14; T.A. McCahagan, *Cartesianism in the Netherlands, 1639-1676. The New Science and the Calvinist Counter-Reformation*, Ph.D. Thesis University of Pennsylvania, (Microfilm copy Ann Arbor, 1978), pp. 321-47. Naturally the intervention in favour of the Voetians elsewhere had political effects as the urban factions were an important factor in Dutch politics; cf. D.J. Roorda, *Partij en factie. De oproeren van 1672 in de steden van Holland en Zeeland. Een krachtmeting tussen partijen en facties*, Groningen, 1961, pp. 4-36. For political reasons William III had to make use of the local factions and the connections between the factions throughout the Netherlands; cf. S. Groenveld, '"J'équipe une flotte très considérable". The Dutch Side of the Glorious Revolution', in R.A. Beddard (ed.), *The Revolution of 1688* (provisional title for the forthcoming publication at Oxford of the 1988 Andrew Browning Lectures).

[55] D.J. Roorda, 'De Republiek in de tijd van Stadhouder Willem III', in *Algemene Geschiedenis der Nederlanden*, VIII, Haarlem, 1979, p. 282. Cf. *idem*, 'Willem III, de Koning-Stadhouder', in *Rond Prins en patriciaat. Verspreide opstellen*, pp. 118-42; M. van der Bijl, 'Willem III, Stadhouder-koning: Pro religione et libertate', in *Achter den tijd. Opstellen aangeboden aan Dr. G. Puchinger*, Haarlem, 1986, pp. 162-67.

[56] G. Burnet, *History of His Own Time: From the Restoration of Charles II to the Treaty of Peace at Utrecht in the Reign of Queen Anne*, II, London, 1847 (new ed.), pp. 438-39. Cf. K.L. Sprunger, *Dutch Puritanism. A History of English and Scottish Churches in the Netherlands in the Sixteenth and Seventeenth Centuries*, Leiden, 1982, p. 453.

[57] J. Reitsma and J. Lindeboom, *Geschiedenis van de Hervorming en de Hervormde Kerk der Nederlanden*, 5th ed., 's-Gravenhage, 1949, p. 334; O.J. de Jong, *Nederlandse kerkgeschiedenis*, 3d ed., Nijkerk, 1986, p. 243.

[58] RA Utrecht, Staten van Utrecht, 232:46, Resoluties, 8 June 1695. Cf. *ibid.*, Classis Utrecht, 6, Acta Classis, 13 and 14 August, art. 11 and the annexed copy of the printed version of the resolution. Professor J.K. Cameron drew my attention to a similar pursuit of peace and quiet in Scotland. William Carstares—who had studied in Utrecht for some years and, like Burnet, was closely involved in the preparations for the Glorious Revolution—rendered assistance to William III in his policy with respect to the Church of Scotland. Cf. A.I. Dunlop, *William Carstares and the Kirk by Law Established* (The Chambers Lectures, 1964), Edinburgh, 1967.

VOWS MADE IN STORMS …
TWO UTRECHT PROFESSORS AMONG
ORANGISTS AND PATRIOTS

Johanna Roelevink

'God save the Batavian Republic and protect our august Prince-Stadholder. The Lord establish our city and return liberty to all and the former privileges to the people.' Christophorus Saxe, professor of antiquities and letters in the University of Utrecht, wrote these politically ambiguous words in 1786 in the draft of an oration which was never to reach the final stages.[1] Years before he had made a similar false start, but this time exalting the Stadholder as the 'Eminent head of the Republic'.[2] If these orations had actually been delivered and printed, they would have been in strong contrast with the one that Saxe wrote in 1798, for by then he had openly joined the Patriots.

One of his colleagues who must have been listening to this last effort with growing resentment was Gisbertus Bonnet, the senior professor of theology, an unwavering Orangist, who together with Saxe had weathered all the storms of the Patriot revolution in Utrecht in the last quarter of the eighteenth century. Some aspects of this revolution will be dealt with by looking at the personal struggle of these two professors, one a theologian in the Netherlands Reformed Church, the other a Lutheran proponent who had turned to classical scholarship.[3]

The city of Utrecht in the eighteenth century ranked fourth in the Republic with about 35,000 inhabitants. Though Protestants predominated, there was a Roman-Catholic minority of about thirty percent. Forty percent of the comparatively wealthy population was engaged in economic and social services, whereas another forty percent earned a living in industry. But as in most parts of the Dutch Republic at the time, things were not going well. Industry was in decline and so was the main social service, the University. Yet, it still drew students from the surrounding provinces as well as from the protestant parts of Germany, from England, Scotland and Hungary and its reputation for religious orthodoxy and sound learning was high.[4]

Utrecht was one of the hotbeds of Patriotism. On 10 December 1785 the city became, in the words of Simon Schama, the very first revolutionary commune.[5] The University played a leading role in this process, for like elsewhere in the Netherlands professors, students and young graduates took more than a fair share in the learned and journalistic output of Patriotism. More particularly Utrecht University had been foremost in encouraging the study of medieval and modern Dutch law. It is therefore hardly surprising that so many Patriot political leaders, including Pieter Paulus, Joan Derk van der Capellen tot den Poll, Quint Ondaatje and Bernd Bicker, had taken their degrees there.[6]

Orangism had an intellectual stronghold in Utrecht too, with Rijklof Michaël van Goens, a very learned and incisive political debater. A more abiding Orangist influence was exercised by the theological faculty of which Gisbertus Bonnet was the leading member. Having made a distinguished career as a minister, he was appointed professor in 1761. An asset to his profession, Bonnet would certainly have got the opportunity to fill prestigious posts elsewhere. But in 1764 he promised to stay in Utrecht in return for higher wages and the very unusual guarantee that at his death his widow would get a pension.[7]

Bonnet was a sound if not very prolific scholar of national reputation and a warmly appreciated teacher. Popular with the students, he took a sincere interest in them.[8] He preached regularly in a simple, appealing style and was widely acclaimed for it. Moreover, Bonnet was the heart and soul of several circles which met regularly to study the Bible and to talk over recent theological developments. As a theologian Bonnet belonged to the orthodox tradition, but in many ways he was not an intolerant man. Sometimes he preferred moderation to the point of vagueness. That, at least was the view of his friends in The Hague, who once complained that he did not commit his thoughts to paper, not even in a letter, playing the 'politique' again.[9] Nevertheless Bonnet quite vigourously expressed his opinions when he thought it really mattered and he honestly tried to stick to a consistent set of principles. Bonnet stressed the importance of a personal knowledge of Christ, but at the same time placed great emphasis on natural theology and natural law. He held that reason, tainted as it was by sin, would testify to the truth, though not to the fundamental goodness of things. All in all this champion of orthodoxy was not as untainted by the Enlightenment as many church-people liked to think.

The life of Bonnet's colleague Christophorus Saxe had been very different.[10] Born and bred in Saxony he studied classical languages and theology at the University of Leipzig. Like so many Lutheran proponents who did not manage to secure a post, he had to earn his living as a tutor. In 1748 he came to the Netherlands in that capacity with the children of the secretary of the Prince of Orange and in due time exchanged them for the offspring of a patrician in Utrecht. These employers used their influence at court to help Saxe along. In 1753 the widow of Stadholder William IV procured his appointment as professor of antiquities and letters in Utrecht. It was rather a mixed blessing for Saxe was foisted upon two colleagues who already taught these subjects and made it quite clear that they did not appreciate this move. But instead of lying low, Saxe made matters worse by starting an unholy row over borrowed manuscripts with professor Petrus Burmannus Secundus, who, unlike Saxe, was anything but an Orangist. While a war of pamphlets gathered strength, Saxe alienated many fellow-philologists in his attempts to hide the fact that he himself was in the wrong. But the political overtones of the conflict saved him from exposure. As it was friends in high places as well as the town council managed to gain control over the situation without interfering too much.

Unfortunately Saxe commanded no outstanding scholarship, success as a teacher or great personal charm to compensate for his quarrelsomeness. His most important asset was a wide knowledge of literary history (in the eighteenth century sense of bibliography)[11], of Roman antiquities and of classical archaeology. He was the first to introduce this last subject into the Dutch university curriculum and one of those who immediately appreciated the outstanding contribution which Winckelmann was making to the history of art.[12]

In the University Saxe's teaching did not really catch on, but in 1778 it was his good fortune to become the only professor who taught Latin and history. The students had the choice between attending his lectures or dropping these subjects. Socially, Saxe did make some acquaintances among the Dutch, like the ubiquitous Orangist Tydeman family, but he never gives the impression of feeling really at home in Utrecht. He was much closer to his German correspondents than to the Dutch. One reason may have been that he was and remained a Lutheran and married a lady from that same church. Saxe was wise enough not to proclaim his anti-Calvinist feelings in public[13], but his teaching lacked the edge which the orthodox Calvinists would have liked. Certainly his religious background detracted greatly from his value as patron within the church and within the world of higher education. And indeed he had a strong personal conviction that it was a great handicap to be a dissenter.[14]

When the Patriot movement gathered strength in the 1780s, the cautious Bonnet avoided politics as much as possible[15] and with apparent success. He had no past to conquer. Moreover Orangists were still in the majority both in the University senate and in the native population of the city. As long as they did not advocate their point of view too openly, the Patriots left them well alone. But when the more radical Patriots in December 1785 established a revolutionary town council which was not recognized by the Stadholder and the provincial government, a clash seemed inevitable. In February 1786, when riots kept the magistrates on their toes, a new letter for a day of prayer caused great strain. The Orangist minister Jacobus Hinlopen confided his anxiety to a good friend and complained about being so very restricted in praying and preaching. Contrary to the usual procedure the consistory decided 'for certain reasons' not to hold a meeting to discuss this matter.[16] But nothing much happened.

During 1786 however a still more radical town council was established. In March 1787 this magistracy felt strong enough to decree that the clergy should pray for the present reigning lawful magistrates.[17] So far they had simply done so for the magistrates without any specification. But now a decision had to be taken which involved Bonnet too. He was not technically a minister in the city, but as a professor of theology he had to take services regularly. Moreover he had just been elected an elder.[18] Bonnet must have had an authoritative voice in the discussions of the consistory. The outcome was a private declaration of the Orangist ministers that they would neither confirm nor deny the lawfulness of the present magistrates, because the congregation was not at one in the matter. This straight answer, which did not compromise the consistory itself and preserved its unity, seemed to settle it all. No immediate action was taken by the town council.[19]

But they were only biding their time. March 28th was to be a day of prayer and thanksgiving. Again the consistory decided not to discuss their common strategy on this point. It was one thing to keep silent but quite another to reach a unanimous conclusion, for the one Patriot minister, undoubtedly supported by the radical professor of theology IJsbrand van Hamelsveld, would never have consented to open defiance of the powers that be.[20] But this time the magistrates actively pursued the matter by asking for a written statement that the letter had been received. The consistory, however, kept its head and, having notified the town council of the arrival of the letter, again left action to the Orangist ministers. They declared to the town council that they could not go any further than a pledge not to use expressions which would hurt anyone.[21] Getting no definite answer, the Orangist ministers again bravely prayed for the magistrates in general. Only minister Schouw, who had been persuaded at the last moment to withdraw his signature, did otherwise. But immediately afterwards he collapsed, crying dismally that he had sinned against his conscience.[22]

It was clear that the magistrates would think twice before attacking the Orangist clergy with its many supporters in the city. Moreover,

Utrecht became increasingly aware of its dangerous position in case the Stadholder should send an army against it. There must also have been concern about the University. The number of students had dwindled during the unrest and several professors tried and succeeded in getting away. If Bonnet did so too, that would spell disaster because most theological students would leave with him.[23] The danger was far from imaginary. The University of Franeker did in fact call Bonnet, but he kept his promise to stay in Utrecht, without telling the magistrates. That way he probably forfeited an increase of wages, but his line was that he would not ask favours of a government he did not approve of. His reward came when in September 1787 the Prussians brought the Orangists back to power.[24]

Saxe was far less happy with that event, for he had come down on the side of the Patriots. Right through the 1770s he had been an Orangist, reaping the financial harvest of the protection of the court. Up to 1785 he dedicated books to the Stadholder. The draft of the oration he had hoped to deliver in 1786 still contained some bland praise for the prince, according to the prevailing political atmosphere. But by then Saxe had already thrown in his lot with the Patriots. In June 1783 he was asked by a 'Societas Armiferae Antesignani' to provide a device for a banner. This society is to be identified with the Utrecht Patriot freecorps Pro Patria et Libertate, founded in February of that year. Though the freecorps in the end preferred a more terse device in stead of the ones proposed by Saxe, he was apparently in sympathy with the principles it stood for. There are signs that in 1784 he criticized the ancestors of the present Stadholder in his lectures on Dutch history, but this last piece of evidence is in itself far from conclusive. In any case he must have destroyed most of his notes afterwards. In November 1785 he wrote to a German friend that Utrecht had grown impatient with its former slavery. Later on he allowed himself to be appointed *rector magnificus* by the revolutionary commune and was delighted when his son Frederik became a professor of law.[25]

It is difficult to probe Saxe's motives for joining the Patriots. He certainly never liked court life, but neither was he a radical democrat. Yet a letter to an unknown fellow professor, written in August 1786, shortly after many councillors had been removed by radicals, is most revealing. Saxe stated that it was not up to him to judge the wisdom of this. We, he said, just have to accept those in office who have sworn to keep the law.[26] But before we dismiss Saxe as a mere time-server, it is necessary to look at other circumstances of a religious and private nature.

In the local Lutheran Church, as elsewhere, there were two parties: the conservatives who preferred a German pastor and the more enlightened who wanted a Dutch one.[27] The struggle was intertwined with politics. The Orangist government had always championed the Germans, while the Patriots supported the Dutch side which Saxe also favoured. For although he was conservative as a scholar and teacher, he seems to have been more liberal in his theology. So Saxe, who certainly was a deeply religious man, had at least one motive to join the Patriots.

But the strongest inducement most probably was Saxe's son Frederik, who had studied law in Utrecht. He was a pupil of the Patriot professor Johannes Henricus Voorda and a member of the freecorps. In 1784 he took his doctor's degree together with the radical Johan van Lidt de Jeude, who was to be one of the ringleaders in the revolt.[28] If Frederik Saxe was not persuasive enough himself, paternal ambition did the rest. For in January 1786 father Saxe suggested to the magistrates that his son be appointed professor extraordinary in civil law. This came to nothing. But when Voorda was appointed to the revolutionary town council, Frederik applied for the succession. He offered to give free lectures in the meantime, while twenty-four students demanded his appointment.[29] The offer was accepted, to the detriment of an Orangist professor of law. But the town council looked for a more experienced teacher than young Saxe who was fobbed off with an extraordinary professorship without pay. Instead, Johan Valckenaer, a professor who had had to leave the University of Franeker because of his Patriotism, was made most welcome in Utrecht.[30]

Meanwhile Frederik's father acted as *rector magnificus* in 1787. In this capacity he showed much zeal by offering to confer a doctor's degree on a newly appointed professor of philosophy, Pieter Nieuwland, because the proper man to do the job had left the city for the summer. But Saxe, as a professor of languages had no right to act in that way and even the most unwavering Patriot in the senate, Van Hamelsveld, was not slow to point this out. In fact Nieuwland was never able to give an inaugural oration for the day after this debate the Prussians entered Utrecht. Next Saxe found himself complimenting the Orangist magistrate on behalf of the University and getting a very sour answer indeed.[31]

Most Patriots had remained in the city and escaped trouble, while only the diehards took flight, like Van Hamelsveld, who left a Sunday morning congregation of five waiting in vain, while the reader droned away one Bible chapter after the other. Saxe, now in his early seventies, also remained in office. But all appointments of the former 'pretense magistraat' were annulled and Frederik Saxe lost his newly won professorate. For his aged father it only remained to settle into the old routine and to grumble about bad times and fewer students in his lecture room. The new magistrates did not deign to pay for the printing of his rectoral oration let alone showing him other favours.[32] His son Frederik was not averse to leaving for Germany if a suitable professorate would become available there. But his father was not very sanguine about that. Yet they were in fact luckier than could have been expected. Within a few years Frederik was appointed professor at the Athenaeum of Deventer.[33] And though rumour had it that he would rather have served a Patriot government, his love for that good cause did not induce him to suffer with his friends.[34] Meanwhile the German Lutherans in Utrecht managed to get the sort of vicar they desired, despite a request of the opposition which was only signed by the female members of the Saxe household.[35] The wily old fox kept out of everything.

But victory was ahead. In 1795 the French brought the liberty Saxe had looked forward to so eagerly. When the new municipality asked all civil servants to show their commissions, Saxe was the first and, as it turned out, the only professor to comply at once.[36] In the event nobody lost his job, although the former Patriot professors were invited back on the same terms. One of them was Frederik Saxe, who had recently been dismissed in Deventer for his political—anti-Patriot!—feelings. Incidentally, his bid for a paid professorate in civil and natural law was turned down, but he did become a judge in the Court of Utrecht in 1796.[37] Saxe himself was made secretary of the senate and afterwards *rector magnificus* for the fourth time. He paid a handsome tribute to the new government by pronouncing an oration, entitled *In legis regiae patronos*.[38] Saxe started with an exposition of all the well worn arguments against royal absolutism, drawing on the Bible and the classics. But then he went out of his way to describe the vices of personal rule, a thinly veiled comment on the stadholders and on the enemies of France. Saxe topped this with warm praise for the liberators and for the new municipality, publicly referring to a recent increase of his wages. And indeed Saxe was now one of the best paid professors in the University, which was highly unusual for a teacher of languages and history.[39] He also proudly signed himself Christoph Saxe at the very top of a request of the Enlightened Lutherans for a Dutch pastor.[40] They were successful.

In the meantime Bonnet and his friends, only deserted by William Laurence Brown, the vicar of the English Church at Utrecht and a professor in ethics and natural law, who left for Scotland in 1794, faced their first test. It was the inevitable thanksgiving day. The government had deliberately chosen Sunday 8 March, 'Prinsjesdag', the birthday of Stadholder William V. The previous Sunday the letter for the prayer day had been duly read from the pulpit in some churches while the congregation registered dissent by the blowing of noses, the shuffling of feet or walking out.[41] The next Sunday most people stayed at home. But that course was not open to the ministers. They again tried to avoid trouble by not saying anything much. In fact, eight of them did not read the letter at all. But this strategy did not cut any ice with the government. The ministers, including Bonnet, were summoned to come to the town hall where they were severely rebuked. An inquiry brought to light that only J. Hinlopen, who liked to speak his mind, had preached against the state. He lost his office.[42]

But this was not all. On 10 March, Bonnet, as a regent of the *Diakonieschool*, was supervising exams. At about seven o'clock in the evening two members of the Commission for Education turned up, in the company of two armed French soldiers. Not deterred, the presiding minister Gerhard Masman refused them access without the support of the consistory. Masman was sent home immediately, while the others were kept waiting for a considerable time.[43] Masman lost his office temporarily and the diakonie had to comply.

Trouble was ahead in the University as well. In May 1796 the professors, as civil servants, were required to declare their allegiance to the new government, stating that they would never support the Orangists in word or deed. Bonnet and two other theologians flatly refused to do this, thereby risking their office. Students intervened for them, and the senate with its secretary Saxe in particular, tried to save the situation, alleging that the departure of these teachers would irreparably damage the University. In the end the three only promised obedience without making any political confession. Again the reputation of the theological faculty and the importance of the University to the city had saved heads. In October 1797 the government finally required a declaration of submission and a promise to further its causes in so far as an individual's profession required it. Bonnet applied for exemption, but in the end he complied, again with a declaration of his own making which was duly accepted.[44]

So Bonnet was allowed to continue in his office and he retired when the opportunity was offered in 1804, eighty-one years old. He died in 1805, two years before Saxe, who had also retired in 1804, but grudgingly for he refused to see why a nonagenarian could not teach as well as any.[45] So, while they did not survive to see the Kingdom of the Netherlands, Bonnet and Saxe remained in office right through all the upheavals of the Patriot and the Batavian revolution.

Though neither of them was politically active, they could not help being involved. Why did Bonnet and Saxe act as they did? Was it an archetypal difference between a politically and religiously orthodox Orangist and a liberal Patriot? Or merely a difference between the theologian of the Netherlands Reformed Church and a Lutheran dissenter? No doubt there is some truth in both statements[46], but they should not be overaccentuated. Was the social gap between Bonnet and Saxe sufficiently wide to explain a difference in political attitude? In fact, the labelling of social groups as Orangists or Patriots had proved to be a very hazardous occupation, not to mention the difficulty in defining the many varieties of Patriotism and Orangism. So no easy explanation is at hand.

But in this particular case there was a difference in mental make-up. Bonnet was well to do, childless, part of the social life of the city and a highly admired clergyman and professor. Saxe on the other hand, was comparatively poor, leaving no money to support his widow and his three unmarried daughters. Always very conscious of being a foreigner and a dissenter, he could only find security in a government which would guarantee his position. As an enlightened Lutheran he was not sure of the esteem of the majority of his co-religionists. So Saxe, always trying to be obedient to the God-appointed government, clung to his office by using flattery and persuasion, and by keeping silent when necessary. In fact, his behaviour was very complex.

Bonnet did not feel insecure. Storms did not affect his vows and allegiances in any way. Like the majority of his contemporary fellow preachers in any church, he did not like to talk politics in the pulpit. As an Orangist whose persuasion was well known, he behaved with the quiet dignity, the timely political moderation and the necessary firmness which seem to have characterized most Orangist ministers during this whole period. Utrecht had set the example in 1786 and 1787, the Orangist part of the church followed suit during the oppression by the French. For while the Dutch Lutheran church did in the end split into two churches, the Dutch Reformed Church, as exemplified by men like professor Jona Willem te Water and Hiëronymus van Alphen, for good or for worse, held out in a silent but determined rebellion.[47]

Of course Bonnet as well as Saxe benefited from the fact that the Dutch revolution was moderate and remarkably free from bloodshed. Therefore we must own that if their lives, their homes or the wellbeing of others had been at stake, the tale might have been quite different.

[1] University Library Utrecht, MS O F 12-5, Annotationes variae, unfinished Oratio sesqui saecularis Academiae nostrae natalis causa, f. 23. On 27 February 1786 the town council decided that professor Rau was to deliver the festive oration (G.W. Kernkamp, *Acta et decreta senatus, vroedschapsresolutiën en andere bescheiden betreffende de Utrechtsche academie*, III, Utrecht, 1940, p. 176).

² University Library Utrecht, MS O F 12-2, Annotationes variae, ff. 32-45, draft of an 'Oratio genethliaca in honorem ... Guilielmi Frederici ... primi eius natalis diei causa'. Prince William's first birthday was on 24 August 1773. The town council apparently never considered commissioning an oration for this occasion.
³ On Dutch patriotism, see S. Schama, *Patriots and Liberators. Revolution in the Netherlands 1780-1813*, New York, 1977. For some recent reappraisals, see F. Grijzenhout, W.W. Mijnhardt and N.C.F. van Sas (eds.), *Voor vaderland en vrijheid. De revolutie van de patriotten*, Amsterdam, 1987; Th.S.M. van der Zee, J.G.M.M. Rosendaal and P.G.B. Thissen (eds.), *1787 De Nederlandse revolutie?*, Amsterdam, 1988; H. Bots and W.W. Mijnhardt (eds.), *De droom van de revolutie. Nieuwe benaderingen van het patriottisme*, Amsterdam, 1988.
⁴ On the University, see G.W. Kernkamp, *De Utrechtsche universiteit 1636-1936*, I, *De Utrechtsche Academie 1636-1815*, Utrecht, 1936; J. Roelevink, *Gedicteerd verleden. Het onderwijs in de algemene geschiedenis aan de universiteit te Utrecht, 1735-1839*, Amsterdam/Maarssen, 1986; J.A. Cramer, *De theologische faculteit te Utrecht in de 18e en het begin der 19e Eeuw*, Utrecht, 1936. On the city of Utrecht, A. van Hulzen, *Utrecht in de patriottentijd*, Zaltbommel, 1966; R.E. de Bruin, *Burgers op het kussen. Volkssoevereiniteit en bestuurssamenstelling in de stad Utrecht, 1795-1813*, Zutphen, 1986; R.E. de Bruin, *Revolutie in Utrecht. Studenten, burgers en regenten in de Patriottentijd (1780-1787)*, Utrecht, 1987.
⁵ Schama, *Patriots*, p. 100.
⁶ C.J.H. Jansen, *Natuurrecht of Romeins recht. Een studie over leven en werk van F.A. van der Marck (1719-1800) in het licht van de opvattingen van zijn tijd*, Leiden, 1987; J. Roelevink, 'Perkamenten blindgangers? Patriotten, prinsgezinden en de archieven van hun overheden', in *Droom van de revolutie*, pp. 71-82; J. Hartog, *De patriotten en Oranje van 1747-1787*, Amsterdam, 1882.
⁷ On Bonnet, see A. van den Ende, *Gisbertus Bonnet. Bijdrage tot de kennis van de geschiedenis der gereformeerde theologie in de achttiende eeuw*, Wageningen, 1957; A. de Groot, 'Gisbert Bonnet', *Biografisch lexicon voor de geschiedenis van het Nederlands protestantisme*, II, pp. 78-80. On the efforts of Leiden University to secure the services of Bonnet, as well as on the subsequent pension, *Acta*, II, pp. 572-75.
⁸ The surviving part of his correspondence testifies to this (Utrecht University Library, MS 15 A 13, Papers of G. Bonnet).
⁹ Utrecht University Library, MS 15 A 13, Papers of G. Bonnet, letter from Johannes Eusebius Voet to Bonnet, The Hague, 2 February 1764. Again a student, Jean Louis Verster, writes on 3 March 1777 to Bonnet that he is grateful because he had always been taught moderation, not partiality.
¹⁰ On Saxe, see Roelevink, *Gedicteerd verleden*, pp. 160 ff.
¹¹ Roelevink, *Gedicteerd verleden*, pp. 195, 196.
¹² *Ibid.*, pp. 192, 232.
¹³ Royal Library, The Hague, MS 74 D 13 II, Saxe to C.A. Klotz, 27 July 1764: daily he hears the altercations of the Calvinists, but he firmly holds the Lutheran doctrine about Holy Communion, whatever they may reason; Royal Library, The Hague, MS 74 D 14 III, Saxe to J.A. Cramer, 31 August 1781: Saxe never joins theological discussions among colleagues and only touches upon the simplicity and perspicuity of the Christian doctrine in his lectures on rhetoric. Privately he laughs at the technical terms and the theological squabbles. To Th.Ch. Harles Saxe complains that the Calvinists, and the Gomarists more in particular stick to their privilege as the public religion (Royal Library, The Hague, MS 74 D 14 II, Saxe to Harles, 1 August 1772).
¹⁴ G.W. Kernkamp (ed.), 'Johann Beckmann's dagboek van zijne reis door Nederland in 1762', *Bijdragen en mededeelingen van het Historisch Genootschap*, 33 (1912), p. 421: Saxe tells his German visitor Beckmann '... es sey allemal böse und gefährliche Sache wenn man sacris publicis alienus sey' (see also p. 424, where another professor says as much about Saxe).
¹⁵ There is no evidence that Bonnet ever brought up politics in his sermons, not even when dealing with such obvious texts as 'The Lord reigneth' (G. Bonnet, *Verzameling van leerredenen*, 4 vols., 1774, 1776, 1782 and 1792; University Library Utrecht, MS 15 C13;

Mijnard Tydeman, reports of sermons attended in Utrecht, 1777-1783, 1784-1794, 1789, 1795 and 1813-1814. The reports are admittedly very short from 1784 onwards, but strong language would have been noted appreciatively by this fellow Orangist). The well known Patriot Van der Capellen tot den Pol was appalled by the lack of political engagement in the average minister of the Reformed church; see M. Evers, 'Angelsaksische inspiratiebronnen voor de patriottische denkbeelden van Joan Derk van der Capellen', in *Nederlandse Revolutie*, p. 217.

¹⁶ Leiden University Library, MS BPL 945, Jacobus Hinlopen to Mijnard Tydeman, 6 February 1786; City Archives, Utrecht, Archives of the Netherlands Reformed Church, no. 15, Acta van de bijzondere kerkeraad, 1762-1786, 13 February 1786.

¹⁷ Van Hulzen, *Patriottisme*, p. 263.

¹⁸ City Archives Utrecht, Archives of the consistory of the Netherlands Reformed Church, no. 24, Acta van de grote kerkeraad, 1763-1801, 4 July 1785; no. 15, Acta van de bijzondere kerkeraad, 1762-1786, 12 September 1785.

¹⁹ Van Hulzen, *Patriottisme*, p. 265.

²⁰ City Archives Utrecht, Archives of the Netherlands Reformed Church, no. 16, Acta van de bijzondere kerkeraad 1787-1803, 12 maart 1787.

²¹ Van Hulzen, *Patriottisme*, p. 264.

²² City Archives Utrecht, Martens papers, no. 319, D.J. Martens, Verhaal gebeurtenissen 1786-1787, p. 79 (printed as 'Eenige aanteekeningen wegens het gebeurde te Utrecht in 1786 en 1787', *Kronijk van het Historisch Genootschap* 26 (1870), p. 452.

²³ *Acta*, III, p. 192; Roelevink, *Gedicteerd verleden*, pp. 166, 167.

²⁴ *Acta*, III, p. 199. On 20 october 1787 both Bonnet and Pieter Bondam, a distinguished professor of law, received a delegation of the magistracy to thank them for their ignoring the revolutionary government.

²⁵ Royal Library, The Hague, MS 74 D 14 III, f. 939; the banner was to show a hand with a sword and an olive branch. As device Saxe proposed: 1. *Pax armorum non expers*; 2. *Armorum usu tuta pax*; 3. *Armorum exercitia justae pacis altrix*; 4. *Brachii fortitudo solidae pacis custos*. According to Van Hulzen, *Patriottisme*, p. 64, Pro Patria indeed had one such banner, with the equally menacing but more telling motto *Ad utrumque paratus*. The lecture notes (Utrecht University Library, MS 5 N 6, Historia Batava), possibly date from 1784, but there are loose leafs with stronger comments. On 15 November 1785 Saxe in a letter to Harles referred to '... nostra ... urbe ... pristinae servitutis impatiente ...' (Royal Library, The Hague, MS 74 D 14 III). Saxe was appointed *rector magnificus* in March 1787 (*Acta*, III, p. 189). For Frederik Saxe's professorate in January 1787, see *Acta*, III, p. 183

²⁶ Royal Library The Hague, MS 74 D 14 III, between f. 986 and f. 987, Saxe to a fellow professor, undated (August 1786): 'Opportunum sane non est, nos de utrorumvis consulum continuandorum, an recens creatorum optione facienda judicare. Certent ipsi utriusque partis Consules inter se jure et legibus. Nostrum est, accipere, qui reapse nobis dati sunt, et qui reapse in leges civitatis jurarunt. Ideoque more et instituto maiorum gratulandum esse censeo iis Consulibus quos hesterna populi comitia jusserunt.' Even in 1798 Saxe stated in an oration (see note 39): 'Immo non ea est vera popularis respublica, quae vulgo dicitur cuiuscunque multitudinis, omnes rumorum et concionum ventos colligentis, sed ubi loci, census, atque ordinis cives ad iusta comitia vocati leges ferunt, optimos et mente et animo sui vicarios creant, junctimque cum his et per eos saluti publicae communiter consulendum esse putant, adeoque civitas et popularii, et optimo status genere confusa est modice.'

²⁷ City Archives Utrecht, Archive of the Evangelical Lutheran Church, no. 18, Resolutions of the large and the small consistory, 1755-1796, and no. 66, Papers concerning the appointment of ministers and the lawsuit of J.P. Griesenbeck. On the Dutch Lutheran Churches, see C.Ch.G. Visser, *De Lutheranen in Nederland tussen Katholicisme en Calvinisme, 1566 tot heden*, Dieren, 1983.

²⁸ *Acta*, III, pp. 162-64.

²⁹ *Acta*, III, pp. 176, 183, 192-93.

³⁰ Johan Valckenaer, a Franeker professor, had no choice but to resign for political

reasons, which he did on 15 May 1787. Of course this martyr, an experienced teacher, was preferred to Frederik Saxe. On Valckenaer and on Franeker in particular, see I. Schöffer, 'Een kortstondig hoogleraarschap. Johan Valckenaer in Leiden, 1795-1796', in S. Groenveld, M.E.H.N. Mout and I. Schöffer (eds.), *Bestuurders en geleerden*, Amsterdam/Dieren, 1985, pp. 193-208, and S. Zijlstra, 'Patriotse professors. Opkomst en undergang fan it patriottisme oan de Fryske hegeskoalle', in W. Bergsma, C. Boschma, M.G. Buist and H. Spanninga (eds.), *For Uwz lân, wijv en bern*, Leeuwarden, 1987, pp. 99-110. At the end of his own inaugural lecture, delivered on 31 May 1787, which was non-political, Frederik Saxe expresses his debts to his teacher and his wish that Voorda may work to the advantage of the city and burghers; *Oratio de utilitate et jucunditate historiae juris civilis*, pp. 27-28.

[31] City Archives Leiden, Tydeman Papers, professor Pieter Bondam to Mijnard Tydeman, 16 September 1787. Professor Rossijn being absent, his colleagues Oosterdijk Schacht, Segaar, Bondam and Van Hamelsveld voted unanimously against Saxe's proposal which was termed a 'res novi exempli'. This small matter did, of course, not get into the minutes of the senate. On 18 September 1787 the senate, including Saxe, was graciously received by the Stadholder. Afterwards they went to the town council. According to Bondam Saxe was none too pleased with the reply (City Archives Leiden, Tydeman papers, Pieter Bondam to Mijnard Tydeman, 18 September 1787). My attention was drawn to this letter by L. van Poelgeest, whom I would like to thank.

[32] On Van Hamelsveld, see City Archives Leiden, Tydeman papers, P. Bondam to M. Tydeman, Sunday 16 September 1787. On Saxe's state of mind, see a letter from Saxe to Harles, Utrecht, 3 November 1788: 'Nullus enim remedio locus est, nisi cum interitu optimatium, sensu quippe Ciceroniani. Propterea magno animo ferendum quicquid corrigere est nefas' (Royal Library The Hague, MS 74 D 14 III). On 28 October 1789 Saxe wrote to the same sympathetic correspondent: 'Taedet me publica rerum et literarum forma. Nullos habeo vigiliarum academicarum socios, nisi dominis subparasitantes ...' and 'linguam et calamum compescere debeo. Est enim apud nos libertas vincta catenis.' In the same letter he refers to the refusal to print his oration.

[33] Saxe to Harles, 6 April 1788 (the bad news) and 28 October 1789 (the good news). On 3 November 1788 the anxious father had written: 'Ambitionem servilem odit filius meus, nec adduci potest ut Idola adoret' (Royal Library, The Hague, MS 74 D 14 III). For the appointment in Deventer, see J.C. van Slee, *De Illustre School te Deventer 1630-1878, hare geschiedenis, hoogleeraren en studenten, met bijvoeging van het album studiosorum*, 's-Gravenhage, 1916, p. 145.

[34] Royal Library The Hague, MS 128 G 24, H.W. Tydeman, Biography of Mijnard Tydeman (copy), p. 106: F. Saxe had been appointed by the Orangists to replace the (Patriot) Van der Marck, but he would rather have served their adversaries.

[35] The request, signed by Anna Juliana Saxe-Novisadi, Sophia Saxe, Anna Juliana Saxe, Johanna Ernestina Saxe and many others was handed in to the Lutheran consistory on 9 December 1788. For a copy of the request with the names of the signers, City Archives Utrecht, Archives of the Evangelical-Lutheran Church, no. 18, Resoluties van de grote en de kleine kerkeraad, 1755-1796.

[36] *Acta*, III, p. 258. It turned out that professors were not meant to do so.

[37] J.A. Wijnne and L. Miedema (eds.), *Resolutiën van de vroedschap van Utrecht betreffende de Academie*, Utrecht, 1900, p. 485; *Acta*, III, p. 257.

[38] Chr. Saxe, *Oratio honoraria in legis regiae patronos*, Trajecti Batavorum, 1798.

[39] *In legis regiae patronos*, pp. 78, 83-84; Roelevink, *Gedicteerd verleden*, p. 169.

[40] City Archives Utrecht, Archives of the Evangelical Lutheran Church, no. 66, Papers on German and Dutch ministers, 1772-1800, undated request (presented to the consistory on 23 February 1795; Archives Lutheran Church, no. 18, Resoluties van de grote en de kleine kerkeraad, 1755-1796). Among the thirty-nine signatures are also those of Anna Juliana Saxe-Novisadi, Sophia Saxe, A.J. Saxe and J.E. Saxe.

[41] City Archives Utrecht, Martens papers, no. 319, David Jan Martens, Verhaal van de gebeurtenissen te Utrecht in de jaren 1795-1796, p. 13.

[42] *Acta*, III, pp. 247-48; De Bruin, *Burgers*, p. 48. On Hinlopen, see P.J. Buijnsters, *Hiëronimus van Alphen (1746-1803)*, Assen, 1973, p. 56.

[43] City Archives Utrecht, Martens papers, no. 319, David Jan Martens, Verhaal van de gebeurtenissen te Utrecht in de jaren 1795-1796, p. 12; De Bruin, *Burgers*, p. 48. On Gerhard Masman, see *Biografisch lexicon voor de geschiedenis van het Nederlandse protestantisme*, I, Kampen, 1978, p. 165.

[44] *Acta*, III, pp. 263-64, 266-67, 270-72; 278-81, 295-96.

[45] Roelevink, *Gedicteerd verleden*, pp. 171ff.

[46] Ph.H. Breuker, 'Eelko Alta as Patriot', in W. Bergsma *et al.*, *For Uwz lân, wyv en bern*, Leeuwarden, 1987, p. 62, claims that there is no correlation between orthodoxy/Orangism and liberalism/Patriotism. J. den Boer, 'Vrijkorpsen in Friesland', *ibid.*, p. 84, states that contemporaries nevertheless did see one. For a balanced discussion of this point, see J. van den Berg, 'Hervormden, dissenters en de patriottenbeweging', in *1787 De Nederlandse revolutie?*, p. 124.

[47] Te Water writes in his autobiography that he always tried to combine honesty with prudence, because anybody who did not promise to obey the new administration and the new laws would be forced to leave the country; *Levens-berigt van Jona Willem te Water ... door hem zelven vervaardigd*, p. 367 ff. Buynsters, *Van Alphen*, p. 285, states that Van Alphen disapproved of any political resistance to the new regime in 1795, but also of any form of cooperation. Another cautious man was Gerard Kuypers, see D. Nauta, 'Gerard Kuypers', in *Opera minora. Kerkhistorische verhandelingen over Calvijn en de geschiedenis van de kerk in Nederland*, Kampen, 1961, pp. 117 ff. R.A. Flinterman, in *Biografisch lexicon voor de geschiedenis van het Nederlands protestantisme*, II, p. 454, takes a dim view of Te Water's behaviour, but though not very muscular, it was commonplace among Orangists and his unwavering political views were well known.

INDEX